SAT
Literature

Heather M. Hilliard, MS
Jessica Egan, MS
John Keefe, MS

XAMonline

To obtain permission(s) to use the material from this work for any purpose including workshops or seminars, please submit a written request to:

XAMonline, Inc.
21 Orient Avenue
Melrose, MA 02176
Toll Free: 1-800-301-4647
Email: info@xamonline.com
Web: www.xamonline.com
Fax: 1-617-583-5552

Library of Congress Cataloging-in-Publication Data
Hilliard, Heather

SAT Literature/Heather Hilliard ISBN: 978-1-60787-573-4

1. SAT   2. Study Guides   3. English

Disclaimer:

Printed in the United States of America

SAT Literature
ISBN: 978-1-60787-573-4

Table of Contents

About the Authors

Earning her bachelor's degree in New Orleans and her two masters degrees from the University of Pittsburgh, **Heather M. Hilliard** serves as an Adjunct Professor for her undergraduate alma mater, Tulane University. From teaching - both at the collegiate level as well as special courses at a leading independent high school - to her corporate endeavors, she has consciously focused aspects of her career and volunteerism on education. She has received several commendations for her achievements, has been inducted into the national honor society for public health and is one of fewer than 1,000 internationally Certified Emergency Managers in the world. She has published on a variety of topics and edited textbooks as well as other fiction and non-fiction work and focuses on strategic communications and improvements for clients - including writing and editing for XAMonline preparation content and tests including Advanced Placement exams, CLEP materials, and the SAT.

With a Master's Degree in English Education from Florida State University, **Jessica Egan** has expertise in the areas of literature, linguistics, and educational psychology. Jessica has worked as an instructional technologist and has experience in teaching secondary English, English as a Second Language (ESL), college-level composition and Adult Basic Education (ABE). She has authored lesson plans, teacher certification materials, and test preparation texts.

John Keefe is an author and editor from Chicago, Illinois. A graduate of Columbia College Chicago, John Keefe has written fiction and non-fiction for publications such as Chicago Literati, Hair Trigger Magazine, and websites like Cracked.com. He is also an actor and playwright."

SECTION I:

Introduction

Chapter 1: Introduction

How the SAT Subject Tests Work

SAT SUBJECT TESTS ARE COLLEGE ADMISSION EXAMS ON SPECIFIC SUBJECTS. THESE ARE the only national admission tests where you choose the tests that best showcase your strengths and interests. There are 20 SAT Subject Tests in five general subject areas and each subject test is an hour long. They are all multiple choice and scored on a 200-800 scale.

The SAT Subject tests are generally given six times in any given school year, on the same days and in the same test centers as the SAT — but not all 20 tests are offered on every SAT date. You can take one, two, or three Subject Tests on any test date but you can't take the SAT and any SAT Subject Tests on the same day.

When you take an SAT Subject Test, you are doing more than showing off your strengths. Some colleges require or recommend that you take the SAT Subject Tests, especially if you are applying to take specific courses or programs.

Even if a college doesn't require a Subject Test, the school may accept them and use them in admissions to get a more complete picture of applicants. Some colleges use Subject Tests to place students into the appropriate courses, so you may be able to fulfill basic requirements or to get credit for introductory-level courses.

The SAT Subject Tests cover material that is taught in high school courses at many schools. Faculty at individual schools review the exams to ensure that they cover the important material currently taught in their courses and are appropriate for their schools to accept the SAT Subject Test for possible introductory-level course exemption.

If the college decides to give you credit, it will record the number of credits on your permanent record, thereby indicating that you have completed work equivalent to a course in that subject. If the college decides to grant exemption without giving you credit for a course, you will be permitted to omit a course that would normally be required of you and to take a course of your choice instead.

When to Take Subject Tests

In general, The College board recommends that students should take SAT Subject Tests right after completing the recommended classes, because the material will still be fresh in your mind. In some cases, it may be much earlier than the main SAT test — the spring of your freshman or sophomore year.

If you're thinking of applying early decision or early action to any college, note that many colleges advise that you take the SAT Subject Tests by October or

November of your senior year. For regular decision applications, some colleges will accept SAT Subject Test scores through the January administration. Check with the college you're interested in to find out its deadlines. If you are not sure when you should schedule your SAT Subject Tests, talk to your school counselor or teacher to figure out the timing that works best for you.

Because the SAT Subject Tests are based on high school course work, the best way to prepare for them is by learning the material taught in the corresponding classes and using the textbooks that you're already using for those classes.

If you're doing well in these courses or taking advanced level courses (such as honors, dual enrollment, Advanced Placement, IB), Subject Tests are an excellent opportunity for you to show your understanding of the subject area.

This guide will help give reminders and pointers about the tests, so that you can achieve the highest score possible!

Where to Take the Examination and How to Register

While there are differences with some of the SAT Subject Tests, the SAT Literature Test is typically administered on paper and is approximately 60 minutes long, with 60 questions that match passages in the exam. Questions are multiple-choice and they test your reading comprehension as well as figurative language. It looks at your understanding of tone, theme, and imagery.

While you may be able to register via computer, there are certain instances when students need to register for any SAT Subject Tests by mail (also known as paper registration) if:

Requesting testing closer to home.

Requesting Sunday testing for the first time.

Paying by check or money order (payable to "The College Board").

Younger than 13 years old.

Unable to upload a digital photo as part of the online registration process.

Taking the test in Ghana. See other policies for test-takers in certain countries.

Registering through an SAT international representative.

You might need to include other items along with your paper registration form, depending on your reason for mailing in your registration. Check with The College Board to see what may need attached.

You must include a recent photo with your paper registration form. This photo will become part of your Admission Ticket, and test center staff will compare it to your photo ID to ensure security on test day.

Lastly, when you fill out the form, you'll need a College Board code for your high school (or the home-school code, 970000) and your test center. You might also need codes for the colleges you want to send scores to, your intended college major, and your country. You can find the listing of these codes online at The College Board (or your school counselors likely know the school's code if you are taking it there).

Accommodations for Students with Disabilities ─────────────

If you have a documented disability, you may be eligible for accommodations when you take the SAT Subject Tests and other College Board tests. Some available accommodations are extended time, extra and extended breaks, and reading and seeing accommodations (for example, large-type test books or Braille test books).

Accommodations must be approved by the College Board's Services for Students with Disabilities. School accommodations are not the same thing as College Board accommodations. Scores will be canceled if accommodations are used without College Board approval.

It can take up to seven weeks for accommodations to be approved. If you plan to take Subject Tests in October, for instance, talk to your counselor to start the process in the spring of the previous school year — well before summer break.

Check your Admission Ticket. If you've been approved for accommodations, they should be noted on the ticket. If they're not, call 212-713-8333 to ensure approved accommodations are added to your registration.

Also, if you need assistance or have questions about how The College Board works to meet your needs, contact Services for Students with Disabilities (SSD) program at 212-713-8333 for information about accommodations.

Changing Subject Tests on Test Day ─────────────────────

In general, you can take a different test from the one for which you are registered — the test booklet contains all Subject Tests available that day, so just take the ones you want. But if you want to take Language with Listening Tests, you have to register for it and can't change your mind to take it that day because they require special equipment.

If you decide to take fewer tests on that day, just turn in your answer sheet before the next test begins. Remember, though, that once you start answering a test, you can't decide not to take it — you'll have to cancel all tests taken that day to avoid having it scored.

You can add a test on test day, if it's being given on that day — but you can't add a Language with Listening Test. You'll be billed for the tests you add.

Test Day Checklist ────────────────────────────────

There are only a few things you really need to bring on test day and a lot of things you need to leave at home.
- Your Admission Ticket
- Acceptable photo identification
- Two No. 2 pencils with erasers
- If you're taking a Subject Test in Mathematics: an approved calculator — not needed for SAT Literature
- If you're taking a Language with Listening Test: an approved CD player.

What Not to Bring

- Cellphones
- Any devices, including digital watches, that can be used to record, transmit, receive, or play back audio, photographic, text, or video content (with the exception of CD players used for Language with Listening Subject Tests only)
- Audio players/recorders, tablets, laptops, notebooks, Google Glass, or any other personal computing devices
- Any texting device
- Cameras or any other photographic equipment
- Separate timers of any type

Your school counselor can share a complete list of prohibited devices — just ask to see the Official Student Guide.

Important: Violations Mean Canceled Scores

The Do-Not-Bring list is serious: Your scores will be canceled if you're caught using them, even during breaks. This includes cellphones.

There are some additional recommendations from The College Board that may be helpful to you before you get into this Guide that provides you with additional information to help you do your best.

- Read carefully. Consider all the choices in each question and read all options. Avoid careless mistakes that will cause you to lose points.
- Answer the easy questions first. Work on less time-consuming questions before moving on to the more difficult ones. Questions on each test are generally ordered from easiest to hardest.
- Eliminate answer choices that you know are wrong. Cross them out in your test booklet so that you can clearly see which choices are left.
- Make an educated guess or skip the question. If you have eliminated the choices that you know are wrong, guessing is your best strategy. However, if you cannot eliminate any of the answer choices, it is best to skip the question. You will lose points for incorrect answers but not for skipped ones. Make sure you skip the corresponding question on your answer sheet.
- Keep your answer sheet neat. The answer sheet is scored by a machine, which can't tell the difference between an answer and a doodle. If the machine reads marks that could be two answers for one question, it will consider the question unanswered.
- Use your test booklet as scrap paper. Use it to make notes or write down ideas. What you write in the booklet will not affect your score.
- Circle the questions you skip in your booklet. This will help you keep track of which questions you didn't answer.
- Check your answer sheet regularly. Make sure you are in the right place. Check the number of the question and the number on the answer sheet every few

questions. This is especially important when you skip a question.

- Work at an even, steady pace, and keep moving. Each question on the test takes a certain amount of time to read and answer. Through practice, you can develop a sense of timing to help you complete the test. Your goal is to spend time on the questions that you are most likely to answer correctly.
- Keep track of time. You are given one hour to complete each test. Occasionally check your progress so that you know where you are and how much time is left.
- Remember to always use a No. 2 pencil. All answer sheet circles must be filled in darkly and completely with a No. 2 pencil. If you need to erase an answer, erase it as completely as possible.
- Do not try to erase all of your answers. If you erase all of the answers to one of the tests you take on a given date, all of your tests you take that day will be canceled. Remember that you can choose which scores to send to colleges.

Test Day Important Notes

By familiarizing yourself with what will happen on test day, you can lower your stress levels and focus on the actual test passages and questions.

Arrive at the test center no later than 7:45 a.m., unless your Admission Ticket says otherwise. The doors to the testing rooms close about 8 a.m.

Testing starts between 8:30 and 9 a.m. Once testing has begun, latecomers cannot be admitted.

You are given two five-minute breaks, and you can consume snacks and drinks at these times.

DO NOT take your cell phone with you — there can be serious repercussions if you have it at the test. If you need to coordinate your ride, make sure to set your pick up time and location before test-day.

Wait to be seated. Your seat is assigned, not chosen by you.

So you aren't surprised, the test booklet will contain all of the Subject Tests that will be given on that particular day.

The test supervisor reads all instructions verbatim from a testing manual. He or she can only answer questions about procedure, not about test questions or content.

The test supervisor will tell you when to start and stop each test.

After each hour of testing, the supervisor collects test books and answer sheets from students who are finished testing for the day. If you are taking another test, sit quietly until testing resumes.

Your Score

Your score report gives you a breakdown of your scores and information about what those scores mean. Your score report may help you choose courses in high school or decide what programs or majors you want to pursue in college. It can also help you compare your mastery of a specific subject with that of students across the country and around the world. That could be especially useful to home-schooled students or high school students outside the United States who want to apply to U.S. colleges.

SAT Subject Test scores are kept on file for many years, but only valid for five years. During this period, for a small fee, you may have your transcript sent to another college or to anyone else you specify. Your score(s) will never be sent to anyone without your approval.

If you have a College Board online account, you can see your SAT Subject Test scores as soon as they're available, and can check the access list on The College Board's website. Also on this date, you can call and get your scores by phone for an extra cost.

If you registered by mail and don't have an online account — or if you registered online but asked to be sent a paper score report — you'll get a paper score report in the mail.

When you registered for the test or afterward, you told us what colleges or scholarship programs you wanted us to send your scores to. They'll get your score report shortly after you do. So will your high school.

Interpreting Your Scores _____

SAT Subject Tests are scored in two steps:
- The raw score is established.
- The raw score is converted to the College Board 200 — to 800-point scaled score.

All questions on SAT Subject Tests are multiple choice. To establish the raw score:
- One point is added for each correct answer.
- A fraction of a point is subtracted for wrong answers:
- 1/4 point is subtracted for five-choice questions.
- 1/3 point is subtracted for four-choice questions.
- 1/2 point is subtracted for three-choice questions.
- No points are deducted for unanswered questions.
    - The total points answered incorrectly are subtracted from those answered correctly.
    - If the resulting score is a fraction, it is rounded to the nearest whole number — 1/2 or more is rounded up; less than 1/2 is rounded down.

Converting the Raw Score to the Scaled Score _____

The raw score is converted to the College Board 200 — to 800-point scaled score by a statistical process called equating.

Equating adjusts for slight differences in difficulty between test editions and ensures that:
- A student's score does not depend on the specific test edition she or he took.

- A student's score does not depend on how well others did on the same edition of the test.
- The scaled score is reported to colleges. Total test scores for all Subject Tests are reported on the College Board 200 — to 800-point scale.

Scoring Quality Control

All SAT Subject Tests are multiple-choice, though some have other components to them — the SAT Literature is only multiple choice. The scanning accuracy of the SAT answer documents is very closely monitored, with several quality assurance checks including alignment checks and double scanning of documents. We also control the humidity of the scanning facility to minimize environmental impacts on the system, and we conduct frequent and controlled maintenance of all scanning machines.

If the test-taker's marks conform to the published instructions for marking the answer sheet, the scanning and scoring processes, combined with the quality control procedure, grading machine produces an accurate score.

- Use a No. 2 pencil and a soft eraser. Do not use a pen or mechanical pencil.
- Fill in the entire circle darkly and completely.
- Erase as completely as possible if you need to change an answer.

Score Range

Your test score represents a snapshot in time. If you took the test multiple times, however, that number would likely change — increase or decrease — on each test. This is why The College Board sometimes says a score range better represents your true ability; it considers multiple snapshots of your score instead of just one.

Usually, your scores fall in a range of roughly 30-40 points above or below your true ability. Colleges know this, and they receive the score ranges along with your scores to consider that single snapshot in context.

Because score ranges are the best representation of your abilities, we say that there must be a difference of at least 60 points between your score and another student's score to be able to say that one of you performed better than the other.

Percentiles

Percentiles compare your scores to those of other students who took the test. Say, for example, your Biology Test score is 500. If the national percentile for 500 is 47, then this means you did better than than 47 percent of all high school students who took this test (the most-recent scores are used).

Because different groups of students take different Subject Tests, you can't compare a Biology Test percentile with your SAT Literature Test percentile, as an example.

Average (or mean) scores are based upon the most recent scores of all students of a particular graduating class.

Chapter 2: Details about the SAT Literature Test

The SAT Literature Test gives you the opportunity to highlight your strengths in reading and interpreting literary texts from a variety of historical periods and genres. Taking the test also gives you the opportunity to showcase your interests and enhance your college application.

The College Board also notes that you do not have to get every question correct to receive the highest score (an 800) for the test. So, you do not have to know every topic or have read every work used for questions on the SAT Literature Test to do well. Here are some general facts you should know for this exam.

Knowledge and Skills Required for the SAT Literature Test

Every Subject Test looks at different things, and you need to know what particular skills are being evaluated to help you be prepared for test day. The SAT Literature test evaluates your following things:

- Knowledge of basic literary terminology, such as irony, stanza, image, tone, alliteration, and speaker (highly specialized terms are not covered).
- Understanding of the following literary concepts:
- Overall meaning, including effect and theme
- Form, including structure, genre, and organization
- Use of language, including word choice, imagery and metaphor
- Meanings and connotations of specific words in context
- Narrative voice, including tone and attitude
- Characterization in narrative and dramatic selections

Recommended Preparation

It is best to take the tests when you know you've studied the material. For the SAT Literature Test, there are some background areas that you should have experienced before registering for the exam:

- Three to four years of literary study at the college-preparatory level
- Close, critical reading in English and American literature from a variety of historical periods and genres
- Reading of complete novels and plays — not just excerpts
- Independent, critical reading of poetry, prose, and drama

Topics on the Test

There are six to eight passages with corresponding questions on the test. There are three sets of classifications that describe selections on the test. This will help you know the types of passages you'll be reading.

- American Literature, written by authors from the United States, make approximately 40-50% of the questions
- English (British) Literature, written by British authors, make approximately 40-50% of the questions
- Other Literature (sometimes called "World" Literature), written by authors from around the world, can comprise no questions or up to 10%

Timeframe of Literature Selections

Of the questions in the various countries of origin, there is then a further breakdown of the timeframe when the passages were written:

- Renaissance and 17th century are used in approximately 30% of the questions
- 18th and 19th century writing is used for approximately 30% of the test
  20th and 21st century works make the majority of the test, about 40%

Types of Literature

With so many choices and types of writing, it's important to know what kinds of passages you can expect:

- Prose (primarily fiction and essays) will be 40-50% of the passages
- Poetry (usually entire poems rather than excerpts) also 40-50% of selections
- Drama or other forms rarely are included, but comprise 10% when offered

What To Expect In This Book

You may have heard that the SAT tests are changing — we wrote this guide so you are better prepared for what you'll see in the questions! As you move forward through these next pages, you will see a variety of information. The first section is a review of English concepts that you should know, or at least with which you should be familiar. You will see they are broken down by main topic in the Table of Contents.

We have arranged this book from the more basic components for review to the more detailed chapters on literary periods and genres, and conclude with chapters that may present new information for you. All of these components — even if they seem "too simple" for a SAT review — are keys to success in the multiple choice section on the SAT Literature test. The information should all be reviewed in order for you to have a review of what is most important on your SAT Literature exam for the best grade possible.

You will also find some sample tests at the end of this book. These are designed to give you hands-on experience that simulates the actual exam you will be taking. Each question on these tests has a detailed answer as to why it is correct and why the incorrect answers are wrong. Use this information to help guide your learning. You may also practice by timing yourself as you move through the multiple choice questions to best prepare yourself for the day of the exam.

Additionally, you will also find sample tests in the back of the book to practice what you know and be comfortable with how questions are worded and the types of passage. While these are not necessarily in the same format you will see on the SAT Literature Test, they will help you to assess your knowledge of the different concepts.

Now that all of the test mechanics have been covered, let's get started!

SECTION II:

Reading Comprehension:
Skills You Need
to Succeed

Chapter 3: TECHNIQUES USED IN THE READING COMPREHENSION

THE SAT LITERATURE TEST FOCUSES ITS MULTIPLE CHOICE SECTION ON EXAMPLES OF rhetoric in different styles and eras of literature. Many people throw general language around, and you have probably even said yourself, "Is that a rhetorical question?" However, most people don't understand rhetoric — and if you make the assumption that you do, your test score on this exam will likely suffer.

So, let's review some of the essential foundations of rhetoric and the techniques used in the multiple choice portion of the exam.

What is Rhetoric?

When someone refers to rhetoric, it is a way to describe a manner of speaking or writing that is meant to generate a substantial effect on its audience. Some people say a person uses rhetoric well when they claim "she has a way with words" or perhaps state "he makes a good argument." It may also refer to the study of the way someone speaks or presents words — but for this exam, it is the way an image is created through word choice, emphasis, and the intent to influence beliefs. This counts when you are reading passages in the multiple choice section as well as the passages for your essay prompts (if you choose to take the optional essay portion).

Be cautious, as rhetoric is not just a philosophy being presented, a means of persuasion, or merely speaking well. Rather, it is the intention behind the statements and careful selection of the words used — not just what's said.

Then What are Rhetorical Techniques?

The techniques used in rhetoric are the same things students have been told for years that good essays will answer — who, what, how — as well as the way information is delivered, the actual content, and the method used to convey the message. Two main techniques, or devices, are tropes and schemes.

Tropes are figures of speech that provide an unexpected twist in the meaning of words, and is used when there is a change in words that embellishes or energizes a phrase. The four most frequently used tropes (and the basic, or most essential ones) are metaphor, metonymy, synecdoche, and irony. We define these for you below, so you have a quick reference list. Schemes are the pattern and format of words.

A trope is also sometimes called a "figure of thought" where as when the pattern changes for schemes, it may be called "figure of speech."

How is Rhetoric Created or Used?

There are different ways that people use words to get a point across, as they are trying to persuade listeners to believe in what they are saying. It includes the pace or speed of their delivery, the tone of voice of the speaker (or author) and the interaction with body language as the words are spoken. You can see that rhetoric likely does not work very well on the phone (where other distractions can pull a listener away from a speaker's delivery and there is no way to see the body language); similarly, to be understood well in writing, the author must be very accomplished indeed.

The way to achieve good writing and speaking is through a rhetorical device. It's how the speaker persuades the listener to understand and convert to a different perspective. The primary purpose is for the listener to believe in the argument, though side effects (of emotional response or reaction) are likely to occur depending on the method used by the speaker.

Rhetorical Devices Help Explain Words In Context

Devices or different "mechanisms" are used to convey ideas, and they are very important in successful rhetoric. Here is a partial list of rhetorical devices in alphabetical order, including the most common (the most likely to be used or asked in definitions on the exam).

To help you improve your score, knowing the definitions as well as being able to identify/create examples helps you on the multiple choice section. If you understand these — and don't just memorize them — you will be able to consider the provided answers faster in context with the reading selection, ruling out one if not two answers immediately, then you will be able to select the most appropriate answer from the ones remaining.

On the SAT Literature Test, as opposed to other tests, it's not just memorizing terms and being able to pick the correct definition out of a list of options. Knowing what words mean and how they are used helps you understand figurative language as well as understanding what the author means in context of the passage.

Some of these words on the list are called "sonic" because they depend on sound and they are marked by (s) to help you distinguish them. Others classified as "imagery" because they conjure visions and they are marked by (i) for ease in identification.

Review this partial list and learn what they mean as well as examples of their use in order to improve your ability to understand and answer 60 questions in 60 minutes!

| Alliteration | repetitive initial consonant sounds, usually with an overtone of humor or nonsense; she sells sea shells by the sea shore. Assonance (s) would be the same, though with vowel sounds. |
| Allusion | A reference to a person, literary work, or an event. "He's as fast as The Flash." |

Antanagoge	places a criticism and compliment together
Antonomasia	sing an epithet or nickname instead of a person's true name; "The Lionheart"
Epithet (i)	using an adjective or adjective phrase to describe, and it can be metaphorical or transferred (adjective modifying something it normally doesn't); "lazy road" and "blind mouths", respectively
Euphemism	replacing a harsh plain phrase with a less offensive one; "her elevator doesn't go to the top"
Hypocatastasis (i)	labelling far beyond metaphor or simile; "that snake"
Irony	saying something contrary to make a point, but in rhetoric, it's most often used a device of humor to reduce an option for a course of action; Abraham Lincoln said about an adversary that he "died down deeper into the sea of knowledge and come up drier than any other man he knew."
Metaphor (i)	compares two things without "as" or "like"; "she is a lion"
Metonymy	when a similar word is substituted for the actual or typical word and it can also be when you describe something or a person by describing what's around the item being depicted; like "redneck" to describe someone who lives in a rural area (in a negative way)
Onomatopoeia (s)	words that sound like what they describe; "bang"
Oxymoron	a two word paradox; "near miss"
Simile (i)	compares one object to another with "like" or "as"; "strong as the sun"
Synecdoche	when parts are used to describe a whole (can be a subvarient of metonymy; "a new set of wheels" to describe a new car

Presentation of Information and Ideas

The philosopher Cicero was very effective in persuading listeners to his point of view using various styles, called **rhetoric canons**. This SAT Literature exam will test your understanding of how authors express their points of view — or how their characters present their ideas. These styles, or categories, provide a template of the author's argument as well as a pattern for training in that style. It helps you understand themes and questions The College Board will ask.

There are other various styles, but these are the five examples for structure (the canons) that The College Board may use in the selecting the passage for multiple choice question/answer options. While you don't need to memorize the different methods, recognizing the differences may help you on the exam answer questions about the passage, such as the author's meaning or tone.

Invention	a derivative of Aristotle's theory, this is when the author finds (or "invents") something to say and bases the points on logic. It may include an "if… then" statement or go through reasoning in several paragraphs to explain cause and effect or compare different aspects to get to the author's conclusion. This is generally a brainstorming phase, where the author must consider the audience, what facts are available to use in the presentation, the best Aristotelian method to present those facts, and the time you have to deliver the argument.
Style	refreshingly, Cicero named this exactly what he intends — the style of how something is said — and it's no surprise, with the original root of Latin meaning "elocution." Style is very intentional in rhetoric and should be remembered that the style gives clues to the meaning and position of the author. Style includes grammar, consideration of audience, address of appeal, decorum (appropriateness and "situation"), and ornamental language. Style is more than pathos — it incorporates ethos as well, or persuasion effect.
Arrangement	In this process, Cicero uses all of the tools from Aristotle, beginning with an introduction (using ethos, and appeal to ethics); the next sections of facts, division, proof, refute (employing logos, or logic); the conclusion uses pathos (meaning emotion). The organization brings meaning to the passage — it helps the reader understand content.
Memory	Cicero often had to respond or interact with his audience, and thus this style was intended to continue a path of the speech but giving sensitivity to verbal or other cues) from an audience. It is a psychological component of the rhetoric in addition to the formality of a speech, especially since the most effective speeches in ancient times were totally memorized. Understanding this style may come in handy if the SAT Literature has a drama passage between speakers.

Delivery	very important, though frequently not considered as important as word choice, is how something was said; this is what Cicero termed delivery. As you may have experienced yourself, the way a teacher presents a topic can get you engaged… or not. Delivery can significantly alter the way something is interpreted, thus pathos is integral to the successful delivery. Today, people are very skeptical of someone who has a speech memorized and polished — they almost prefer a little authenticity and "humanness" in a composition (though too rough and the speaker will get criticized for that, too!) You may read character's reactions to a speech in a passage and be asked to provide insight on the SAT Literature Test.

Why Is Any Of This Important?

By identifying the various facets of rhetoric in the multiple choice section and then using the tools of successful experts in rhetoric within your essay responses (if you chose to do the essays), you will be able to achieve your highest possible score.

Strategy for Points: Techniques for Reading Comprehension

- Remember that rhetoric is an author or speaker attempting to persuade a reader or listener to his/her point of view.

- You don't need to know all of the words for rhetorical devices — some lists have more than 160 options! Remember the main de initions as multiple choice questions frequently are given with a statement and you must select the correct answer.

- It is a good idea to know the difference between sonic and imagery — it will likely come in handy during your composition section (though you will not be able to look back at the multiple choice section). Use them at the appropriate times.

- Understanding the uses of rhetoric will help in reading comprehension, to know when there is a play on words or which of the three efforts is being put forth by the author (or speaker) and why.

- The SAT Literature Test uses these rhetorical devices to ask more questions about reading comprehension and literature, but the example passages used will have various types of literature from different eras.

Chapter 4:
DECIPHERING VOCABULARY

THE ENGLISH LANGUAGE HAS A MORE EXTENSIVE VOCABULARY THAN ANY OTHER LANG-uage. English is a language of synonyms, words borrowed from other languages, and coined words — many of them introduced by the rapid expansion of technology. It is important to understand that language is in constant flux, and the English language in particular is constantly evolving with words that are created based on societal trends. Improvements in your vocabulary will increase your ability to correctly identify answers in the SAT Literature Exam.

Register (informal and formal language) is a distinction made on the basis of the occasion and the audience. In written English, a formal register would be used for scholarly works, research papers, literary criticisms, professional conference presentations, and other serious works. When the register is formal, longer sentences, more complex and exact syntax are used, as is more complex vocabulary. This is what will appear on the SAT Literature Test, with the passages and word choices being more complex as you proceed through the exam.

Slang is frowned upon, as are common expressions or colloquialisms and contractions. Informal works or occasions call for a less formal use of language. In inormal setting (such as texting or emailing riends), vocabulary is more casual; slang, colloquialisms, and contractions are used reely. Syntax is more relaxed; sentences are shorter in informal discourse. Informal written communications would include newspaper and magazine articles, popular books, and everyday conversations. You will likely only see this as a component o someone's speech as quoted in a fiction passage or drama.

When preparing for the exam, practicing different tones and incorporating vocabulary will give you to opportunity to familiarize yourself with the proper register. Given your audience (experienced professors creating the exam), you can be certain that formal language will be used throughout the exam. You will need to analyze writing using a formal tone and be able to correctly interpret meanings given the context of the selection.

- A few strategies to read unfamiliar words and to build vocabulary include:
- expand vocabulary through wide reading, listening, and discussing;
- rely on context to determine meanings of words and phrases such as figurative language, idioms, multiple meaning words, and technical vocabulary;
- apply meanings of prefixes, roots, and suffixes in order to comprehend new words;

- research word origins, including Anglo-Saxon, Latin, and Greek words;
- use reference material such as glossary, dictionary, thesaurus, and available technology to determine precise meanings and usage; and
- identify the relation of word meanings in analogies, homonyms, synonyms/antonyms, and connotation/denotation.

But don't focus on just building your vocabulary with flash cards and to have a big list of words you know. It's more important for you to understand how to figure out the words that you don't know, and you can dissect the words to help you understand the meaning if you don't know. Remember, The College Board says you can still score an 800 without answering all questions correctly! Here are tips on "investigating" words.

Root, Base, and Compound Words

Structural elements within words can be used independently to determine meaning. Often including a historical element, root words commonly stem from Latin or Greek origins. Base words are considered language in the simplest form. Compound words create meaning through the combination of two words that are able to stand alone.

Root words: A root word is a word from which another word is developed. The second word can be said to have its "root" in the first. This structural component lends itself to an illustration of a tree and its roots, which can concretize the meaning for students. Typically, root words cannot stand alone.

- Aphostrophe (apho = separate)
- Submerge (sub = under)
- Junction (junct = connect)

Base words: Unlike root words, base words are stand-alone linguistic units that cannot be deconstructed or broken down into smaller words. Prefixes and suffixes are connected to base words to create meaning.

- Retell (base = tell)
- Instructor (base = instruct)
- Sampled (base = sample)

Compound words: Compound words occur when two or more base words are connected to form a new word. The meaning of the new word is in some way connected to the meanings of the base words.

- Everything (every + thing)
- Backpack (back + pack)
- Notebook (note + book)

Prefixes and Suffixes

Prefixes are beginning units of meaning that can be added (affixed) to the beginning of a base word or root word. They are also known as bound morphemes, meaning that they cannot stand alone as words.

Prefix	Meaning	Example
Re-	To do again	Reread
Anti-	Against	Anticlimactic
Uni-	One	Unibrow
Mis-	Incorrect	Misunderstood

Suffixes are ending units of meaning that can be affixed to the end of a base word or root word. Suffixes transform the original meanings of base and root words. Like prefixes, they are also known as bound morphemes because they cannot stand alone as words.

Ending	Original Word	New Word
-s	Road	Roads
-es	Mix	Mixes
-ing	Write	Writes
-ed	Sample	Sampled

Inflectional endings: Inflectional endings are types of suffixes that impart a new meaning to the base word or root word. These endings change the gender, number, tense, or form of the base or root word. Just like other suffixes, these are bound morphemes.

Connotation and Denotation

Denotation is the literal meaning of a word, as opposed to its connotative meaning.

Connotation refers to the ripple effect surrounding the implications and associations of a given word, distinct from the denotative or literal meaning. Connotation is used when a subtle tone is preferred. It may stir up a more effective emotional response than if the author had used blunt, denotative diction. For example, "Good night, sweet prince, and flights of angels sing thee to thy rest," a line from Shakespeare's Hamlet, literally refers to death; connotatively, it renders the harsh reality of death in gentle terms such as those used in putting a child to sleep.

Informative connotations are definitions agreed upon by the society in which the learner operates. A skunk is "a black and white mammal of the weasel family with a pair of pineal glands which secrete a pungent odor." The Merriam-Webster Collegiate Dictionary adds ". . . and offensive" odor. The color, species, and glandular characteristics are informative. The interpretation of the odor as offensive is affective.

Affective connotations are the personal feelings a word arouses. A child who has no personal experience with a skunk and its odor will feel differently about the word skunk than a child who has smelled the spray or been conditioned vicariously to associate offensiveness with the animal denoted skunk. The fact that our society views a skunk as an animal to be avoided will affect the child's interpretation of the word. In fact, it is not necessary for one to have actually seen a skunk (that is, have a denotative understanding) to use the word in either connotative expression. For example, one child might call another child a skunk, connoting an unpleasant reaction (affective use) or, seeing another small black and white animal, call it a skunk based on the definition (informative use).

Figurative Devices

Figurative language allows for the writer to use words or expressions with a meaning that is different from the literal interpretation. Figures of speech add many dimensions of richness to our writing and allow many opportunities for worthwhile analysis. Skillfully used, a figure of speech will help a reader see more clearly and focus upon particulars. Listing all possible figures of speech is beyond the scope of this list.

For purposes of building vocabulary and increasing your reading comprehension, a few are sufficient. Understanding how these devices can be used will help you read the passages quickly and understand them accurately, so you can answer 60 questions in 60 minutes easily.

Parallelism: The arrangement of ideas in phrases, sentences, and paragraphs that balance one element with another of equal importance and similar wording. Here is an example from Francis Bacon's *Of Studies*:

"Reading maketh a full man, conference a ready man, and writing an exact man."

Euphemism: The substitution of an agreeable or inoffensive term for one that might offend or suggest something unpleasant. Many euphemisms are used to refer to death to avoid using the word, such as "passed away," "crossed over," or "passed."

Hyperbole: Deliberate exaggeration for dramatic or comic effect. Here is an example from Shakespeare's The Merchant of Venice:

Why, if two gods should play some heavenly match

And on the wager lay two earthly women,

And Portia one, there must be something else

Pawned with the other, for the poor rude world

Hath not her fellow.

Bathos: A ludicrous attempt to portray pathos — that is, to evoke pity, sympathy, or sorrow. It may result from inappropriately dignifying the commonplace, using elevated language to describe something trivial, or greatly exaggerating pathos.

Oxymoron: A contradiction in terms deliberately employed for effect. It is usually seen in a qualifying adjective whose meaning is contrary to that of the noun it modifies, such as "wise folly."

Irony: Expressing something other than and often opposite of the literal meaning, such as words of praise when blame is intended. In poetry, it is often used as a sophisticated or resigned awareness of contrast between what is and what ought to be and expresses a controlled pathos without sentimentality. It is a form of indirection that avoids overt praise or censure. An early example is the Greek comic character Eiron, a clever underdog who by his wit repeatedly triumphs over the boastful character Alazon.

Malapropism: A verbal blunder in which one word is replaced by another similar in sound but different in meaning. This term comes from Sheridan's Mrs. Malaprop in The Rivals (1775). Thinking of the geography of contiguous countries, she spoke of the "geometry" of "contagious countries."

Other Syntax Devices

Synonyms and antonyms: A synonym which means the same thing as another word and can substitute for it in certain contexts. Diversifying vocabulary in your writing by incorporating synonyms will improve your writing, giving you the best chance for a high score on the written sections for AP exams.

Original word	Synonyms
Smart	Intelligent, bright
Required	Necessary, mandatory
Many	Numerous

An antonym represents a meaning opposite tsat of a given word.

Original word	Antonym
Optional	Required
Before	After
Complex	Simple

Analogies

A comparison between two things, an analogy illustrates an idea by means of a more familiar idea that is similar or parallel to it. These devices are commonly found in passages (from a variety of time periods — and they can be in any of the genres presented), and studying vocabulary and literary devices will help you in breaking down meaning to find the correct answers.

As you read through options for analogies in the multiple choice sections, it's important to keep in mind that you're looking for the most logical answer. Beware of questions that have multiple options that make sense, and try to zero in on the "best" answer.

Also, it's best to go with your gut answer while determining the correct option for analogies; overthinking will lead to second guessing, and you could waste valuable test time if you continue to mentally run through the possibilities.

Most commonly, direct analogies would be laid out like this:

An apple is to fruit as _____ is to vegetable.

    A. Celery

    B. Water

    C. Organic

    D. Hydroponic

The correct answer is A. The clear answer for the above question is Celery (A). You may find analogies on exams that stem from cause/effect, part of a whole, and characteristics (similar or complete opposite).

Idioms

An **idiom** is a word or expression that cannot be translated word for word in another language, such as "I am running low on gas." By extension, writers use idioms to convey a way of speaking and writing typical of a group of people. Some idioms are passed down from one generation to the next, but not all. Because language is constantly evolving, some idioms are left behind while new phrases are used to parallel the common society.

For example, the saying "burn the midnight oil," meaning, working late into the night, has died off. This may have been a common saying around the time oil lamps were used, but technology has evolved to the point this saying would be arbitrary to our current society.

Examples:

Birthday suit

Down the drain

Show off

At the drop of a hat

Taste of your own medicine

Piece of cake

Keep an eye on it

Long shot

Play it by ear

Raining cats and dogs

An arm and a leg

Sick as a dog

Silver lining

Last straw

Get the ball rolling

Dialect

Dialect, also referred to as regionalism, includes usages that are peculiar to a particular part of the country. A good example is the second-person plural pronoun you. Because the plural is the same as the singular, speakers in various parts of the country have developed their own vocabulary solutions to be sure that they are understood when they are speaking to more than one "you."

In the South, "you-all" or "y'all" is common. In the Northeast, one often hears "youse." In some areas of the Midwest, "you'ns" can be heard. Similar to idiomatic expressions, dialect evolves to incorporate societal trends and expands from year to year.

Jargon

Jargon is a specialized vocabulary. It may be the vocabulary peculiar to a particular industry such as computers or of a field such as religion. It may also be the vocabulary of a social group. The jargon of bloggers comprises a whole vocabulary that has even developed its own dictionaries.

The speaker must be knowledgeable about and sensitive to the jargon peculiar to the particular audience. That may require some research and some vocabulary development on the speaker's part. For example, technical language is a form of jargon. It is usually specific to an industry, profession, or field of study. Sensitivity to the language familiar to the particular audience is important.

Strategy for Points: Avoiding Vocabulary Errors

- Avoid using the pronunciation of a word, which often results in improper spelling. Test day is not a great time to incorporate vocabulary words that you are not 100% confident in; therefore, if you find yourself trying to sound a word out, skip that word and try using something you're more familiar with.

- Varying vocabulary is a great way to diversify your writing. Because you will be developing a written response to portray concise, strong writing, you do not want to take away from your message by using the same words over and over again. Look back over the synonym and antonym section to refresh your memory for substituting and expanding the words used in your written responses. Switching up words, phrases, and methods of emphasizing will give you the best opportunity for a high score.

- Stick to words that you know. Now is not the time to try to add in a fancy word to make your writing seem college ready. It's best to use words that you are familiar with (in both meaning and usage) than to take a risk and end up losing points because you have used a word incorrectly.

- Use context clues to define words that are unknown. This will assist you when reading multiple choice questions, particularly definitions and analogies, as well as poetry selections that you may not be familiar with.

- Flashcards can be a great way to prepare you for unknown words. You may pick up on a root, or a common prefix or suffix that will help you in selecting correct answers on the day of the test. But don't forget to study how to decipher the meaning of words and how they are formed, as 'investigation' can help you when you are uncertain of the answer.

Chapter 5:
LITERARY PERIODS

ALL THROUGHOUT HISTORY, THE POLITICS OF EACH CULTURE ARE REFLECTED IN ITS literature. Developments in technology, philosophy, and language can be charted through familiarity with each culture's body of work. The SAT Literature Test has a focus on English language literature, specifically that of the United States and the British Isles, but an understanding of major developments in world literature is also essential. By knowing the major works, authors, and themes of each literary period, you can demonstrate a fuller understanding of the literary canon that shaped the world we live in today.

This chapter can act as a refresher to each literary period throughout the world's literature. For the SAT Literature Test, it isn't as important to do more in-depth research of specific literary works as you study for the test — that will be necessary for your AP English Literature Exam (and for writing the best essays with strong examples, but that's for another time). An understanding of the historical context of these works is also important and you can use the date they list to remind you of the time period, and that may provide clues to the right answers.

With the two main types of literature being American and British, and the main era of writing being the 20th and 21st century, by focusing efforts here you can help yourself understand modern writing and get many of these questions correct. The next block is fairly evenly split, but Renaissance and 17th century literature would be British (or perhaps a World question) as America wasn't colonized yet. 18th and 19th century literature, then, may be weighted more toward American authors since the previous 200 years would be covered by British authors.

When you know what to expect, it's easy to map out what you'll see. Here's how you can refresh yourself with important authors in the literary periods as well as the time periods in which those authors wrote.

American Literature

The earliest literature to come out of North America was produced by the various indigenous tribes that inhabited the continent before European settlers appeared. These stories were almost always oral tellings, passed down from generation to generation, dealing with themes such as the interconnectedness of nature and a reverence for family and tradition. After European colonization began, Native American stories took on somber tone as they lamented the destruction of their people and culture.

The Colonial Period of American literature, by contrast, was written down instead of told orally, and was deeply Christian and neoclassical in style. In the 1630s, the first printing presses were built by colonists in the New World, and they created writings that borrowed heavily from British literary canon. Colonists were often taught proper English grammar and spelling, and their works depicted the struggles of early colonial life, always with an emphasis on order, family, and religion. William Bradford's Mayflower Compact recounted the daily hardships of colonization during the harsh winter in Massachusetts, whereas **Anne Bradstreet** explored colonial daily life through poetry. **Captain John Smith** is sometimes considered the first author of the New World due to his journals recalling his earliest days on the new continent.

Values at this time were distinctly Puritan, emphasizing the church as the center of all daily life. Indeed, much of the writing produced at this time was intended simply to be read aloud during sermons. It wasn't until the Revolutionary Period in the mid-1700s that works of a more political nature began to appear.

In 1775, **Thomas Paine**, a philosopher and agitator, wrote a pamphlet that would go on to become the top-selling piece of American literature of all time. Common Sense was an incendiary piece of writing, detailing in clear, simple prose the need for rebellion against British rule. The pamphlet's fierce rhetoric stirred the hearts of the colonial upper class, and its concise style meant it could be read aloud in taverns and town squares so that even the illiterate could hear Paine's words. **John Adams** would later say, "Without the pen of the author of Common Sense, the sword of Washington would have been raised in vain." Common Sense epitomized this period of American literature, emphasizing freedom from Britain and the need to forge a new identity as Americans.

Among the educated elite, Enlightenment was the watchword of the day. Enlightenment thinkers criticized the religious and political dogma they had been raised with, insisting a new social order based on reason was necessary to modernize the human race. Some Enlightenment thinkers, like **Benjamin Franklin**, explored new concepts of morality outside of Puritanism – Franklin's Poor Richard's Almanack was a collection of wit and wisdom that detailed Franklin's concepts of common virtue in an entertaining style. Many of Franklin's aphorisms from this book ("A penny saved is a penny earned") survive to this day.

The Revolutionary Period also produced stirring oration – **Patrick Henry's** "Speech to the Virginia House of Burgesses" produced the timeless quotation "Give me liberty or give me death!" This directness was a necessary component of Revolutionary writing, as it needed to be accessible to even the uneducated and illiterate citizens the upper class wished to recruit.

Even the Declaration of Independence exhibits characteristics of good Revolutionary literature. Written by **Thomas Jefferson**, it offers neoclassical style, direct prose, and plenty of irresistible quotations that deliver a unified political message.

The 1800s saw the rise of the Romantic Period in American literature. Romanticism was considered very liberal and radical for its time, a reaction to the Industrial

Revolution and the increasing scientific rationalization of nature. Romanticism focused on intense emotions, such as awe, horror, love, lust, and depression, and found artistic beauty in the wonders of nature. American Romanticists also lionized their own exploits – the trials against the Indians, Manifest Destiny, and the triumphs of Revolutionary heroes like George Washington. Later critics would characterize Romanticism as naïve, but the influence of the movement on world literature was indelible.

Washington Irving was an early American Romantic, creating folk tales like "The Legend of Sleepy Hollow" and "Rip Van Winkle", which largely rejected British influence in favor of a new American consciousness. The Romantic period also saw a rise in poetry intended to be read as cozy fireside entertainment. "Fireside Poets" such as **James Russell Lowell, Oliver Wendell Holmes,** and **John Greenleaf Whittier** wrote of scenarios familiar to Americans at the time, such as the harshness and beauty of New England winters. Henry Wadsworth Longfellow wrote longer poetic epics like The Song of Hiawatha and The Courtship of Miles Standish which could thrill as well as educate.

Another prominent American Romantic author is Edgar Allan Poe. Among the first authors to make his living solely by writing, Poe's influence has been felt around the world. With short stories like "Murders in the Rue Morgue", Poe invented the genre of detective fiction, and works like "The Cask of Amontillado" pioneered in the genre of horror. His works explored topics of depression and family strife, drawing heavily upon his own struggles. He had a major influence on other genres like science fiction and mystery, and he's considered one of the all-time masters of the short story, helping to establish it as a major literary form.

Meanwhile, **Nathaniel Hawthorne** offered some of the first true criticisms of the Puritan lifestyle that had been so prominent in Colonial times. The Scarlet Letter is considered his masterwork, depicting the public shaming and ostracization of Hester Prynne, a Puritan woman accused of adultery. Though a fundamentally Romantic book, it eschews much of the wide-eyed naiveté common to the movement, focusing more on the grim realities of human nature.

This political bend in Romantic literature was pushed further by the "Transcendentalists" – **Henry David Thoreau** and **Ralph Waldo Emerson** created this subgenre of Romanticism which sought beauty in the simplicity of nature and freedom from the struggles of society. Both authors were intensely political and anti-government, this being reflected in the works Walden and the anti-authoritarian screed "On the Duty of Civil Disobedience". In Walden, Thoreau painted an attractive portrait of his time living simply in the bounty of nature. The book mixes social commentary, satire, and observations of the natural world to great effect.

But perhaps the single most prominent work of American Romantic literature is **Herman Melville's** *Moby Dick*. The timeless story pits mad Captain Ahab against the whale that took his leg, casting their struggle as a battle between man and nature, or perhaps man against the very universe itself. Melville explores a heightened dialect in the book, harkening back to the works of Shakespeare or the ancient Greeks, which rejects realism in favor of operatic emotion. Though unappreciated in its time, the story is now considered among the best novels ever produced by an American.

As the Romantic Period faded in the 1850s with the American Civil War, a new Realist Period began to take hold. Americans felt Romantic writings no longer reflected the grim realities o lie during wartime, and so began producing simpler, more grounded literature, replete with imagery and often expressing cynicism and dissatisfaction.

Walt Whitman was among the early Realist pioneers. His poetry made use of simple images, and was very prose-like. He's considered the "Father of Free Verse" or his influential style, which shirked much o the established rules o poetry or the time. **Emily Dickinson** is also sometimes considered a Realist. A reclusive woman, Dickinson's body of work is deeply introspective, focusing on intense sensory input and attention to detail which reflects her apprehension of the outside world.

But no one captured the sentiment of post-Civil War America quite like Mark Twain. The pen name of **Samuel Longhorn Clemens**, Twain is considered by many to be America's first great humorist, penning works o staggering wit that oozed nostalgia, appealing to both young readers and old. His works explore the American South during the Reconstruction period, drawing on his own childhood and adventures as a river boat worker for inspiration. His works, like The Adventures of Huckleberry Finn, also explore racial themes and are considered controversial to this day.

Other authors of note include **Stephen Crane**, whose book, *The Red Badge of Courage*, offered a realistic depiction of a soldier's life during the Civil War. He also wrote *Maggie: A Girl of the Streets*, a cynical tale of a poor woman who turns to prostitution. **Upton Sinclair's** work is similarly unromantic, with books like *The Jungle* exposing the deplorable working conditions of Chicago meat packers. Sinclair was considered a major agitator in his time. He also wrote *Oil!*, which criticized the greed of American oilmen and proved extremely controversial due to its depiction of a sexual encounter in a motel.

20th Century literature is nearly 50% of the SAT Literature test. It is very diverse due to the rise of mass media, and can be divided into the realms of fiction, poetry, and drama. Among the greatest American dramatists is **Eugene O'Neill**, who won an unprecedented four Pulitzer Prizes for Drama for his works. Deeply personal, O'Neill's works reflect his own struggles with depression, alcoholism, and family dysfunction that bordered on abuse. His masterpiece is Long Day's Journey Into Night, a semi-autobiographical tale of a family being slowly torn apart by substance abuse and their own incompatible egos. **Tennessee Williams** is another giant of American drama, penning classics like Cat On a Hot Tin Roof and A Streetcar Named Desire, which deal with issues of sexuality, gender, and mental illness. Both dramatists evoked the Realist style from decades earlier, creating terse and sometimes pessimistic deconstructions of modern American life through the lenses of volatile families and failed careers.

Of poetry, the 20th masters would be **Maya Angelou, Langston Hughes**, and **Robert Frost**. Angelou was a Civil Rights activist who wrote stunning poems and memoirs on themes of racism and gender, with the autobiographical *I Know Why the Caged Bird Sings* detailing her growth from an insecure and abused young woman into an independent firebrand. Hughes, likewise, wrote detailed accounts of the African-American experience. He was a leading figure in the Harlem Renaissance, a movement in the 1920s that gave a voice to black writers in New York City, many of whom would go on to become massively influential. Meanwhile, Frost's poems are more traditional, detailing the beauty of the natural world he experienced growing up in rural New England and the joys of simple living. His work "The Road Less Traveled" is among the most well-known and acclaimed poems of all time.

But prose fiction has always had the largest reach and biggest influence, and many 20th century American authors have penned works that continue to change the world. In 1925, **F. Scott Fitzgerald** published *The Great Gatsby*, considered by many to be perhaps the greatest American novel. The book follows wealthy socialite Jay Gatsby as viewed through the eyes of his friend and confidante Nick Carraway, as Gatsby tries in vain to leverage his vast wealth and influence towards winning back the woman of his dreams. The book is considered the ultimate satire on the American Dream, exploring the vacuity of wealth and material gains that so many Americans strive for.

Meanwhile, the works of **Ernest Hemingway** and **John Steinbeck** explored the struggles of the lower classes. Steinbeck's *The Grapes of Wrath* follows the doomed Joad family during the Great Depression as they try time and again to carve out a better future for themselves, being stopped at every turn by greedy opportunists and exploitative businessmen. Steinbeck wrote in a very colloquial dialect that made his works extremely popular, but Hemingway took it even farther, pioneering a new style involving simple words and short declarative sentences that emphasized action and image rather than introspection. He wrote philosophical tales of fate like The Old Man and the Sea and also wartime narratives like A Farewell to Arms and The Sun Also Rises, which were inspired by his own experiences in WWI.

And lastly, **William Faulkner** pioneered in the Southern Gothic genre, exploring grotesque scenarios involving poverty, mysticism, or outcast characters in the American South. Faulkner's work described the lingering effects of slavery and the erosion of traditional Southern institutions in an absurdist and experimental style. *As I Lay Dying* and *The Sound and the Fury* are considered his masterpieces.

Since the beginning, American literature has focused largely on issues of class, race, religion, and the struggle for independence, be it from oppressive institutions, economic inequality, or bigotry. Knowing this and recognizing excerpts from well-known works may help you answer questions about theme or tone for these passages. The so-called "pioneer spirit" can still be found in contemporary American iconography, the cowboys and superheroes that Americans enjoy reflect a fierce belief in the power of the individual and the need to struggle against life's unfairness. Much world literature focuses on groups, on collectives or movements, but it is not uncommon for American stories to focus on one character only and tell a more universal tale through their experiences. From the earliest pioneer tales to modern stories of the empty promises of the American Dream, the United States has proved itself a powerhouse in the world of literature.

British Literature

The myriad varieties of literature found throughout the world are too numerous to explore in any book, but for the purposes of SAT Literature study, some of the most significant literary accomplishments can be summarized. Remember, there is no substitute for in-depth research. Read reviews, summaries, criticisms, or even the works themselves to get a fuller understanding of the power these stories have held in whatever culture they may have sprung from.

The most significant direct influence on American literature comes rom our neighbors across the Atlantic in the British Isles. During the Anglo-Saxon period between the 8th and 11th centuries, the English language was still coming into its own as a unique dialect separate from Latin or German. Among the earliest works in the English language is Beowulf, an epic poem describing the exploits of its titular hero as he attempts to slay the monstrous creature, Grendel. Beowulf's author is not known, and the story likely originated as an oral telling that distorted real historical events into the realm of fairy tale.

The medieval period lasted until the 15th century and introduced many other stories that have become an essential part of British consciousness. **Thomas Malory's** *La Morte D'Arthur* is one o the first Arthurian legends, describing the exploits o King Arthur, Guinevere, Sir Lancelot, and the rest o the Knights o the Round Table which have made an indelible mark on world literature. But **Geoffrey Chaucer's** *Canterbury Tales* is the true apex of medieval British literature. The book, which follows a group of pilgrims engaged in a storytelling contest as they travel to a famous shrine, featured an unprecedented mastery of common language and a massive cast of characters from all walks of life who painted an ironic and critical view of English life. Chaucer introduced many new words and phrases into the English language with Canterbury, and his view of English life as seen through the eyes of worldly lower class laborers has proven invaluable to historians ever since.

Of course, no mention of British literature is complete without Shakespeare and his contemporaries who worked during the Renaissance Era of the 14th through 17th centuries. Considered by many to be the greatest writer in the English language, **William Shakespeare** produced thirty-nine plays and over one hundred sonnets, ranging from broad comedies to heartfelt tragedies and bloody historical tellings. Shakespeare was a master of iambic pentameter, a poetical meter with each line having five iambs or "eet", each containing a stressed and unstressed syllable. This style of verse was said to mimic the beating of the human heart, and it leant

Shakespeare's prose much lively energy that has proved attractive to actors and readers for centuries. Shakespeare was also a great wit and an incredible craftsmen of language. No other author has contributed more words to the English language than Shakespeare. His contemporaries, such as Christopher Marlowe and John Webster, also experimented wildly with new forms of vernacular storytelling, often repackaging ancient Greek tales for popular consumption.

In the 17th century, British literature largely focused on religious concerns. **John Milton**, a staunch Puritan, gave *Paradise Lost* to the world. The epic poem details the fall of the archangel Lucifer from heaven and his subsequent rebellion against God. The work proved so influential that it is sometimes mistaken for Biblical canon. **John Bunyan's** *The Pilgrim's Progress* is also staunchly religious, telling of a man's journey towards heaven after death. For many years, the book was second only to the Bible in terms of sales. **John Donne's** poetry, meanwhile, was more personal and satirical. Common turns of phrase like "for whom the bell tolls" and "no man is an island" come from his works.

18th century British literature became even more intensely political following the revival of the monarchy under Charles II. Neoclassical writing was the rule at this time, as British citizens sought to elevate and reconnect with their past. Notable authors include **Alexander Pope**, a poet who dabbled in a variety of neoclassical forms, and **Robert Burns**, a Scotsman who explored common Scottish brogue in his poems such as "To A Mouse". But **William Blake** came to be viewed as the eminent voice of this generation – a notably progressive thinker with decidedly anti-church politics, Blake's work fought for the dissolution of gender roles and more critical views towards religion. He was a friend and contemporary of Thomas Paine, and the two shared many views popular amongst Enlightenment figures at this time.

The works of Blake help usher in an era of Romanticism in British literature in the 1800s. The "First Generation" of Romantics included **William Wordsworth** and **Samuel Taylor Coleridge,** who collaborated *Lyrical Ballads,* a collection of experimental poems like "Rime of the Ancient Mariner" which epitomized the Romantic style and essayed Wordsworth's philosophical belief that men are inherently good but often become corrupted by society. The Second Generation of Romantics include **John Keats**, **Lord Byron**, and **Percy Bysshe Shelley**, who churned out sonnets, epics, and narrative poems featuring gorgeous prose and keen wit. Byron's *Don Juan* is a masterpiece of British satire, and his autobiographical *Childe Harold's Pilgrimage* is exceedingly self-deprecating. Shelley's works feature remarkable sensory detail – his poem "Ozymandias" describes a traveler who discovers a monument to some forgotten king whose grand empire has crumbled to dust. Keats' works display maturity far beyond his years, as the poet died at the tender age of 25.

The Romantic era also saw the rise o the some o the first prominent emale authors in British history, creating a feminist perspective that was often missing from literature until that point. **Jane Austen** is the most popular author from this time, and her works, such as Pride & Prejudice and Mansfield Park, provided realistic characters and cutting social commentary that have endured in popularity even to the present day. **Charlotte and Emily Bronte** were sisters and professional rivals, who wrote Jane Eyre and Wuthering Heights respectively, two grand Romantic novels focusing on duplicity and unrequited love amongst the landed gentry of England. All of these authors struggled against societal expectations of women during this time, and many critics less were than generous with their reviews, leading another prominent author of this time, **Mary Ann Evans**, to write under the alias of George Eliot to get a fairer appraisal of her work.

The rise of printed media in the 1800s created a diverse range of literature in Britain, ranging from the sharply satirical to the proudly adventurous. Great satirists like **Oscar Wilde** skewered the manners and customs of the upper class to a greater degree than ever before, earning scorn from censors and traditionalists while keeping readers enraptured. It was also a great time for young adult literature – **Robert Louis Stevenson's** *Treasure Island* wove action-packed tales of high adventure that appealed to young readers. Still other authors focused their attentions on social commentary, such as **Rudyard Kipling**, who crafted many fables and parables that taught valuable lessons in *The Jungle Book*. **Charles Dickens's** works were more critical, deconstructing Victorian values of greed and decadence, focusing his attentions on the downtrodden orphans and lower class laborers who suffered during the Industrial Revolution. He also wrote immensely popular potboilers such as *A Christmas Carol*, which helped re-popularize the Christmas holiday and has never once been out of publication since its first printing.

This experimentation and variety has continued in the 20th century, in which Britain has firmly established itself as a major force in world literature. Remember, 20th Century literature is nearly 50% of the SAT Literature test. Irish authors **James Joyce** and **Samuel Beckett** pioneered Modernist literature, which remixed and recontextualized existing dramatic forms in absurd, experimental new ways. Beckett's *Waiting for Godot* is among the most influential plays ever written, examining the tragedy and comedy of the human condition via two clownish vagabonds contemplating their own inability to accomplish anything of note. The play is a landmark work of Absurdist and Post-Modern theater, two experimental styles that pushed the limits of what audiences could expect from the stage.

Joyce's Ulysses is considered by many critics to be perhaps the greatest English language novel – it experiments and invents in nearly every literary style, using a dreamlike stream-of-consciousness narrative of a man's madcap journey through Dublin on a single day. The works of **George Orwell** are more political. A former police officer in English-occupied Burma, Orwell's works are fiercely anti-ascist, providing stark warnings about the dangers o totalitarianism. His science-fiction/dystopian novel 1984 is considered his masterpiece, telling the tale of a common man's struggle against his brutally conformist society led by the mysterious dictator, "Big Brother".

British literature has flitted between proud lionization o their own accomplishments and self-deprecating laughter at their failings. Traditions of satire and wordplay run deep in English writings, from the comedies of Shakespeare with their puns and double entendres, to the biting, controversial ironies of Oscar Wilde. Still other authors have sought to elevate institutions of British life, such as religion or the monarchy. British writings owe a strong debt to the works of the ancient Greeks, whose tragedies and philosophical writings inspired countless English-language works. The body of work produced by these small island nations continues to grow and develop, further establishing their place as a force to be reckoned with in world media.

The SAT Literature Test focuses largely on American and British writings, but a familiarity with other examples of world literature is also useful.

World Literature

The popular writings in this category come mainly in two areas — the earliest literature (before 16th century) and then in the 20th/21st century. While no one can predict with certainty that the four centuries in between will not have a sample of work, with only 60 questions being asked, it is pretty safe to say either very early or very recent writing will appear if there is a passage from world literature on your exam.

Among the most important authors from the rest of the European continent, ancient Greek philosophers such as **Sophocles, Euripedes**, and **Aeschylu**s wrote many tragedies that have formed the backbone of much of Western literature. Greek tragedies focus largely on the failings of the main character, on their pride (or "hubris") that causes them to subvert the natural order of things and earn the ire of the gods, which eventually leads to their downfall (a "catharsis" or cleansing). Most plays contain a mythic or religious component, and many end with direct intervention from the gods themselves (termed a "deus ex machina", a sudden ending where a godlike figure appears and re-establishes order). Important Greek tragedies include Oedipus Rex, Medea, and Antigone. The epics of **Homer** are also noteworthy, which include The Iliad and The Odyssey, epic poems that described the exploits of brave Greek warriors and their struggles against each other and the gods themselves. Homer is sometimes considered the first great European author, and his influence cannot be overstated.

French literature has also proven massively influential to American writers, with much of their work being deeply Romantic and socially conscious, exploring the country's long history of revolution, monarchy, and military triumph. **Victor Hugo** is considered to be perhaps the premiere French author, penning heartbreaking tragedies like *The Hunchback of Notre Dame* and *Les Miserables* that explored the suffering of outcasts and the lower class, in a similar manner to Charles Dickens across the English Channel. The works of **Alexandre Duma**s are more pulpy and readable, oten classified as swashbucklers or tales o high adventure. Dumas' works include The Three Musketeers and The Count of Monte Cristo, focusing on tales of revenge, rebellion, and complex love triangles. His works have been translated into over 100 languages and have ormed the basis or countless adaptations into film and theater.

The greatest author from the Slavic nations would have to be **Franz Kafka**. Though largely unnoticed during his lietime, Kaka is now considered one o the most important figures in 20th century literature, writing accounts o depression, anxiety, and isolation that blended the realistic and surreal. He was among the first authors to criticize bureaucratic institutions, with works like *The Trial* and *In the Penal Colony*, which eature characters being tormented by shady government figures or reasons that are never fully explained. He also delved into more fantastical subject matter with works like *The Metamorphosis*, a tale of a traveling salesman who awakens one day to find he has been transormed into a massive bug. The term "Kakaesque" is common in literary criticism today, describing situations in which a main character is being persecuted for unclear reasons and has no clear method of rectifying their terrible situation.

Russian literary greats include **Leo Tolstoy**, who described Napolean's capture of the city of Moscow in *War and Peace*, and **Fyodor Dostoyevski**, who wrote *The Brothers Karamazov,* a satirical and philosophical depiction of the dissolving relationship between three brothers and their father which eventually culminates in murder. Tolstoy also wrote *Anna Karenina*, a prime example o Realist fiction, ollowing the exploits of its titular heroin as she pursues a doomed affair with a wealthy count. The 20th century gave **Vladimir Nabokov** to the world, the controversial author of such works as *Lolita*, which describes the relationship between a literarily-minded pedophile and his stepdaughter. Nabokov's works are replete with sensory detail and are sharply ironic, offering many cutting observations about the American culture that Nabokov gradually assimilated into. **Anton Chekov** is considered Russia's prime dramatist, giving the world stories like *Uncle Vanya* and *The Cherry Orchard* which stretched the limits of actors' abilities and paved new ground for concepts like subtext and psychological realism in theater.

These works form much of the basis for the Western canon of literature. One can study these works for a lifetime and not scratch the surface of the stories available, but for the purposes of the SAT Literature Test, a functional understanding of "Western literature", a good comprehension of the primary titles or eras, and authors will suffice.

Strategy for Points: Literary Periods _____

- If nothing else, understand the following literary periods – Colonial, Revolutionary, Romantic, then Realist, and Contemporary or 20th Century. Most of these periods contain numerous sub-movements as well.

- Literary movements were affected and were affected by major events in American history. The Colonial era inspired literature that was religious and orderly, the Revolution created an era of political agitation. Romanticism harkened back to simpler times before industry and reason removed much of the wonder from life, and Realism reminded us of the grim realities of the Civil War. Literature is always a reflection of the time period that creates it.

- Familiarize yourself with the works of the major names in American literature, such as Hemingway, Faulkner, Poe, Melville, Fitzgerald, or Twain. Even if the test does not require you to analyze these authors directly, a familiarity with their work will prove useful for comparisons, and it will help you answer questions faster with the topics of these authors spreading through more works that you may see.

- It's not enough to merely state that a work belongs in a certain literary period. You must demonstrate why, often with explicit references to the text.

- Most great works of literature are considered to have pioneered in some respect, to have shirked what came before and created something innovative and new. Knowing what literary period preceded a work can help you select the right answer and be quicker in contextual analysis.

Chapter 6: Prose

Unlike Poetry (covered in the next chapter), prose does not contain metrical structure. While it follows the normal grammatical rules for the language, prose includes a more literal, natural way of speaking or presenting descriptions of characters or situations. It's straightforward and does not follow a rhyme scheme.

You will have at least one excerpt from a famous work of prose included in the multiple choice passage of your SAT LiteratureTest — and likely three or four passages. By familiarizing yourself with the difference between poetry and prose and the various styles of each, you will set yourself up for the best probability of a high score. Being familiar with the context from the time period and the author's background will be instrumental in creating strong support for your responses.

Poetry Versus Prose

Poetry follows a structure with metric or rhyme scheme, while prose does not have a standard style of writing. In addition, poetry often leads the reader to read between the lines, while prose has a much more literal approach. There is minimal critical thinking involved when it comes to reading a piece of prose — you are simply reading a story. You do not have to continuously question the author's intention or the intended meaning of the piece.

If you were to write a piece in both poetry and prose formats and put them beside one another, they would represent the same idea using extremely different formats. Take a look at the two examples below, Emily Dickinson's famous poem The Carriage, and Life by Charlotte Brontë.

Example 1: The Carriage
    Because I could not stop for Death –
    He kindly stopped for me –
    The Carriage held but just Ourselves –
    And Immortality.
    We slowly drove – He knew no haste
    And I had put away
    My labor and my leisure too,

For His Civility –

We passed the School, where Children strove

At Recess – in the Ring –

We passed the Fields of Gazing Grain –

We passed the Setting Sun –

Or rather – He passed us –

The Dews drew quivering and chill –

For only Gossamer, my Gown –

My Tippet – only Tulle –

We paused before a House that seemed

A Swelling of the Ground –

The Roof was scarcely visible –

The Cornice – in the Ground –

Since then – 'tis Centuries – and yet

Feels shorter than the Day

I first surmised the Horses' Heads

Were toward Eternity –

                -Emily Dickinson

Example 2: Life

As I look back on my life, I cannot help but think about lost opportunity and what it will be like when I leave this world. (She dies and is buried in a cemetery where she will stay for eternity.)

Life, believe, is not a dream

So dark as sages say;

Oft a little morning rain

Foretells a pleasant day.

Sometimes there are clouds of gloom,

But these are transient all;

If the shower will make the roses bloom,

O why lament its fall?

Rapidly, merrily,

Life's sunny hours flit by,

Gratefully, cheerily,

Enjoy them as they fly!

What though Death at times steps in

And calls our Best away?

What though sorrow seems to win,

O'er hope, a heavy sway?

Yet hope again elastic springs,

Unconquered, though she fell;

Still buoyant are her golden wings,

Still strong to bear us well.
Manfully, fearlessly,
The day of trial bear,
For gloriously, victoriously,
Can courage quell despair!
— Charlotte Brontë

I think it's critical to understand that even if you're having a bad day, your outlook and attitude can help you be happy. Everyone should strive to live life in the moment and enjoy the good times because time passes by faster than you'd expect.

Prose Categories

Fictional prose: The most common example of fictional prose is a novel. Using a narrative form of writing, fictional prose has been used to tell tales of adventure, erotica, and mystery. Other examples include romance and short story.

Nonfiction prose: Nonfiction prose is based on facts, but it may also include fictional elements. It is used to be informative and persuasive, yet it does not include any scientific evidence to support its claims. Examples include: journal entry, biography, and essay.

Heroic prose: Also written in the narrative form, heroic prose has a dramatic style that allows for the works to be recited or performed. The most common form of heroic prose is the legend.

Rhymed prose: The difference between prose and poetry is not always clear. Rhymed prose is written with rhymes that are not metrical and is considered to be an artistic, skilled form of writing across the world. Examples include Rayok in Russian culture, Saj' from Arabic culture, and Fu from Chinese culture.

Prose poetry: Prose poetry can be considered a combination, or fusion, of both poetry and prose. It uses extreme imagery, yet does not include the typical metrical structure or rhyme scheme found in a poem.

Types of Prose

Allegory: A story in verse or prose with characters representing virtues and vices. An allegory has two meanings: symbolic and literal. John Bunyan's The Pilgrim's Progress is the most renowned of this genre.

Epistle: A letter that was not always intended for public distribution, but due to the fame of the sender and/or recipient, becomes widely known. Paul wrote epistles that were later placed in the Bible.

Essay: Typically a relatively short prose work focusing on a topic, propounding a definite point of view and using an authoritative tone. Great essayists include Carlyle, Lamb, DeQuincy, Emerson, and Montaigne, who is credited with defining this genre.

Legend: A traditional narrative or collection of related narratives, popularly regarded as historically factual but actually a mixture of fact and fiction.

Novel: The longest form of fictional prose containing a variety of characters, settings, local color, and regionalism. Most have complex plots, expanded description, and attention to detail. Some of the great novelists include Austen, the Brontë sisters, Twain, Tolstoy, Hugo, Hardy, Dickens, Hawthorne, Forster, and Flaubert.

Romance: A highly imaginative tale set in a fantastical realm dealing with the conflicts between heroes, villains, and/or monsters. "The Knight's Tale" from Chaucer's Canterbury Tales, Sir Gawain and the Green Knight, and Keats' "The Eve of St. Agnes" are representatives.

Short story: Typically a terse narrative, with less development and background about characters; may include description, author's point of view, and tone. Poe emphasized that a successful short story should create one focused impact. Some great short story writers are Hemingway, Faulkner, Twain, Joyce, Shirley Jackson, Flannery O'Connor, de Maupassant, Saki, Edgar Allen Poe, and Pushkin.

Analyzing Prose _____

The analysis of prose, similar to the analysis of poetry, also calls for attention to structural elements so as to discern meaning, purpose, and themes. The author's intentions are gleaned through the elements he or she uses and how they are used. As you read the passages in the multiple choice section, it is important to deeply analyze all structural elements (plot, characters, setting, and point of view). This will assist you in answering the multiple choice questions wisely — and quickly.

Plot: The plot is the sequence of events (it may or may not be chronological) that the author chooses to represent the story to be told--both the underlying story and the externals of the occurrences the author relates. An author may use "flashbacks" to tell the back story (or what went before the current events begin). Often, authors begin their stories in media res, or in the middle of things, and, over time, supply the details of what has gone before to provide a clearer picture to the reader of all the relevant events.

In good novels, each part of the plot is necessary and has a purpose. For example, in Anna Karenina, a chapter is devoted to a horse race Count Vronsky participates in. This might seem like mere entertainment, but, in fact, Count Vronsky is riding his favorite mare, and, in a moment of carelessness in taking a jump, puts the whole weight of his body on the mare's back, breaking it. The horse must be shot. Vronsky loved and admired the mare, but being overcome by a desire to win, he kills the very thing he loves. Similarly, Anna descends into obsession and jealousy as their affair isolates her from society and separates her from her child, and ultimately kills herself. The chapter symbolizes the destructive effect Vronsky's love, coupled with inordinate desire, has upon what and whom he loves.

Other authors use repetitious plot lines to reveal the larger story over time. For example, in Joseph Heller's tragic-comedy Catch-22, the novel repeatedly returns to a horrific incident in an airplane while flying a combat mission. Each time the protagonist, Yossarian, recalls the incident, more detail is revealed. The reader knows from the beginning that this incident is key to why Yossarian wants to be discharged from the army, but it is not until the full details of the gruesome incidents are revealed late in the book that the reader knows why the incident has driven Yossarian almost mad. Interspersed with comedic and ironic episodes, the book's climax (the full revealing of the incident) remains powerfully with the reader, showing the absurdity, insanity, and inhumanity of war. The comic device of Catch-22, a fictitious army rule from which the title is derived, makes this point in a funny way: Catch-22 states that a soldier cannot be discharged from the army unless he is crazy; yet, if he wants to be discharged from the army, he is not crazy. This rule seems to embody the insanity, absurdity, and inhumanity of war.

Characters: Characters usually represent or embody an idea or ideal acting in the world. For example in the Harry Potter series, Harry Potter's goodness, courage and unselfishness as well as his capacity for friendship and love make him a powerful opponent to Voldemort, whose selfishness, cruelty, and isolation make him the leader of the evil forces in the epic battle of good versus evil. Memorable characters are many-sided: Harry is not only brave, strong, and true, he is vulnerable and sympathetic: orphaned as a child, bespectacled, and often misunderstood by his peers, Harry is not a stereotypical hero.

Charles Dickens's Oliver Twist is the principle of goodness, oppressed and unrecognized, unleashed in a troubled world. Oliver encounters a great deal of evil, which he refuses to cooperate with, and also a great deal of good in people who have sympathy for his plight. In contrast to the gentle, kindly, and selfless Maylies who take Oliver in, recognizing his goodness, are the evil Bill Sykes and Fagin — thieves and murderers — who are willing to sell and hurt others for their own gain. When Nancy, a thief in league with Sykes and Fagin, essentially "sells" herself to help Oliver, she represents redemption from evil through sacrifice.

Setting: The setting of a work of fiction adds a great deal to the story. Historical fiction relies firmly on an established time and place: Johnny Tremain takes place in revolutionary Boston; the story could not take place anywhere else or at any other time. Ray Bradbury's The Most Dangerous Game requires an isolated, uninhabited island for its plot. Settings are sometimes changed in a work to represent different periods of a person's life or to compare and contrast life in the city or life in the country.

Point of View: The point of view is the perspective of the person who is the focus of the work of fiction: a story told in the first person is from the point of view of the narrator. In more modern works, works told in the third person usually concentrate on the point of view of one character or else the changes in point of view are clearly delineated, as in Cold Mountain by Charles Frazier, who names each chapter after the person whose point of view is being shown. Sudden, unexplained shifts in point of view — i.e., going into the thoughts of one character after another within a short space of time — are a sign of amateurish writing.

Strategy for Points: Prose _____

- Review prose written by different authors in different eras so you understanding how the context and time period will assist you in identifying pieces in multiple choice questions.
- When reviewing a passage, pay close attention to the point of view in the work that is being used. This will help you in depicting the author's intended message.
- Analyze pieces for rhyme scheme and rhythm when trying to determine if it's poetry or prose, and familiarize yourself with the "poetry vs prose" section at the start of this chapter.
- Read carefully as the prose sections will base answers to the questions on what is literally there or what you need to infer from the passage. It will not bring outside information (other than vocabulary, for instance).
- Build your familiarity with prose pieces that are most likely to appear on the SAT exam, but remember that the most important component is answering the questions within the context of what appears in the exam itself.

Chapter 7: POETRY

POETRY IS THE USE OF WORDS TO CONVEY IMAGE AND EMOTION. POETRY IS OFTEN LESS explicit than prose, relying on implication and suggestion rather than overt statement of fact. Poetry is not always concerned with "realism", often shirking basic tenets of grammar and syntax for better artistic effect.

There are few true "answers" in poetry, as poems are often interpreted in a variety of ways, but certain conclusions can be drawn from a close reading of the text. This is an important skill for the SAT Literature Exam, which will ask questions about general poetic forms, styles, and nomenclature as well as interpretation of meaning, tone, and intent.

Poetic Terminology

Rhyme: Indicates a repeated end sound of lines or words within a poem. Rhymes usually occur at the ends of lines, though they can also be internal.

Example:

"Because I could not stop for Death / He kindly stopped for me / The Carriage held but just Ourselves / And Immortality." – Emily Dickinson, "Because I could not stop for Death".

"Me" and "Immortality" rhyme in this poem, lending a sense o finality to the last line and giving it a pleasing rhythm.

Rhyme scheme: The pattern of rhymes in each line of a poem. Rhyme schemes are usually indicated with letters. Some poets follow strict rhyme schemes, some shirk them entirely, but most employ repetitive rhyme schemes when aesthetically appropriate and then subvert them for stronger effect.

Example:

A wonderful bird is the pelican;
His beak can hold more than his belly-can.
He can hold in his beak
Enough food for a week,
Though I'm damned if I know how the hell-he-can!"
      — Dixon Lanier Merritt

This is an example of a limerick, a short, humorous poem employing a five line rhyme scheme. Limericks always follow an AABBA rhyme scheme – the first two lines rhyme, the next two shorter lines have a different rhyme, and the fifth line calls back to the original rhyme. Limerick structure is intentionally simplistic, highlighting the absurdity of the subject matter and allowing the poet to focus more on wordplay. The B rhymes of the third and fourth lines build anticipation for the final reveal on the fifth line, where the author can reveal a witty subversion.

Slant Rhyme: A slant rhyme is also known as a "near rhyme", "half rhyme" or "lazy rhyme". Slant rhymes sometimes have the same vowel sounds but different consonants, or the reverse. Slant rhymes are sometimes considered childish or uncreative, but many poets of have made use of them in order to avoid clichés, to create disharmony in a piece, or to draw unusual connections between words.

Example:

"When have I last looked on
The round green eyes and the long wavering bodies
Of the dark leopards of the moon?
All the wild witches, those most noble ladies"
    – W. B. Yeats, "Lines Written in Dejection"

"On" and "moon" are slant rhymes, as are "bodies" and "ladies". This could be said to suggest the author's discordant, dejected state of mind. Perfects in a happier poem these rhymes would be clearer and more musical. But not here.

Stanza: A group of lines, offset by punctuation or spacing, forming a metrical unit or verse in a poem.

Example:

"Do not go gentle into that good night,
Old age should burn and rave at close of day;
Rage, rage against the dying of the light.
Though wise men at their end know dark is right,
Because their words had forked no lightning they
Do not go gentle into that good night."
    – Dylan Thomas, "Do not go gentle into that good night".

Each short stanza contains three lines and ends with either "do not go gentle into that good night" or "rage, rage against the dying of the light". This ending rhyme repeats throughout the entire poem, ensuring that each stanza delivers the essential message in a profound and affecting way.

Meter: The basic rhythmic structure of a poem, the "music" of it. Some poetic forms prescribe their own metrical structure, but other poets invented or modified their own.

Example:

Shall I compare thee to a summer's day?
Thou art more lovely and more temperate
 Rough winds do shake the darling buds of May,
And summer's lease hath all too short a date."
    – William Shakespeare, "Sonnet 18".

Almost any poem could be said to have some form of meter, but Shakespeare's "iambic pentameter" is among the most famous styles. This metrical style is divided into "iambs", five of them per line, each containing a stressed and unstressed syllable. The pattern could be described as "ba-BUM, ba-BUM, ba-BUM", not unlike the beating of a heart. This metrical rhythm permeates Shakespeare's work, proving very attractive to actors who appreciate the clear, emphatic delivery.

Alliteration: the use of repeated sounds at the start of words in quick succession. Alliteration is often used to draw attention to specific words or sounds, to lend emphasis to specific aspects of the poem. It can also be used to provide an entertaining and engaging voice to a poem.

Example:

One short sleepe past, wee wake eternally,
And death shall be no more; death, thou shalt die.
    – John Donne, "Death Be Not Proud".

In this poem, the alliterative W and D sounds draw parallels between their respective words, and creating sort of a vocal punctuation for the line. A D sound begins the last line and a D sound ends it, creating a sense of urgency, of continuity and finality in the line.

Assonance: similar to alliteration, except that the repeated sounds are contained within certain words.

Example:

And miles to go before I sleep,
And miles to go before I sleep."
    – Robert Frost, "Stopping by Woods on a Snowy Evening".

The repeated O sounds create a sense of speed and urgency. The sound carries us through the line, creating contrast with the E sound in "sleep", where both the narrator and reader finally rest.

Enjambment: An enjambed line flows into the next without a break. No punctuation divides one line from the next, it simply continues.

Example:

> April is the cruellest month, breeding
> Lilacs out of the dead land, mixing
> Memory and desire, stirring
> Dull roots with spring rain."
>> – T. S. Eliot, The Waste Land.

Eliot's use of enjambment in "The Waste Land" creates a sense of suspense in the poem. The action of breeding, mixing, and stirring are lent equal or superior importance to the actual subjects these actions are done to. The enjambment also creates a slant rhyme as well, with each line ending on an "-ing" until we arrive at "rain".

Free Verse: Poetry that avoids an identifiable meter or rhyme scheme could be said to be "free". The style became more popular amongst avant-guarde, modern, and post-modern poets. It was comparatively rare in classical poetry.

Example:

> i carry your heart with me(i carry it in
> my heart)i am never without it(anywhere
> i go you go,my dear;and whatever is done
> by only me is your doing,my darling)
>> – e e cummings, "i carry your heart with me".

Cummings' style shirked literary conventions, creating poems that challenged traditional assumptions about form and aesthetic appeal through his use of strange capitalization, heavy enjambment, and free verse. Cummings' poems defy clear explanation, but some critics suggest he wrote in this manner to evoke a childish, earnest state of mind.

Metaphor: An indirect comparison between two things, denoting one object or action in place of another to suggest a comparison between them. This is distinct from a simile, which directly compares two things using words such as "like" or "as".

Example:

> "I'm a riddle in nine syllables,
> An elephant, a ponderous house,
> A melon strolling on two tendrils.
> O red fruit, ivory, fine timbers!"
>> – Sylvia Plath, "Metaphors".

Appropriately enough, Sylvia Plath's "Metaphors" contains several playful metaphors used to describe her pregnancy. Plath uses herself as a subject, comparing her pregnant state to an elephant, a melon, and in several ways to a shelter for the life growing inside her. At first the metaphors seem self-deprecating and humorous, but later in the poem, where she calls herself a "means, a stage" and mentions how she's "boarded the train there's no getting off", the metaphors take on darker connotation as they reflect her dehumanization and resigned acceptance that she's become merely an incubator for the child she now carries.

Sonnet: A poetic form that originated in Italy, consisting of fourteen lines which follow a clear alternating rhyme scheme. Conventions of sonnets have shifted through the centuries, and the form has proved popular in England, Italy, and France.

Example:

Do not stand at my grave and weep:
I am not there; I do not sleep.
I am a thousand winds that blow,
I am the diamond glints on snow,
I am the sun on ripened grain,
I am the gentle autumn rain.
When you awaken in the morning's hush
I am the swift uplifting rush
Of quiet birds in circling flight.
I am the soft starshine at night.
Do not stand at my grave and cry:
I am not there; I did not die.
    – Mary Elizabeth Frye, "Do not stand at my grave and weep".

This sonnet showcases much of what is attractive about the form to poets. The simple rhyme scheme is unpretentious and readable, and the poem's format lends itself well to repetition. The repeated "I am's" creating a soothing rhythm, sort of a lullaby quality. The subject matter is bittersweet, as with many sonnets that have explored romance, mortality, or spirituality. The first and last two lines mirror each other, suggesting change and finality. The poem's subject matter insists we not fear the end, and this is reflected in the sonnet's form.

Imagery: Any sequence of words that refers to a sensory experience can be considered imagery. Rather than merely describing the visual aspect of something, imagery often relies on taste, touch, smell, or sound to draw a fuller portrait of the subject.

Example:

Whirl up, sea —
Whirl your pointed pines,
Splash your great pines

On our rocks,
Hurl your green over us —
Cover us with your pools of fir."
  – Hilda Doolittle, "Oread".

Doolittle's poem neatly encapsulates a style known as Imagism, a short-lived movement in the early 20th century that sought to reduce poetic language to its barest components. Each line, each word in this poem reveals something new – Doolittle likens a forest to a sea (or perhaps a sea to a forest), encouraging us to imagine green trees like torrential waves, evoking sound, color, and texture to maintain this dual metaphor. The poem is unique in that there is no "correct" image. Both the sea and the forest are equally valid interpretations of this poem.

Onomatopoeia: A "sound effect", a word that imitates that actual sound it describes. "Buzz" or "hiss" both sound like the actions of buzzing or hissing.

Example:

I chatter over stony ways,
In little sharps and trebles,
bubble into eddying bays,
I babble on the pebbles."
  – Alfred, Lord Tennyson, "The Brook"

The onomatopoeia in Tennyson's "The Brook" evoke the sounds of its subject. The assonant B and T sounds suggest the burbling of a river.

Personification: When human qualities are applied to a non-human entity, such as an animal, an emotion, an object, or something more esoteric.

Example:

Let the rain kiss you
Let the rain beat upon your head with silver liquid drops
Let the rain sing you a lullaby"
  – Langston Hughes, "April Rain Song".

In this poem, Hughes suggests that the rain has the human ability to kiss and to sing. Rather than merely describing pleasant, "realistic" aspects of rain, he personifies it as a friendly, motherly figure to better describe his feelings towards rain.

Couplet: A pair of rhyming lines with the same meter. A "heroic couplet" is a couplet in iambic pentameter that is "self-contained" and not enjambed. Shakespeare often ended his sonnets with a heroic couplet, allowing the piece to build towards a climactic, self-contained final rhyme that delivered the sonnet's chief message.

Example:

Sol thro' white Curtains shot a tim'rous Ray,
And op'd those Eyes that must eclipse the Day;
Now Lapdogs give themselves the rowzing Shake,
And sleepless Lovers, just at Twelve, awake:

   – Alexander Pope, "Rape of the Lock".

Pope's "Rape of the Lock" is a satirical narrative poem written entirely in heroic couplets. The subject matter of the piece, regarding a baron's attempts to gain a lock of a woman's hair, is silly and banal. Thus, the constant use of triumphant, heroic couplets renders the whole thing a bizarre parody.

Narrative poem: Appropriately enough, a narrative poem is a poem that tells a story. It can make use of narrators, characters, plot, setting, and other literary devices, though they often contain more poetic features, such as rhyme, meter, and metaphor. An "epic poem" is a type of narrative poem that's usually lengthy and recounts heroic deeds and mythology.

Example:

By the shore of Gitche Gumee,
By the shining Big-Sea-Water,
At the doorway of his wigwam,
In the pleasant Summer morning,
Hiawatha stood and waited.

   – Henry Wadsworth Longfellow, "The Song of Hiawatha".

Longfellow's epic poem, "The Song of Hiawatha", recalls the mythologized exploits of the titular Native American hero. Hiawatha is based on a few historical persons, but as with much epic poetry, his exploits become something superhuman.

When setting out to interpret a poem and answer multiple choice questions, authorial intention is a good starting point. What message was the author intending to convey with the piece? Read it through a few times, and pause to consider words or references you don't understand. Start with the easy solution, not every poem is a labyrinth of mysterious interpretations. Consider the fact that, in an enduring poem, nothing happens by accident. Each line, each word was selected very carefully by the poet for a specific effect. This will allow you to go deeper off of your original assessment of the poem, and to infer the meaning of unclear references and unusual devices.

Example Analysis

Let's try one. The following is one of the most revered poems in the English canon, "Ozymandias" by Percy Bysshe Shelley. Read it through, and see what your initial reactions are. Try reading it out loud as well. Some poems are better understand when heard.

> I met a traveller from an antique land
> Who said: "Two vast and trunkless legs of stone
> Stand in the desert . . . Near them, on the sand,
> Half sunk, a shattered visage lies, whose frown,
> And wrinkled lip, and sneer of cold command,
> Tell that its sculptor well those passions read
> Which yet survive, stamped on these lifeless things,
> The hand that mocked them, and the heart that fed:
> And on the pedestal these words appear:
> 'My name is Ozymandias, king of kings:
> Look on my works, ye Mighty, and despair!'
> Nothing beside remains. Round the decay
> Of that colossal wreck, boundless and bare
> The lone and level sands stretch far away."

First, let's summarize the literal basics. What is the "story" of this poem? What is the "plot", the actual event being described? Our narrator is unnamed, and the story is told by him second hand, a tale he recalls from some traveler from an "antique land". The traveler describes a two pillars of stone he found in the endless desert, and next to them lay a shattered stone face, well-carved but slowly eroding away. Beside the face is a pedestal telling of some "king of kings", Ozymandias, who declares his "works" would cause even the mighty to despair. What "works" this describes is not clear to the traveler, for they seem to have crumbled to dust in the endless centuries, leaving only sand as far as the eye can see.

On a surface level, this is a simple tale of a stranger remembering a statue he found in the desert. Why is this important? Why did Shelley find this important to recount?

To answer this, we need to look past what is literally stated to find what is implied. We can infer that the pedestal once referred to some grander structure, a monument perhaps, or maybe a castle or city. The face and pillars, at the very least, likely towered above the desert sometime in the past, depicting their fearsome subject for all to see. Surely this Ozymandias must have been wealthy to erect such a large sculpture, and it is telling that he wished to be depicted with a commanding sneer. The face was carved by some sculptor who either feared or greatly revered his subject. Ozymandias fancied himself a conqueror, one who would inspire awe in all who see his monument.

But it did not last. The monument is crumbling, the desert around it is bare. Even this traveler from his "antique land" knows nothing of great Ozymandias except what he read on some plinth in the desert. Why did Ozymandias fade from memory? Who can say? Whatever great and terrible things Ozymandias accomplished, it was not enough to save him or his memory from the ravages of time.

The pedestal thus becomes sadly ironic – whereas once the mighty may have despaired upon seeing a fearsome monument that dwarfed them, today they will despair upon seeing that even the "king of kings", Ozymandias, has been forgotten for all time, his great accomplishments lost to the ages, never to be recalled. Shelley is trying to teach us that even the mightiest of conquerors can die and be forgotten. Time waits for no man.

What poetic devices are on display here? The poem is a sonnet, though not a typical one. There is a rhyme scheme but it is far less pronounced than in most sonnets – it makes frequent use of slant rhymes, such as "stone" and "frown" or "ear" and "despair", and the enjambment o the piece alters its flow, preventing "sing-song" rhymes from appearing. It contains no heroic couplet. The poem also features iambic pentameter, though it is less pronounced than in works such as Shakespeare's. Each line contains five iambs o two syllables each, with exactly one exception: line 10, "my name is Ozymandias", breaks the ten syllable pattern, offering eleven syllables instead. Perhaps this is Shelley's way of drawing attention to that line and to Ozymandias himself. Truly, Ozymandias was so great that even sonnet form could not contain him.

The poem also makes sparing using of alliteration, particularly in the last two lines with "boundless and bare" and "lone and level sands stretch". This seems to be Shelley's substitute for the heroic couplet. Rather than offering a two line rhyme to announce the poem's final thought, he builds more subtly with alliterative turns o phrase that œet the final words "ar away". This is the note he leaves us on. There is nothing in the desert but sand, lone and level, boundless and bare. This is what history remembers and this is what he œrs as his final word on the subject. It is also worth noting that the poem is told second hand – even the narrator is hearing about this from some nameless traveler from a nameless land. He's simply repeating what he heard. The great Ozymandias has been reduced to a half-remembered plaque in some forgotten desert that our raconteur thinks he remembered a stranger describe.

That's a heavy message for such a short poem, and it's Shelley's mastery of poetic forms that allow him to deliver it so forcefully. The SAT Literature Exam will likely require you to interpret a poem along a more specific guideline, such as how it might reflect the styles and forms of a specific movement of poetry. But if you can demonstrate a strong core knowledge of poetic style, you'll have little trouble answering those questions correctly.

Strategy for Points: Poetry _____

- Poetry is not about finding the "correct" answer. Many poems have multiple interpretations, while others are less obscure. Select the best answer of those offered, as sometimes more than one may appear right but there is always the right answer offered.

- You must understand the names and functions of poetic devices. But don't just memorize them, as learning the different techniques will help you answer questions faster and correctly.

- Many poems make references that are far out of the normal subjects to the modern reader. A good understanding of historical references is useful, but not essential. For instance, you need only infer that Ozymandias was a powerful ruler who faded from memory.

- Understand that nothing in a poem happens by accident. Everything, even the most oblique stream-of-consciousness phrases, is selected for a specific effect.

- It is also important to understand how poems fit into broader literary movements. Imagism, post-modernism, avant garde, classical, romantic, all offer unique takes on poetic styles and forms. Knowing generally when they were written may come in handy when answering multiple choice questions.

Chapter 8: Drama

EVEN THOUGH THE TEST HAS LESS THAN 10% OF ITS QUESTIONS USING DRAMA PASSAGES, IT IS IMPORTANT TO UNDERSTAND THE genre. If you can analyze dramatic passages, where tone and meaning can be draped in deep context, then you can work through any passage with speed and accuracy. We review the main points so that you also are prepare early for other courses and your AP English Literature exam if you take that one, too.

Drama is the primary expression of narrative in performance. Any type of creative display involving performers and an audience could be said to have its roots in drama. In Greek, the word **drama** means "action," derived from the verb form *drao*, meaning "to do" or "to act". More specifically, "drama" often refers to a composition of verse or prose, delivered to a live audience, involving characters and a conflict of some sort. Thus, things that are not true drama, such as poems, songs, or real-life situations that contain elements of conflict and high emotion are often said to be dramatic.

Drama is also a unique art-form in that is, by necessity, collaborative — an author needs only a pen and paper to write a story, but a drama requires multiple voices, such as actors, authors, and directors of some kind, to deliver the performance, as well as an audience to receive it. Drama is a fundamental understanding of storytelling that stretches back to the earliest creations in the western canon.

Ancient Greek Drama

The first Western dramatists to record their works were the Greeks, and it is from their experiments that much of our modern dramatic structures are derived. It was the understanding of Greek dramatists like Sophocles, Aeschylus, and Euripides, that drama was governed by the laws of comedy and tragedy, represented by the famous grinning and weeping masks. The Greeks saw a clear delineation between comedy and tragedy, deciding that essentially, a comedy could be defined as a drama with a happy ending whereas a tragedy would have a sad one. This terminology continued up through the Renaissance, where even the works of Shakespeare and Marlowe can be clearly separated into comedies and tragedies. **Comedies**, to the Greeks, were life-affirming romps, often containing satire, clowning, and jokes involving scatological references and innuendo.

Tragedies, on the other hand, were serious business. The "Greek Tragedy" is considered the most enduring gift of the ancient Greeks. The most famous of these is the Oedipus The King, Sophocles' magnum opus, describing the rise and fall of the mighty Oedipus, doomed by fate to slay his father and marry his mother. A common trope in **Greek tragedy** is the prophecy, delivering the will of the gods to the hero via an oracle, which the hero ignores or seeks to defy more often than not. This reveals the hero's hamartia, his fatal flaw that brings about his downfall. For Oedipus, this is hubris, a great pride that sets him above the will of the gods and thus incurs their wrath. In the play, Oedipus was a brilliant man, able to solve the Sphinx's riddle and become king of Thebes, but even his vaunted intellect could not save him from his prophecy. In a fit of blind rage, King Oedipus slays a traveler he meets on the road, later revealed to be his father, Laius. He also unwittingly took his mother, Jocasta, to bride, who bore him four children before their true relationship was uncovered. In true tragic form, the play ends with a catharsis, a cleansing act brought on by extreme emotion: Jocasta hangs herself due to shame, and Oedipus, upon finding the body, takes the pins from her dress and plunges them into his eyes.

These concepts as outlined by the Greeks would go on to define Western drama for millennia, even as drama declined in relevance over the centuries as European languages evolved and borders were drawn. Most performance in Europe up to the Middle Ages was strictly religious in nature: drama amongst the working classes amounted to little more than campfire stories and folk songs, whereas the church dabbled in live re-enactments, feeling they could be a useful imparting Biblical tales to the illiterate masses. High drama for the purposes of entertainment or art was little known. This changed in the 16th century with the rise of vernacular English, or "Middle English", and the flowering of literary giants like Christopher Marlowe, John Webster, and William Shakespeare.

British Dramatists

Considered perhaps the greatest and most influential author in the English language, **William Shakespeare** wrote 39 plays, 154 sonnets, and two long-form poems, displaying a mastery of language that has a larger influence on the Western canon of drama than any other figure. He invented or popularized roughly 1700 words that are in common use to this day (only Geoffrey Chaucer can claim to have created nearly as many), and displayed a stunning deftness with the tropes and forms common in Greek tragedy, immortalizing their styles for centuries to come.

Like the Greeks, Shakespeare divided his works into comedies and tragedies, with a few historical plays belonging to neither category. Shakespeare's tragedies exhibit many Greek forms: in the tragedy of Macbeth, for instance, the plot is set in motion by supernatural forces, though Shakespeare substitutes three meddlesome witches for an oracle. Macbeth, our protagonist, possesses the hamartia of ambition – he seeks to become king of Scotland, and is driven to commit many terrible crimes in this pursuit. In the end, this destroys him, as the honorable MacDuff avenges the deaths of his family by beheading Macbeth in single combat, thus bringing peace and order back to the realm, albeit at a terrible cost. The comedies of Shakespeare, likewise, are light-hearted romps involving romance, wordplay, physical comedy, and numerous innuendos.

Shakespeare dabbled in satire and social commentary, but his works are still fundamentally religious and pro-status quo. More often than not, order is restored through royal decree or divine intervention. Conflicts have a tendency to resolve themselves or peter out entirely, as is the case in Much Ado About Nothing, where the villainous Don John is captured by unnamed soldiers with no help from the main characters. This kind of abrupt conclusion harkens back to another term coined by the ancient Greeks: the deus ex machina, a sudden conclusion brought on by forces not previously established in the play. In Greek plays, it was not uncommon for the action to be resolved by the appearance of a literal god onstage. Zeus may appear, brandishing thunderbolts, to destroy the wicked, punish the prideful, and restore the natural order of things, before disappearing just as suddenly. Even the Greeks considered the deus ex machina to be a hallmark of lazy writing, Aristotle being one of the trope's most famous critics, but the plot device endured in the works of Shakespeare, sometimes as tongue-in-cheek parody, and other times as an earnest expression of the belief that godly order will naturally assert itself, even in bizarre or dangerous situations.

Stylistically, Shakespeare's works reveal an astounding command of the nascent English language. Though he invented many words and phrases that became common to English speakers, his dialogue was intentionally heightened and unrealistic for dramatic effect. Shakespeare wrote in blank verse, a type of poetic style involving regular metrical lines with only occasional rhymes. Each line in blank verse has the same poetic meter, consisting of equal syllables on each line. More specifically, Shakespeare's style of blank verse made use of iambic pentameter, a style innovated by Shakespeare's contemporary **Christopher Marlowe**, which uses ten syllables per line divided into five "feet" consisting of a stressed and unstressed syllable. This creates sort of a galloping or heartbeat cadence for each line, a buh-BUM buh-BUM buh-BUM rhythm that has proved attractive to actors for centuries. The limitations imposed by iambic pentameter are numerous, but Shakespeare mastered the form, creating dialogue that was heightened enough to be dramatic yet witty and ribald enough to be understood and enjoyed by the common listener.

The styles of Renaissance artists like Shakespeare and Marlowe, as well as the Greeks who inspired them, provided much inspiration for English and American dramatists in the centuries to come. The first professional theater company to perform in America, the Lewis Hallam troupe, staged Shakespeare's The Merchant of Venice in Williamsburg, Virginia in 1752. Their run in the colonies was a mild success, though theater companies struggled to find an audience in more conservative areas where Puritan communities considered theater to be, at best, a frivolous distraction and at worst, blasphemy. It was not until after the Revolutionary War, where the populace had been inspired by the fiery orations of leaders like Patrick Henry ("Give me liberty or give me death!") and the lean, aggressive prose of authors like Thomas Paine, that American drama would find its own identity.

American Dramatists

William Dunlap is considered the father of American theater. A painter, historian, and artist, Dunlap produced over sixty plays in his career, many of them being translations of German or French works displaying a broad knowledge of politics and a fierce loyalty to the newly minted American identity. His most famous works include Andre, a tragedy that dramatizes the trial of Major John Andre, a British soldier who was hanged as a spy for his support of Benedict Arnold, and The Italian Father, a comedy which borrowed heavily from the works of English dramatist **Thomas Dekker.**

In the 19th century, American theater was largely melodramatic. American authors mimicked the style of the classical greats who inspired them, creating broad and operatic pieces dealing with issues of class, race, and the American dream. Uncle Tom's Cabin was by far the most popular American play of the 1800s. Due to sparsely-enforced copyright laws and the immense popularity of **Harriet Beecher Stowe's** source novel, many "Tom shows" were performed throughout the United States and England, incorporating elements of heightened soap opera and blackface minstrelsy. Though the novel is staunchly anti-slavery, it resorts heavily to stereotypes, and theaters portrayed these with varying degrees of sensitivity and clownishness. It was not uncommon at this time for white actors to portray black characters, complete with darkened faces and exaggerated African-American dialects, and the various "Tom shows" and minstrel shows this spawned dominated the American theatrical scene for some time. These shows often validated the racist attitudes of Americans instead of challenging them, and they became symbolic of the American South's troubled history with race.

The 20th century saw a flowering of American theater. The Civil War, the Depression, and the rise of mechanization and industry left many Americans nostalgic for simpler times and confused about the modern world they lived in, with its promises of a mythical American Dream. The early quarter of the century was dominated by vaudeville revues featuring circus acts, burlesque, music, and fast-paced comedy. After WWII, American drama would finally discover its own voice in the works of **Eugene O'Neill, Tennessee Williams**, and **Arthur Miller**, each of whom would explore distinctly American themes relating to family, individuality, sexuality, and the failings of a capitalist system.

Eugene O'Neill was born into a family with deep ties to the theater. His father, **James O'Neill**, was considered one of the greatest actors of his generation, at least until he squandered his career playing in a successful production of The Count of Monte Cristo for a full six thousand performances, causing many critics to label him a sell-out. The family James built with his wife, Mary Ellen Quinlan, was rife with dysfunction, alcohol abuse, and emotional manipulation. Eugene dropped out of school at a young age and spent several years at sea, struggling with alcoholism and depression. He became a popular fixture in Greenwich village's literary scene before writing his first play, Beyond the Horizon, in 1920. The play would win the young author a Pulitzer Prize for Drama. O'Neill would earn three more of the prizes over his vaunted career, an unprecedented accomplishment for any author.

Other great works by O'Neill include Strange Interlude, Anna Christie, The Hairy Ape, and his masterpiece, Long Day's Journey Into Night, which depicts in brutal detail the emotional manipulation and substance abuse that turned his childhood into a living hell. O'Neill was among the first authors to explore American vernacular as a legitimate dialect of the theater. His works often dealt with alcoholism and masculinity, and his plays often featured characters who lived on the fringes of society, such as prostitutes, addicts, and homeless people. O'Neill was also the first author to write a major play starring an African-American in a serious role: The Emperor Jones, which was influential in the black literary community despite resorting to stereotypes to get its message across. O'Neill died in 1953 after years of declining health, with his final play, Long Day's Journey, being considered one of the greatest dramatic achievements of all time.

Like his contemporary, **Tennessee Williams** struggled with various addictions and depression throughout his life, channeling these struggles into his plays. Williams was also a closeted homosexual – this revelation, an open secret during much of Williams' career but not formally acknowledged until after his death, has caused many critics to re-evaluate Williams' works from a new perspective. The machismo and violence of many of his male characters, such as the brutish Stanley Kowalski from A Streetcar Named Desire, represents a stern commentary by Williams on the strict gender roles that had caused him to hide his sexuality for much of his life. Williams' was also very close with his sister, Rose, who was diagnosed with schizophrenia at a young age and spent much of her life in institutions. Williams used her as an inspiration for many similar characters, such as the disabled Laura in The Glass Menagerie and even in Streetcar's Blanche Dubois, who suffers a mental breakdown at the end of the play after being preyed upon by the overly masculine Stanley.

Williams other works deal with the identity of the American South and the notion of the "fading Southern belle", an upper class woman struggling with new realities after her money runs out and her looks begin to go. This trope is explored in some of Williams' best works, such as Cat on a Hot Tin Roof, Orpheus Descending, and The Glass Menagerie, in which the mother, Amanda, wishes to recapture her glamorous youth by living vicarious through Laura, whose illness prevents her from socializing.

Williams was also instrumental in advancing the careers of great talents like director Elia Kazan, and actors Kate Hepburn and Marlon Brando, the latter o whom originated the role o Stanley Kowalski, considered by many to be one o the great stage performances of all time.

Arthur Miller's output was largely concerned with the social upheaval of the 1950s. He was forced to testify in front of Senator Joseph McCarthy's House UnAmerican Activities committee to ascertain his supposed communist sympathies, and he became a controversial voice during the period known as the Red Scare. This formed the basis for his classic play, The Crucible, which explores the paranoia of the time by transplanting it back to the Salem Witch Trials. His other great works include All My Sons, a tragic play centering around a family business and WWII, and Death of a Salesman, which follows fading businessman Willy Loman as he slides into obscurity and purposelessness. Miller's works were harshly critical of the American Dream, prompting Sen. McCarthy's interest in attacking Miller's reputation. Miller's career survived the hearings, though he did out several of his contemporaries as communist sympathizers.

Modern American Drama

Remember, approximately 50% of the questions on the SAT LiteratureTest refer to passages taken from 1900 or later, so it is possible that the drama passage is selected from modern American drama. In the latter half of the 20th century, American theater became a dominant cultural force, even as the popularity of the art form was long-since eclipsed by film. The Civil Rights movement of the 1960s spurring many new plays dealing with issues of race, such as Lorraine Hansberry's A Raisin in the Sun, which followed the struggles of a black family in Chicago. The play won a Pulitzer Prize, making Hansberry the first African-American to win the award. Her works were heavily influenced by the Harlem Renaissance of the 1920s, a movement amongst black intellectuals such as Langston Hughes and Zora Neale Hurston to forge a new African-American identity in the United States through artistic and political action in the Harlem neighborhood of New York.

In recent years, American drama has proven to be experimental and uncompromising, displaying a facility with both naturalistic and heightened dialogue as well as finding strong humanity in characters rom all walks o lie. Dominant theatrical voices since the 1950s include David Mamet (Glengarry Glen Ross, Speed-The-Plow), Neil Simon (Lost in Yonkers, The Odd Couple), Henry David Hwang (M. Butterfly), and Tony Kushner (Angels in America). American drama continues to explore themes of sexuality, race, class, and gender as they affect all walks of life. The forms and styles owe a heavy debt to Renaissance artists like Shakespeare and the Greek forerunners that inspired them, but the soul is distinctly American.

Strategy for Points: Drama

- Don't get caught up on Drama for the SAT Literature Test — just review the points or names of famous plays and playwrights so if you get a test with a passage included, you won't be starting from behind.

- Theater has always been closely tied to the culture that creates it. Try to connect theatrical works to the social issues of its time. The works of Williams and O'Neill are concerned with money, important to a generation that survived the Great Depression. The works of Hansberry and Hurston deal with race, just as Civil Rights came into its own.

- Understand the styles of classical artists like Shakespeare and Marlowe. Familiarize yourself with Iambic pentameter, blank verse, and the relationship between poetic language and dialogue they created.

- Many authors drew from elements of their own life. For instance, Williams explored issues of mental illness and strict gender roles, whereas O'Neill dramatized his own struggles with alcohol and family dysfunction.

- Be prepared to analyze text directly. You must be able to identify theme and likely interpret when the play includes a "play on words" — even knowing the type of literary device chosen.

SECTION III:

Analysis Tips for Effective Reading

Chapter 9: Analysis

For the practice exams and on the actual test day, you need to employ strategic reading tactics and critical reading to get the highest score; speed alone will lower your points. Critical reading involves dissecting the text to see the structure of the information presented and classify how things are said — if you were using critical thinking, as you would when completing classwork, you would be trying to validate or would when completing classwork, you would be trying to validate or repudiate what the author says.

Here, you need to just take what the author says as true for multiple choice. You may not like it, but it's how you get more points in multiple choice!

Modes of Each Text (or Passage)

The various pieces that you are asked to read do three things — the text states something, the text describes something, and the text means something. You need to use the various components of this guide and your lessons in English to determine what an author means by looking at the words chosen, the tone used, and any bias the author may readily present.

When you break down all the words to what you need for a thorough analysis, you can handle all the reading passages and multiple choice questions very well. Analysis is what to look for in the passages for the multiple choice selections — remember, it's not about finding the deeper meaning o the literary passage. This test doesn't have time to get into all of that!

Types of Passages

It's fairly easy to spot problem solving selections, as they literally solve a problem. You could be given a passage that explains how a science project was conducted, or the techniques used to file through samples rom an archeological site. There is usually a chronological progress to these passages, and you need to pay attention to the order in which information is presented in addition to what facts or numerical descriptions apply to which steps in a process. These passages tend to lure people towards thinking they can rapidly answer the questions following the selection, but will focus on descriptive words to get you to "just pick" and not think.

Reading comprehension passages typically have several complex paragraphs, especially in the SAT Literature Test. Just by looking at the passage, without any additional investigation, you should be able to determine that it is about comprehension. This means that while the testers do not intend to trick you, they likely will try to pick something that deals with a character's state of mind or an interaction between people that has an "unknown" aspect that isn't covered in much detail so that all students taking the test are being judged on comprehension — NOT what they memorized through class work.

When given critical reasoning options, these are typically shorter passages that will use persuasive arguments to reach an unstated conclusion. Most often, one of the questions will include "what was the author trying to convey" type of selection. In critical reasoning, you need to determine what the author is trying to state or prove, and it helps to figure out what assumption is made during the passage.

Types of Questions

Regardless of the type of passage provided, there are several kinds of questions to evaluate your reading skills when under time constraints.

The first kind of question is inference — by the passage suggesting ideas or presenting information that perhaps can be linked to a "position" or a belief held by a character or author, you need to determine what the author was trying to persuade you to believe. These multiple choice questions nearly always have an absolute wrong answer — a closely-worded option to the best answer, but uses words opposite of the structure in the passage or by throwing in an "absolute" — never, always, not, et cetera. It could also have an option that is way off topic from the main idea in the passage. You can go back to the paragraph in the passage to select the right answer, but read carefully so you don't pick the absolute wrong one.

The second way they test materials presented and your knowledge of what was presented in the passage. By giving details and facts in a passage, perhaps a very descriptive passage of the organization of a room from a character's viewpoint, the test coordinators can overwhelm you with lots of different kinds of information. This frequently happens in passages with a lot of numbers or many items of the same kind in a passage, and the multiple choice answer options will give numbers that are close to each other — and again, there will be at least one option that is the opposite of what you should answer and like one that is totally contrived, not to be found anywhere in the passage at all. These do not only deal with numbers, but those are the simplest to identify as they look to see if you can decipher the content of the passage.

Also, questions may be written to test your ability to induce or reason through an assumption begun by an author. This includes cause-and-effect scenarios, where the question asks "if" and the answer options present "then" finishing options based on the facts presented in the passage. Another way to look at this is making a prediction based on what the author presented. A possible question could ask what is likely to happen next between two characters — and you need to select the best answer based on the information given in the passage. You will have to use reasoning to answer the assumption sort of questions and ensure you follow the path established by the author of the passage, not just what you think would be the correct way to solve a problem.

Similar to assumption and inference is sequential analysis — but the difference here, and it is a slight difference but one you should be able to recognize — is when a set of instructions is given, results are posted yet the question reviews a slightly different set of information following the same set of instructions. You need to be able to follow through ordered steps to get to the right answer. This could be dance steps described in Victorian era, a servant's daily chores, or any number of options in literary examples. The point is that you need to follow the instructions of the author and not select the answer that you think sounds best or makes the most sense according to what you are accustomed to doing.

There are also some seemingly simpler questions on the exam in the multiple choice section that may cause you to miss points because they seem so easy that you don't really pay attention to them. These story line questions make you slow down and answer what you actually read, not what your mind thinks you read. You will be in a hurry on the exam, but remember you really do have enough time to answer all the questions thoughtfully. When faced with story detail questions, go back and find the exact point in question — the multiple choice answers will have four options that read very similar to one another and then the one odd-ball that is not like anything you read previously.

Other Important Aspects of Analysis

Knowing the ways passages are constructed as well as how questions are written are not the only things tested on the multiple choice section in this SAT exam. The other areas of this guide have incorporated literary periods, vocabulary, details on various genres — and these will all be tested throughout the various multiple choice questions of the exam.

Strategy for Points: Analysis

- Every multiple choice question usually includes one "trap" — you can determine which kind of trap depending on the style of the question.
- You cannot answer questions in multiple choice based on your previous classwork or what you think you know — your experience can hurt you in multiple choice. You must answer passages based only on what's presented in front of you. All of the questions can be answered by the information presented.
- Story line questions are frequently thought by test-takers to be the easiest and these are questions usually missed because they rely on memory instead of taking a few extra — and well rewarded — seconds to check the story facts and select the right answer.
- Bias from an author can provoke an emotional response from you, but don't let it distract you from your goal of answering the questions accurately.
- Some instructors recommend "test taking approaches" such as read the passage's questions (not the answer options) before you actually read the

passage, so you can pre-sort the information as you read it according to the questions that will follow. This may allow you to erase or eliminate the trap answer choices because if you know the question first, you can be specific about your attention as you read the passage. However, you need to know whatever is the best work method for you — now is not the time to change your good habits just because you think your score will improve. In all likelihood, making a change close to a test will add stress and possibly even bring down your score.

Chapter 10: Understanding Long Passages

When you are writing, you are trying to convey a message to the reader and persuade them to see your point of view. When The College Board selects passages, they want to make choices that will test your ability to understand how things are organized and if you understand the author's intentions.

Understanding how literary passages are organized can help you read them more accurately and get more questions right. With The College Board using longer passages, you should not rely on your memory to get answers right — figure out the best mapping method for you to use sparingly while drawing attention to main ideas. It may be underlining parts of sentences, boxing main ideas, circling key adjectives that give hints about tone or other methods to pull out a few key pieces of information.

Mapping a Passage

As an author begins to write, he or she forms an outline (or "mind map", if that's a more comfortable term for you). For more difficult passages, you can organize your thoughts and highlight where certain things are located in the passage, should you need to go back and read sections to answer the questions. These notes help you track on paper instead of in your head (that makes it too easy for errors, and the hard copy allows you to look quickly at the answer).

When reading the selection in the test, you may ask yourself 'what questions does this raise for me?' and write the answers down in a list. Perhaps there are obvious messages conveyed in the text, and you could circle the main idea (for example), or the answer to a question the author asks. Don't forget, you can mark any large topics or themes of the book, such as gender issues, good versus evil, or the individual versus society — again, these are all favorites on exams. You can make a box, a circle, or draw a line to the margin to find something quickly as you answer questions.

Short Well-Organized Essays

The structure of any passage, regardless of length, is fairly consistent and expected by readers. Every passage will have a theme, main idea, thesis, or topic the author has chosen to present. It is a very strong possibility that one of the questions asked will have you select the theme of the passage.

The next several paragraphs the passage may compare-and-contrast organizational ideas that give "counterpoints" to show how an idea is not correct.

Lastly, you need to identify a concluding statement in the last paragraph (which does not always say the same thing as the main idea of the passage in the same way), and bring the ideas together. Often, these last lines of a passage may give strong indications about tone or conflict from the passage.

We'll review some points about each of these to help you improve your reading comprehension by using passage organization — be they character development descriptions, conversations, or event narration.

Introduction and Main Idea or "Thesis"

The traditional passages that The College Board selects begin with the main idea early in the first paragraph. Even when it's not the beginning o a book or poem (or longer poems), It is this topic idea that answers a question or expresses the writer's position, lays an argument, and presents brief highlights of how the writer plans on support for that argument or present ideas to support the theme and tone.

The most common introduction sentences (usually two at the beginning of this paragraph) begin to set the tone and topic for a reader. It doesn't always clearly and plainly state what the reader will learn, but will give you an idea of the topic so you can watch for the theme through the passage.

The College Board will select material that may not be amiliar, but you can figure out what's being said because the author has used a map for the whole work to convey messages. In the first five sentences or so, you should know what the passage discusses, identify the tone, and identify the type of passage you are reading.

Body: Persuasive Supportive-Style

In prose passages, an author may persuade a reader. He or she may support statements of a character with details about an event. There may be generalizations made by a character — either in conversation or third-person narration — about other characters or events in the scene.

In these kinds of excerpts on the SAT Literature Test, you will have key words that describe emotion. Knowing what the words themselves mean is important, but the context in which they are used will be typical questions from The College Board.

You may be asked, "What words in the above passage support the main idea that Frankenstein doesn't like boundaries?" You shouldn't expect that words about fences or lines to be there but phrases describing isolation or alienation from society would help support the main idea of the passage.

Be careful, however. If you have read the book, you don't want to use your outside knowledge of the book to make assumptions to answer the questions. Use information in the passage to select the best multiple choice answer. But, knowing the storyline and themes that you know may help you comprehend the passage faster as well as not stumble over words used in certain literary periods.

Body: Persuasive Compare-and-Contrast Style

If the author of the passage has used a Compare-And-Contrast argument then you will be able to read opposing points of view. In the SAT Literature Test, this may happen if a Drama or Prose passage is chosen, when two characters are having a conversation. When it is done property, one of the "sides" builds support the main idea of the passage.

This structure can be written with descriptions or conversations following a back-and-forth (point/counterpoint fashion) or all of one point of view then the all opposing point of view (block all of one side of the argument and then block all of the other side of the argument).

I you find that you are reading a passage comparing two people and how they performed their jobs — authors, politicians, characters or whomever — the block method is probably what is used. It may be an essay style using such phrases as "compared to Author A, Author B said…" or "unlike Author A, Author B thought it important to focus on…" to related the blocks to each other.

These types of passages will almost always ask you for facts about which person held what belief. You have to follow the discuss or narratives and know what the author presents or the ideas of a character. The author may your "favoritism" for one argument over another — but what matters is that you follow the "conversation" or narration so you can answer the questions below — and refer to the passage if needed.

Conclusion Section

The final piece o a story is always the most memorable — or good or bad. But, there will be at least one question about the argument presented by the author where you need to infer his or her opinion and where the passage is leading you as the reader.

There may be a restatement of the main idea or reinforcement of the tone of the passage. For example, in Frankenstein, we may wrap the conclusion around the main sentence or this paragraph as "The monster was a maniestation o personal flaws — shame, alienation, outrageous ego — and Shelley compelled the reader to reflect on how environment/nature shapes the development of a person and society's acceptance of things that are different."

This statement takes the reader back to what was included in the body, but in a different phrasing and actually gives the action item of how to read the story without asking a question. A strong conclusion practically begs the reader to ask himself or herself if he/she was smart enough to think of it in this light, which was just presented.

Special Notes about Organization of Supporting Information

How the information is provided in the author's passage to present the supporting ideas may vary.

For instance, sometimes there is a chronological order that needs to be followed. You cannot ice a cake beore you bake it; nor can you easily or successully discuss the

Boston Tea Party without revealing aspects of the origin or impetus for the fighting. For The College Board to determine your ability to read lengthy passages, they may provide a recipe or an instruction guide.

Used in fiction quite frequently, there may be events that indeed happened in a certain order because there is a pinnacle event — one that culminates the reader's experience in a grand climatic moment. Murder mysteries typically are written in chronological order, but give special consideration to the actual event that is the reason for the book. This type of passage may have questions asking readers to interpret tone or theme or pick out a detail to rephrase using different words.

Through historical analysis pieces, there is almost a reverse chronology to present the supporting facts of the main idea (such as the 'title' of that episode or the type of crime being investigated). Timing of events are still important, but review of data and information has to be researched in order to determine the correct order of events and answer questions accurately.

Strategy for Points: Understanding Longer Passages _____

- Longer passages take longer time. Read carefully, but making sparing marks for main ideas or change in narration tone may help when you get to the questions.
- The passages selected will likely be written in a "boring" or "safe" format — they may be longer, but this is a test of time management NOT speed reading.
- Don't let foundation (punctuation, grammar, vocabulary and syntax) mechanisms trip you up. If it is an older passage that uses less-than-familiar terms, get through the passage and know that you need to leave time to return to answer each question accurately.
- Make sure you mark any transition portions, even with a dash in the margin, so you know when speakers change or big ideas are stated. Use the method that works best for you.
- As you read each paragraph, continue asking yourself "so what" or "how does this support the main idea" to make sure you relate everything to the main point. If you find that it doesn't match what you think the main point is, perhaps you picked the wrong main point so double check the sentences again. Typically when we read in a rush, we skip words — and the SAT Literature will try to trip you up if you don't read accurately

Chapter 11: Tricky Writing

FAR TOO OFTEN, ENGLISH COURSES FOCUS ON ANALYZING CONTENT AND NOT ON REFINING it. Too many students have become obsessed with using lots of big words and rushing through assignments (including reading passages in the SAT Literature Test). The SAT Literature Test is intended to measure one's ability to understand various eras of literature in the English language.

Understanding how to review and critique work will serve you well when you are presented with a piece of literature you must analyze. Don't be afraid to mark the areas of a passage that are important or that you may not understand clearly. Existing early drats o the works o Kaka, Hemingway, and Shakespeare are nearly blacked out by jagged corrective lines and exes.

To comprehend better, some people read aloud — it slows down your eyes and actually gives your brain time to process the passage. Information entering through the ears passes through a different part of the brain than information that enters solely through the eyes. While you can't read aloud, even if you mouth the words with no sound, it may help you improve comprehension.

But sometimes, the authors leave in difficult passages or œct and to make a statement about theme, tone, or for other purpose. You may get an example of one of these in a prose passage or a poetry example for the SAT Literature Test.

Redundancy and Superfluous Detail

Redundancy is used by "literature giants" to draw attention to something in particular. It is a useful rhetorical device, and if the passage has phrases (or just words) repeated, there is a reason and you can be sure there is a question about it.

Superfluous detail is a similar issue. Authors are chronic over-explainers, eager to paint each scene with microscopic description. Embellishing descriptive words are included to make a point, either in a character's conversation or narrative, there is a reason The College Board has selected it.

Passive Voice

Passive voice plagues persuasive writing and it doesn't help to convince readers of a point very quickly. However, if it's used in a passage with conversation, know that the passive voice (just by using it) helps convey uncertainty and a non-authoritative person. The College Board would have picked the passage to ask at least one question about the character or situation in which the passive voice is used.

Similarly, if a passage is peppered with prevarications like "I believe" or "in my opinion" or "seems to be" or "it appears as if", then that is saying something about the character speaking — this wouldn't be used much outside of a conversation. It may indicate a mystery or a character making some analysis based on facts that may or may not be in the passage. Pay attention when the passive voice is used.

Excessive Punctuation

This is an issue that goes beyond incorrect grammar, but can be used as a device for emphasis or distraction — of the reader or by a character in a scene to distract other characters.

If you are reading a piece that uses a plethora of commas, it is difficult to read and you may be tempted to correct the punctuation. Don't get distracted! Know the context of use (conversation and who's speaking) to help you make inferences about the person or how hey speak.

Also, the serial comma (or Oxford comma) remains controversial amongst editors and writers, with no clear consensus on its usefulness or aesthetic appeal. Most American style guides, such as Strunk & White or The MLA Style Manual, suggest using a serial comma whenever possible. To them, "carrots, peas, and grapes" (with the serial comma before "and") is superior to "carrots, peas and grapes" (with no serial comma). Canadian or British style guides often recommend against using the serial comma, and thus confusion abounds.

Strategy for Points: Tricky Writing

- There is only one point — focus on the context and not the content in this case. It will help you manage your time wisely.

SECTION IV:

Sample Tests

Sample Test One

Section I

Multiple Choice Questions. Time: 60 minutes.

Instructions: This sample exam gives passages from known writings (fiction, poems, non-fiction/history, biographies, drama and more) over the past five hundred years. While the student taking the exam is not expected to have read the material or have familiarity with the passage prior to the exam, the test taker is expected to have the essential knowledge from schoolwork to answer the questions included herein.

At the end of the test passages and answers, there is an answer key and a "rationale" key for each question. Take the test without referencing these guides. For questions that you guess the answers or get wrong, the rationale is provided to help you see how test makers frame answers to questions or explain pieces of information with which you are unfamiliar.

As with the SAT Literature Test, the passages are taken primarily from American and British Literature—though at least one question, just as in the actual exam, is taken from another area of literature. Within the questions of the SAT Literature Test, the mixture of genre types falls typically almost 80-90% between poetry and prose and the remaining on drama. The entire test is balanced between three main eras—Renaissance/17th Century, 18th/19th Century, as well as 20th/21st Century. The test includes three main classifications — American Literature, British Literature, and World Literature. American and British Literature typically account for 80-90%, with

1-2 passages from India, Ireland, Canada, Africa, and/or the Caribbean.

The SAT Literature Test allows 60 minutes to take the exam of approximately 60 ques-tions. Time yourself during the exam, but as you practice, focus more attention on accurately answering questions as the total number of correct answers impacts your score, not how many you skip or get wrong. If you skip any questions, make sure that you also skip that line on the answer sheet—or you may spend a lot of time erasing and redoing your answer key.

These passages do not actually appear on the SAT Literature exam, but are meant to show how the exam is written and the various range of questions, answers, and key knowledge points required in order to pass the SAT Literature exam. Read each ques-tion carefully and provide the best answer choice.

Questions 1-8. Read the following passage carefully before you decide on your answers to the questions.

On the domestic front, life was not easy. England was not a wealthy country and its people endured relatively poor living standards. The landed classes – many of them enriched by the confiscated wealth of former monasteries – were determined in the interests of profile to convert their arable land into pasture for sheep, so as to produce the wool that supported the country's chief economic asset, the woolen cloth trade. But the enclosing of the land only added to the misery of the poor, many of whom, evicted and displaced, left their decaying villages and gravitated to the towns where they joined the growing army of beggars and vagabonds that would become such a feature of Elizabethan life. Once, the religious houses would have dispensed charity to the destitute, but Henry VIII had dissolved them all in the 1530s, and many former monks and nuns were now themselves beggars. Nor did the civic authorities help: they passed laws in an attempt to ban the poor from towns and cities, but to little avail. It was a common sight to see men and women lying in the dusty streets, often dying in the dirt like dogs or beasts, without human compassion being shown to them. 'Certainly, wrote a Spanish observer in 1558, 'the state of England lay now most afflicted.' And although people looked to the new Queen Elizabeth to put matters right, there were so many who doubted if she could overcome the seemingly insurmountable problems she faced, or even remain queen long enough to begin tacking them. Some, both at home and abroad, were the opinion that her title to the throne rested on very precarious foundations. Many regarded the daughter of Henry VIII and Anne Boleyn as a bastard from the time of her birth on 7 September 1533, although, ignoring such slurs on the validity of his second marriage, Henry had declared Elizabeth his heir.

1. **Why was land confiscated from the poor?**

   (A) The town wanted to build a new monastery.

   (B) To create pastures for sheep, ultimately increasing the export of wool.

   (C) The town wanted to create housing for monks and nuns.

   (D) Queen Elizabeth wanted to expand her property.

   (E) The poor did not pay their taxes.

2. **A vagabond is a _____.**

   (A) Wanderer

   (B) Prisoner

   (C) Poor person

   (D) Rich person

   (E) Fighter

3. **Why didn't the poor have shelter with the churches?**

   (A) They were already filled with beggars.

   (B) Religious houses have never offered shelter to the poor.

   (C) They were also being used to raise sheep.

   (D) Henry VIII had dissolved them all in the 1530s.

   (E) Queen Elizabeth dissolved them all in the 1530s.

4. **How were civic authorities unsuccessful?**

(A) Poor people remained within city limits

(B) Public service funds ran out

(C) Public housing plans extended deadlines

(D) Churches did not open their doors to the poor

(E) The poor overthrew them to gain their land back

5. **What is a synonym for precarious?**

(A) Strong

(B) Careful

(C) Risky

(D) Determined

(E) Illegitimate

6. **What is the author's view towards Queen Elizabeth?**

(A) Doubtful

(B) Vengeful

(C) Resentful

(D) Supportive

(E). Confident

7. **How is the English culture portrayed in this passage?**

(A) Religious

(B) Elitist

(C) Racist

(D) Diverse

(E) Spiritual

8. **What is Elizabeth's relationship to Henry?**

(A) Wife

(B) Cousin

(C) Lover

(D) Daughter

(E) Niece

Questions 9-13. Read the following passage carefully before you decide on your answers to the questions.

William Wordsworth—I Wandered Lonely As A Cloud

I wandered lonely as a cloud
That floats on high o'er vales and hills,
When all at once I saw a crowd,
A host, of golden daffodils;
Beside the lake, beneath the trees,
Fluttering and dancing in the breeze

Continuous as the stars that shine
And twinkle on the milky way,
They stretched in never-ending line
Along the margin of a bay:
Ten thousand saw I at a glance,
Tossing their heads in sprightly dance

The waves beside them danced; but they
Out-did the sparkling waves in glee:
A poet could not but be gay,
In such a jocund company:
I gazed—and gazed—but little thought
What wealth the show to me had brought:

For oft, when on my couch I lie
In vacant or in pensive mood,
They flash upon that inward eye
Which is the bliss of solitude;
And then my heart with pleasure fills,
And dances with the daffodils.

9. **The permanence of stars as compared with flowers emphasizes**

(A) the impermanence of life.

(B) the permanence of memory for the poet.

(C) the earlier comparison of the sky to the lake.

(D) that stars are frozen above and daffodils dance below.

(E) the similarity of the inward eye with the fleeting bliss of solitude

10. **The scheme of the poem is**

   (A) ballad.

   (B) Scottish stanza.

   (C) Spenserian stanza.

   (D) quatrain-couplet.

   (E) sonnet.

11. **What is a literary device used in the last two lines of the first two stanzas?**

   (A) Simile

   (B) Metaphor.

   (C) Personification.

   (D) Allegory.

   (E) Paradox.

12. **As used in this poem, the best choice for a synonym of jocund means**

   (A) pleasant.

   (B) vapid.

   (C) lonely.

   (D) jovial.

   (E) sad.

13. **What literary device is used in Line 9, "They stretched in never-ending line."**

   (A) hyperbole.

   (B) onomatopoeia.

   (C) epithet.

   (D) irony.

   (E) anecdote.

Questions 14-19. Read the following selection and answer the questions below, selecting the best choice of the options presented.

My Bondage and My Freedom

Disappearing from the kind reader, in a flying cloud or balloon (pardon the figure), driven by the wind, and knowing not where I should land--whether in slavery or in freedom--it is proper that I should remove, at once, all anxiety, by frankly making known where I alighted. The flight was a bold and perilous one; but here I am, in the great city of New York, safe and sound, without loss of blood or bone. In less than a week after leaving Baltimore, I was walking amid the hurrying throng, and gazing upon the dazzling wonders of Broadway. The dreams of my childhood and the purposes of my manhood were now fulfilled. A free state around me, and a free earth under my feet! What a moment was this to me! A whole year was pressed into a single day. A new world burst upon my agitated vision. I have often been asked, by kind friends to whom I have told my story, how I felt when first I found myself beyond the limits of slavery; and I must say here, as I have often said to them, there is scarcely anything about which I could not give a more satisfactory answer. It was a moment of joyous excitement, which no words can describe. In a letter to a friend, written soon after reaching New York. I said I felt as one might be supposed to feel, on escaping from a den of hungry lions.

14. **When the author writes "escaping from a den of hungry lions," what type of literary device is he using?**

    (A) Simile.

    (B) Personification.

    (C) Metaphor.

    (D) Hyperbole.

    (E) Irony.

15. **What is the author's theme in this passage?**

    (A) Anger at being a slave.

    (B) Numb, as one might be supposed to feel.

    (C) Confusion at the new things he is seeing.

    (D) Self-discovery after flight from slavery.

    (E) None of these describe his tone.

16. In context of the passage, the opening phrase "to the kind reader" used by the author sets what kind of opening tone?

    (A) Friendly

    (B) Condescending

    (C) Boisterous

    (D) Prideful

    (E) Meek

17. The author of this book relays his own experiences fighting slavery. Why does he fight against it. What is the theme of the book?

    (A) Slavery is unnatural.

    (B) Slavery wasn't needed as an economic engine.

    (C) Slavery was morally acceptable.

    (D) Slavery enabled him to see the light of day.

    (E) Slavery made time move too quickly.

18. What does the author figuratively mean by "hurrying throng"?

    (A) The people that bump into him walking past him.

    (B) His blurred vision from bright sunlight.

    (C) The New York tradesmen rushing to their jobs.

    (D) The busy middle class.

    (E) The bustling crowd of free people.

19. What is the author's tone in this passage?

    (A) Cautious

    (B) Enlightened

    (C) Exuberant

    (D) Nervous

    (E) None of these apply

Questions 20-25. Read the following selection and answer the questions below, selecting the best choice of the options presented.

A Bird Came Down the Walk
                —Emily Dickinson

A bird came down the walk:
He did not know I saw;
He bit an angle-worm in halves
And ate the fellow, raw.
And then, he drank a dew
From a convenient grass,
And then hopped sidewise to the wall
To let a beetle pass.

He glanced with rapid eyes
That hurried all abroad,—
They looked like frightened beads, I thought;
He stirred his velvet head

Like one in danger; cautious,
I offered him a crumb,
And he unrolled his feathers
And rowed him softer home

Than oars divide the ocean,
Too silver for a seam,
Or butterflies, off banks of noon,
Leap, plashless, as they swim.

20. **What type of literary device is used in the author's phrase, "drank a dew"?**

    (A) Allusion.

    (B) Foreshadowing.

    (C) Juxtaposition.

    (D) Satire.

    (E) Alliteration.

21. **The author describes action beginning in line 15 of the bird's flight. What type of literary device is used?**

   (A) Simile.

   (B) Metaphor.

   (C) Irony.

   (D) Satire.

   (E) None of these are correct.

22. **What literary device is used when the bird's eyes are compared to frightened beads?**

   (A) Reverse Personification.

   (B) Metaphor.

   (C) Simile.

   (D) Allegory.

   (E) Paradox.

23. **What does the dash at the end of line 12 represent?**

   (A) A change in focus from the bird to the water.

   (B) An abrupt change for the bird.

   (C) An emotional shift from fear to fascination.

   (D) It only shows the middle of the poem.

   (E) None of these accurately describe the meaning of the dash.

24. **What is the author's tone in this poem?**

   (A) She takes the perspective of the bird.

   (B) The author's tone is harsh toward potential prey.

   (C) The tone is factual, describing the actions of a bird.

   (D) Ornithology fascinated the author and she uses flowery language to describe it.

   (E) The author's tone is gentle and respectful demeanor regarding nature.

25. **What is a potential meaning of the allegory used by the author?**

   (A) It could reveal the author's perceptions of God.

   (B) The allegory could be looking at the author's view of marriage.

   (C) The author could reveal the hierarchy between man and beast.

   (D) Descriptions of the forces of nature could parallel emotions.

   (E) There is no allegory used as a literary device in this poem.

Questions 26-32. Read the following selection and answer the questions below, selecting the best choice of the options presented.

A man is born into this world with only a tiny spark of goodness in him. The spark is God, it is the soul; the rest is ugliness and evil, a shell. The spark must be guarded like a treasure, it must be nurtured, it must be fanned into flame. It must learn to seek out other sparks, it must dominate the shell. Anything can be a shell, Reuven. Anything. Indifference, laziness, brutality, and genius. Yes, even a great mind can be a shell and choke the spark.

"Reuven, the Master of the Universe blessed me with a brilliant son. And he cursed me with all the problems of raising him. Ah, what it is to have a Daniel, whose mind is like a pearl, like a sun. Reuben, when my Daniel was four years old, I saw him reading a story from a book. And I was frightened. He did not read the story, he swallowed it, as one swallows food or water. There was no soul in my four-year-old Daniel, there was only his mind. He was a mind in a body without a soul. It was a tory in a Yiddish book about a poor Jew and his struggles to get to Eretz Yisroel before he died. Ah, how that man suffered! And my Daniel enjoyed the story, he enjoyed the last terrible page, because when he finished it he realized for the first time what a memory he had. He looked at me proudly and told me back the story from memory, and I cried inside my heart. I went away and cried to the Master of the Universe, 'What have you done to me? A mind like this I need for a son? A heart I need for a son, a soul I need for a son, compassion I want for my son, righteousness, mercy, strength to suffer and carry pain, that I want from my son, not a mind without a soul!'"

Reb Saunders paused and took a deep, trembling breath. I tried to swallow; my mouth was sand-dry. Danny sat with his right hand over his eyes, his glasses pushed up on his forehead.) He was crying silently, his shoulders quivering. Reb Saunders did not look at him.

26. According to the passage, what was the goal behind raising Danny in silence?

(A) For the speaker to be cruel.

(B) The speaker thought he was being noble.

(C) The narrator believed by being harsh, he was right.

(D) The speaker wanted other people to think they were normal.

(E) He wanted to develop Danny's compassion and soul.

27. What is the author doing when using italics?

(A) The author is using short words to mean big things.

(B) The author signifies the important things in a person's life.

(C) The speaker is listing the attributes of his son.

(D) The speaker shows what his son understood in the stories.

(E) None of these things apply to those words.

28. When Reb's mouth went "sand-dry," this is an example of:

(A) a parody.

(B) an allusion.

(C) a synecdoche.

(D) a metaphor.

(E) an oxymoron.

29. Throughout the book, Reuven had been the peripheral narrator. Who is the narrator in this section?

(A) It is still Reuven.

(B) It is Reb.

(C) It is Danny.

(D) It is a third person narrator.

(E) It is Eretz Yisroel.

30. The passage of this book is written as:

(A) the denouement.

(B) the complication.

(C) the climax.

(D) the suspense.

(E) the introduction.

31. What is the theme of this passage?

(A) Recounting the last moments of an old man's life.

(B) The discussion of coming marriage of Danny.

(C) The symbolism of reading as an alternative for family interactions.

(D) The adoption of Reuven by Reb.

(E) Another example of Jews suffering to get further in life.

32. What is the writing style used by this author in this passage?

(A) Expository

(B) Didactic

(C) Persuasive

(D) Descriptive

(E) Theatrical

Questions 33-40. Read the following selection and answer the questions below, selecting the best choice of the options presented.

Okonkwo and his fellow prisoners were set free as soon as the fine was paid. The District Commissioner spoke to them again about the great queen, and about peace and good government. But the men did not listen. They just sat and looked at him and at his interpreter. In the end they were given back their bags and sheathed machetes and told to go home. They rose and left the courthouse. They neither spoke to anyone nor among themselves.

The courthouse, like the church, was but a little way outside the village. The footpath that linked them was a very busy one because it also led to the stream, beyond the court. It was open and sandy. Footpaths were open and sandy in the dry season. But when the rains came the bush grew thick on either side and closed in on the path. It was now dry season.

As they made their way to the village the six men met women and children going to the stream with their waterpots. But them wore such heavy and fearsome looks to them, but edged out of the way to let them pass. In the village little groups of men joined them until they became a sizable company. They walked silently. As each o the six men got to his compound, he turned in, taking some of the crowd with him. The village was air in a silent, suppressed way.

Ezinma had prepared some food for her father as soon as news spread that the six men would be released. She took it to him in his obi. He ate absent-mindedly. He had no appetite, he only ate to please her. His male relations and friends had gathered in his obi, and Obierika was urging him to eat. Nobody else spoke, but they noticed the log stripes on Okonkwo's back where the warder's whip had cut into his flesh.

33. **Who is the protagonist of this story?**

    (A) Obierika

    (B) Ezinma

    (C) Okonkwo

    (D) The District Commissioner

    (E) Okonkwo's wife

34. **What is the name of this book?**

    (A) Obi

    (B) Things Fall Apart

    (C) Let the Circle Be Unbroken

    (D) Ashes and Dust

    (E) The Rainy Season

35. **What category of literature does this book represent?**

   (A) Romantic.

   (B) Victorian.

   (C) Modernism.

   (D) Transcendentalism.

   (E) Post Colonial.

36. **The main character of the book appears to have what occur throughout the book?**

   (A) He is a champion of his village.

   (B) He shows that he is good provider for his family.

   (C) He represents the disintegration of his society against the change.

   (D) The village doesn't support him.

   (E) The courthouse is targeting him to get rid of the village.

37. **The narrative structure of this passage is:**

   (A) simple narrative.

   (B) cause and effect.

   (C) chronological.

   (D) inductive.

   (E) deductive.

38. **The literary style of the book is:**

   (A) comedy.

   (B) tragedy.

   (C) drama.

   (D) exploration.

   (E) quest.

39. **How is this passage narrated?**

   (A) First person.

   (B) Second person.

   (C) Third person.

   (D) Omniscient observer.

   (E) None of these.

40. What is the main idea of this passage?

(A) The village members continue to carry out the traditions of their ancestors.

(B) There is a drought affecting crops and village life.

(C) The interpreter was sharing with them a new way of life.

(D) The government and church were coming together for the people.

(E) People are resistant to change, and the village and protagonist illustrate it.

Questions 41-47. Read the following selection and answer the questions below, selecting the best choice of the options presented.

Mornings, he likes to sit in his new leather chair by his new living room window, looking out across the rooftops and chimney pots, the clotheslines and telegraph lines and office towers. It's the first time Manhattan, from high above, hasn't crushed him with desire. On the contrary the view makes him feel smug. All those people down there, striving, hustling, pushing, shoving, busting to get what Willie's already got. In spades. He lights a cigarette, blows a jet of smoke against the window. Suckers.

41. The subject in this passage is:

(A) a character, and seems to be the lead of the story.

(B) a supporting character.

(C) has an attitude of a criminal.

(D) is female.

(E) has been poor his whole life.

42. What kind of description is the author providing of this scene?

(A) Backstory of the character.

(B) A characterization of what the character is like.

(C) A narrative in the first person.

(D) The unreliable narrative about a character.

(E) The author is using a persuasive argument.

43. What types of words are "striving, hustling, pushing, shoving, bustling"?

(A) Adjectives

(B) Adverbs

(C) Nouns

(D) Gerunds

(E) Verbs

44. **If you had to explain the phrase "crushed him" in the paragraph above and context of the paragraph, what would be the best appropriate explanation?**

(A) The city sustained him with all the opportunity available.

(B) The city called to him to be part of its life.

(C) The city complimented him for everything he has achieved.

(D) The city had energized him to get what he felt he deserved.

(E) The city smothered him with all its offerings.

45. **Replacing the word "smug" with an antonym in context would have which of the following used?**

(A) Sleepy

(B) Prideful

(C) Humble

(D) Self-satisfied

(E) Elated

46. **When the author uses the phrase, "In spades," which of the following is best representing what he is referencing?**

(A) The large apartment in which Willie is living.

(B) The personal satisfaction of accumulated wealth.

(C) Modern comforts in his home.

(D) The loved ones surrounding him.

(E) None of these is representative.

47. **By using the introductory word "Mornings," the author achieves what?**

(A) An optimistic tone for the passage.

(B) A simple description of time of day, or chronology for the passage.

(C) It's the start of the book, so he sets the passage at "day one."

(D) A and C

(E) None of these.

Questions 48-52. Read the following selection and answer the questions below, selecting the best choice of the options presented.

"Mother," said little Pearl, "the sunshine does not love you. It runs away and hides itself, because it is afraid of something on your bosom. . . . It will not flee from me, for I wear nothing on my bosom yet!"

"Nor ever will, my child, I hope," said Hester.

"And why not, mother?" asked Pearl, stopping short. . . . "Will it not come of its own accord, when I am a woman grown?"

—*The Scarlett Letter*

48. **What kind of description is the author providing of this scene?**

   (A) A symbolic, metaphorical description that provides a backstory of the main character

   (B) A characterization of what the character is like

   (C) A narrative, with the end of the selection giving thoughts in the first person

   (D) The unreliable narrative about a character

   (E) The author is using a persuasive argument

49. **What does the "sunshine" represent?**

   (A) Light

   (B) Hope

   (C) Purity

   (D) Heaven

   (E) Good luck

50. **The author portrays the attitude of the character Pearl as:**

   (A) condescending

   (B) loving

   (C) disrespectful

   (D) innocent

   (E) resentful

51. "Will it not come of its own accord, when I am a woman grown?"
What is the author implying that Pearl is asking for?

(A) If the scarlet letter will be handed down to her when she becomes a woman.

(B) If she will become pregnant when she becomes mature enough.

(C) Whether or not she will get divorced when she marries.

(D) If she will find true love when she grows up.

(E) If her mother will share this symbol with her when she is old enough.

52. Which of the following best describes the author's message?

(A) Little girls are oblivious to the world around them.

(B) Daughters always question things that their mothers do.

(C) Growing up means losing your innocence.

(D) The world will know when you have sinned.

(E) None of the above.

Questions 53-60. Read the following selection and answer the questions below, selecting the best choice of the options presented.

In a village of La Mancha, the name of which I have no desire to call to mind, there lived not long since one of those gentlemen that keep a lance in the lance-rack, an old buckler, a lean hack, and a greyhound for coursing. An olla of rather more beef than mutton, a salad on most nights, scraps on Saturdays, lentils on Fridays, and a pigeon or so extra on Sundays, made away with three-quarters of his incom(E) The rest of it went in a doublet of fine cloth and velvet breeches and shoes to match for holidays, while on week-days he made a brave figure in his best homespun. He had in his house a housekeeper past forty, a niece under twenty, and a lad for the field and market-place, who used to saddle the hack as well as handle the bill-hook. The age of this gentleman of ours was bordering on fifty; he was of a hardy habit, spare, gaunt-featured, a very early riser and a great sportsman. They will have it his surname was Quixada or Quesada (for here there is some difference of opinion among the authors who write on the subject), although from reasonable conjectures it seems plain that he was called Quexana. This, however, is of but little importance to our tale; it will be enough not to stray a hair's breadth from the truth in the telling of it.

You must know, then, that the above-named gentleman whenever he was at leisure (which was mostly all the year round) gave himself up to reading books of chivalry with such ardour and avidity that he almost entirely neglected the pursuit of his field-sports, and even the management of his property; and to such a pitch did his eagerness and infatuation go that he sold many an acre of tillageland to buy books of chivalry to read, and brought home as many of them as he could get. But of all there were none he liked so well as those of the famous Feliciano de Silva's composition, for their lucidity of style and complicated conceits were as pearls in his sight, particularly when in his reading he came upon courtships and cartels, where he often found passages like "the reason of the unreason with which my reason is afflicted so weakens my reason that with reason I murmur at your beauty;" or again, "the high heavens, that of your divinity divinely fortify you with the stars, render you deserving of the desert your greatness deserves." Over conceits of this sort the poor gentleman lost his wits, and used to lie awake striving to understand them and worm the meaning out of them; what Aristotle himself could not have made out or extracted had he come to life again for that special purpose. He was not at all easy about the wounds which Don Belianis gave and took, because it seemed to him that, great as were the surgeons who had cured him, he must have had his face and body covered all over with seams and scars. He commended, however, the author's way of ending his book with the promise of that interminable adventure, and many a time was he tempted to take up his pen and finish it properly as is there proposed, which no doubt he would have done, and made a successful piece of work of it too, had not greater and more absorbing thoughts prevented him.

53. **The author's tone in this piece can best be described as...**

   (A) Heroic

   (B) Comedic

   (C) Florid

   (D) Epic

   (E) Mysterious

54. **The line "were as pearls to his site" is an example of a...**

   (A) Metaphor

   (B) Analogy

   (C) Simile

   (D) Allegory

   (E) Conceit

55. **Our main character's attitude towards reading can best be described as...**

   (A) Lackadaisical

   (B) Unusual

   (C) Illiterate

   (D) Obsessive

   (E) Joyous

56. The passage "the high heavens, that of your divinity divinely fortify you with the stars, render you deserving of the desert your greatness deserves" contains several examples what poetic device?

(A) Alliteration

(B) Onomatopoeia

(C) Diction

(D) Resonance

(E) Enjambment

57. According to the text, who is Count Belianis?

(A) A historical champion

(B) A fictional character

(C) A competing nobleman

(D) A romantic rival

(E) A dead family member

58. The passage "it will be enough not to stray a hair's breadth from the truth in the telling of it" characterizes the previous passage as...

(A) Essential

(B) Metaphorical

(C) Unimportant

(D) Esoteric

(E) Bland

59. What are the two defining traits of the main character described above?

(A) Laziness and obsessiveness

(B) Ignorance and piousness

(C) Diligence and valor

(D) Prideful and vain

(E) Curious and kindhearted

60. **The final sentence of this excerpt is an example of...**

(A) Satire

(B) Foreshadowing

(C) Interstitial

(D) Subtext

(E) Premonition

ANSWER KEY

Question Number	Correct Answer	Your Answer
1.	B	
2.	A	
3.	D	
4.	A	
5.	C	
6.	A	
7.	B	
8.	D	
9.	B	
10.	D	
11.	C	
12.	D	
13.	A	
14.	C	
15.	D	
16.	B	
17.	A	
18.	E	
19.	C	
20.	E	
21.	B	
22.	C	
23.	B	
24.	E	
25.	A	
26.	E	
27.	B	
28.	B	
29.	B	
30.	C	

Question Number	Correct Answer	Your Answer
31.	A	
32.	C	
33.	C	
34.	B	
35.	C	
36.	A	
37.	C	
38.	B	
39.	D	
40.	A	
41.	A	
42.	C	
43.	E	
44.	E	
45.	C	
46.	B	
47.	A	
48.	A	
49.	C	
50.	C	
51.	D	
52.	C	
53.	B	
54.	C	
55.	D	
56.	A	
57.	A	
58.	C	
59.	A	
60.	B	

Questions 1-8. Read the following passage carefully before you decide on your answers to the questions.

On the domestic front, life was not easy. England was not a wealthy country and its people endured relatively poor living standards. The landed classes – many of them enriched by the confiscated wealth of former monasteries – were determined in the interests of profile to convert their arable land into pasture for sheep, so as to produce the wool that supported the country's chief economic asset, the woolen cloth trade. But the enclosing of the land only added to the misery of the poor, many of whom, evicted and displaced, left their decaying villages and gravitated to the towns where they joined the growing army of beggars and vagabonds that would become such a feature of Elizabethan life. Once, the religious houses would have dispensed charity to the destitute, but Henry VIII had dissolved them all in the 1530s, and many former monks and nuns were now themselves beggars. Nor did the civic authorities help: they passed laws in an attempt to ban the poor from towns and cities, but to little avail. It was a common sight to see men and women lying in the dusty streets, often dying in the dirt like dogs or beasts, without human compassion being shown to them. 'Certainly, wrote a Spanish observer in 1558, 'the state of England lay now most afflicted.' And although people looked to the new Queen Elizabeth to put matters right, there were so many who doubted if she could overcome the seemingly insurmountable problems she faced, or even remain queen long enough to begin tacking them. Some, both at home and abroad, were the opinion that her title to the throne rested on very precarious foundations. Many regarded the daughter of Henry VIII and Anne Boleyn as a bastard from the time of her birth on 7 September 1533, although, ignoring such slurs on the validity of his second marriage, Henry had declared Elizabeth his heir.

1. **Why was land confiscated from the poor?**

    (A) The town wanted to build a new monastery.

    (B) To create pastures for sheep, ultimately increasing the export of wool.

    (C) The town wanted to create housing for monks and nuns.

    (D) Queen Elizabeth wanted to expand her property.

    (E) The poor did not pay their taxes.

    The correct answer is B.

    This is stated directly in the paragraph in the opening lines.

2. A vagabond is a _____.

(A) Wanderer

(B) Prisoner

(C) Poor person

(D) Rich person

(E) Fighter

The correct answer is A.

Using your vocabulary, should should know this; but it can also be narrowed down from the passage, where you would be able to guess between C and A.

3. Why didn't the poor have shelter with the churches?

(A) They were already filled with beggars.

(B) Religious houses have never offered shelter to the poor.

(C) They were also being used to raise sheep.

(D) Henry VIII had dissolved them all in the 1530s.

(E) Queen Elizabeth dissolved them all in the 1530s.

The correct answer is D.

Again, this is stated directly in the paragraph. This test looks at your reading comprehension in addition to your knowledge of vocabulary and literary terms.

4. How were civic authorities unsuccessful?

(A) Poor people remained within city limits

(B) Public service funds ran out

(C) Public housing plans extended deadlines

(D) Churches did not open their doors to the poor

(E) The poor overthrew them to gain their land back

The correct answer is A.

Using a statement in the passage, "It was a common sight to see men and women lying in the dusty streets, often dying in the dirt like dogs or beasts," it shows through analysis that they were still in the city. To eliminate the other answers, there is no indication of (B) or (C) in the passage; (D) is incorrect as the previous question reminded you that the churches were closed, and: (E) is incorrect because again, there is no indication in the passage that situation occurred.

5. **What is a synonym for precarious?**

(A) Strong

(B) Careful

(C) Risky

(D) Determined

(E) Illegitimate

The correct answer is C.

This is a test of your vocabulary, but you should be able to use clues in the paragraph if you aren't sure of the answer.

6. **What is the author's view towards Queen Elizabeth?**

(A) Doubtful

(B) Vengeful

(C) Resentful

(D) Supportive

(E). Confident

The correct answer is A.

Indications of this are found toward the end of the passage "there were many who doubted" and the author continues to explain those doubts.

7. **How is the English culture portrayed in this passage?**

(A) Religious

(B) Elitist

(C) Racist

(D) Diverse

(E) Spiritual

The correct answer is B.

By using contextual analysis, you can see how King Henry VII favored land-holders even early in the passage and the description of their life, "enriched by the confiscated wealth of former monasteries."

8. **What is Elizabeth's relationship to Henry?**

(A) Wife

(B) Cousin

(C) Lover

(D) Daughter

(E) Niece

The correct answer is D.

This is explained directly in the passage, after the description of the illegitimacy of the daughter of Anne Boelyn.

Questions 9-13. Read the following passage carefully before you decide on your answers to the questions.

William Wordsworth—I Wandered Lonely As A Cloud

I wandered lonely as a cloud
That floats on high o'er vales and hills,
When all at once I saw a crowd,
A host, of golden daffodils;
Beside the lake, beneath the trees,
Fluttering and dancing in the breeze

Continuous as the stars that shine
And twinkle on the milky way,
They stretched in never-ending line
Along the margin of a bay:
Ten thousand saw I at a glance,
Tossing their heads in sprightly dance

The waves beside them danced; but they
Out-did the sparkling waves in glee:
A poet could not but be gay,
In such a jocund company:
I gazed—and gazed—but little thought
What wealth the show to me had brought:

For oft, when on my couch I lie
In vacant or in pensive mood,
They flash upon that inward eye
Which is the bliss of solitude;
And then my heart with pleasure fills,
And dances with the daffodils.

9. The permanence of stars as compared with flowers emphasizes

(A) the impermanence of life.

(B) the permanence of memory for the poet.

(C) the earlier comparison of the sky to the lake.

(D) that stars are frozen above and daffodils dance below.

(E) the similarity of the inward eye with the fleeting bliss of solitude

The correct answer is B.

The key word in option A is opposite in meaning and the relationship of the verbs in (D) are not correctly aligned for the comparison. (E) is not part of the poem at all. If you don't know the answer between (B) and (C), look back at the poem—and there is no comparison of sky to lake, so that gives you the right answer.

10. The scheme of the poem is

(A) ballad.

(B) Scottish stanza.

(C) Spenserian stanza.

(D) quatrain-couplet.

(E) sonnet.

The correct answer is D.

While this may not be one of the typical questions on the test, it is incorporated so you remember to look at general literary definitions. You can also figure this out by looking at quatrain, which has the base that means "four" and couplet means "two"—that is the same pattern as the poem. (E) isn't right because a sonnet is one verse of specific length; a ballad is the manner of telling a story so it isn't (A). There are particular components of (B) and (C), but if you get to this stage and use the root words, you may be able to guess the right answer if you don't know.

11. What is a literary device used in the last two lines of the first two stanzas?

(A) Simile

(B) Metaphor.

(C) Personification.

(D) Allegory.

(E) Paradox.

The correct answer is C.

When an inanimate or non-human objects is given person-like traits, it's call personification. You should be familiar with all of the words that are given as options in this multiple choice question— review them in the guide for refresher.

12. **As used in this poem, the best choice for a synonym of jocund means**

    (A) pleasant.

    (B) vapid.

    (C) lonely.

    (D) jovial.

    (E) sad.

    The correct answer is D.

    This is a question that tests vocabulary—you should be able to eliminate choices (A), (C), and (E). If you don't know what jocund means, or either vapid or jovial, this is how they are testing for reading comprehension. Jovial is happy and that fits into the structure of the passage within context.

13. **What literary device is used in Line 9, "They stretched in never-ending line."**

    (A) hyperbole.

    (B) onomatopoeia.

    (C) epithet.

    (D) irony.

    (E) anecdote.

    The correct answer is A.

    Knowing what common literary terms mean will allow you to eliminate at least (D) and (E), if not also (B) Between (C) and (A), you could guess, but if you understand either of the definitions, you will pick the correct answer. Review definitions if you can't eliminate at least three of the word answer choices.

Questions 14-19. Read the following selection and answer the questions below, selecting the best choice of the options presented.

My Bondage and My Freedom

Disappearing from the kind reader, in a flying cloud or balloon (pardon the figure), driven by the wind, and knowing not where I should land--whether in slavery or in freedom--it is proper that I should remove, at once, all anxiety, by frankly making known where I alighted. The flight was a bold and perilous one; but here I am, in the great city of New York, safe and sound, without loss of blood or bone. In less than a week after leaving Baltimore, I was walking amid the hurrying throng, and gazing upon the dazzling wonders of Broadway. The dreams of my childhood and the purposes of my manhood were now fulfilled. A free state around me, and a free earth under my feet! What a moment was this to me! A whole year was pressed into a single day. A new world burst upon my agitated vision. I have often been asked, by kind friends to whom I have told my story, how I felt when first I found myself beyond the limits of slavery; and I must say here, as I have often said to them, there is scarcely anything about which I could not give a more satisfactory answer. It was a moment of joyous excitement, which no words can describe. In a letter to a friend, written soon after reaching New York. I said I felt as one might be supposed to feel, on escaping from a den of hungry lions.

14. **When the author writes "escaping from a den of hungry lions," what type of literary device is he using?**

   (A) Simile

   (B) Personification.

   (C) Metaphor.

   (D) Hyperbole.

   (E) Irony.

   The correct answer is C.

   The author uses the "den of hungry lions" to parallel to people in the room in the poem. Of the words in the answer choices, you should at least have memorized the meaning of (A), (B) and (C).

15. **What is the author's theme in this passage?**

   (A) Anger at being a slave.

   (B) Numb, as one might be supposed to feel.

   (C) Confusion at the new things he is seeing.

   (D) Self-discovery after flight from slavery.

   (E) None of these describe his tone.

   The correct answer is D.

   Recall that it is extremely rare that "always" or "never" options are correct. Of the four remaining, review the passage. There is no descriptions that make the reader interpret numbness or confusion. Narrowing it down to (A) and (D), there are key words that show rather than anger, the character is exhibiting (D).

16. In context of the passage, the opening phrase "to the kind reader" used by the author sets what kind of opening tone?

   (A) Friendly

   (B) Condescending

   (C) Boisterous

   (D) Prideful

   (E) Meek

   The correct answer is B.

   If you were answering too quickly, you may think A is the correct answer. But look at the context. The speaker is pandering to the listener.

17. The author of this book relays his own experiences fighting slavery. Why does he fight against it. What is the theme of the book?

   (A) Slavery is unnatural.

   (B) Slavery wasn't needed as an economic engine.

   (C) Slavery was morally acceptable.

   (D) Slavery enabled him to see the light of day.

   (E) Slavery made time move too quickly.

   The correct answer is A.

   There is no proof that the author believes (B) is true, nor any of the other answers. Remember, it's not what you believe but what the author is stating or leading you to believe and that's how you must answer. If you read too fast, you may have thought (B) was the correct answer, but notice the answer is actually negative. Read carefully.

18. What does the author figuratively mean by "hurrying throng"?

   (A) The people that bump into him walking past him.

   (B) His blurred vision from bright sunlight.

   (C) The New York tradesmen rushing to their jobs.

   (D) The busy middle class.

   (E) The bustling crowd of free people.

   The correct answer is E.

   The middle three options are not correct, but A could possibly be accurate. However, there is nothing in the passage that should lead you to think he was bumped into by people passing him. Don't make assumptions or you won't select the right answer.

19. What is the author's tone in this passage?

(A) Cautious

(B) Enlightened

(C) Exuberant

(D) Nervous

(E) None of these apply

The correct answer is C.

While the feeling of the character may be D, there are more cues that point to (C) being the right answer.

Questions 20-25. Read the following selection and answer the questions below, selecting the best choice of the options presented.

A Bird Came Down the Walk
—Emily Dickinson

A bird came down the walk:
He did not know I saw;
He bit an angle-worm in halves
And ate the fellow, raw.
And then, he drank a dew
From a convenient grass,
And then hopped sidewise to the wall
To let a beetle pass.

He glanced with rapid eyes
That hurried all abroad,—
They looked like frightened beads, I thought;
He stirred his velvet head

Like one in danger; cautious,
I offered him a crumb,
And he unrolled his feathers
And rowed him softer home

Than oars divide the ocean,
Too silver for a seam,
Or butterflies, off banks of noon,
Leap, plashless, as they swim.

20. **What type of literary device is used in the author's phrase, "drank a dew"?**

(A) Allusion.

(B) Foreshadowing.

(C) Juxtaposition.

(D) Satire.

(E) Alliteration.

The correct answer is E.

These are all basic literary device words and you should know the definitions of these most-frequently used terms.

21. **The author describes action beginning in line 15 of the bird's flight. What type of literary device is used?**

(A) Simile.

(B) Metaphor.

(C) Irony.

(D) Satire.

(E) None of these are correct.

The correct answer is B.

Remember, absolute answers, such as ones that give "always" or "never" or "none" are typically incorrect. Of the remaining options, you should know these definitions, especially the difference between simile and metaphor.

22. **What literary device is used when the bird's eyes are compared to frightened beads?**

(A) Reverse Personification.

(B) Metaphor.

(C) Simile.

(D) Allegory.

(E) Paradox.

The correct answer is C.

While these types of questions are not likely to come back-to-back in the actual exam, they were placed in repetitive order here to show you that you need to remain focus, answer each question and move forward.

23. What does the dash at the end of line 12 represent?

(A) A change in focus from the bird to the water.

(B) An abrupt change for the bird.

(C) An emotional shift from fear to fascination.

(D) It only shows the middle of the poem.

(E) None of these accurately describe the meaning of the dash.

The correct answer is B.

In context, the bird goes from drinking and allowing a beetle to pass to abruptly being wary. That is the opposite of (C), but many students who rush through the test may select that option. Literally, (D) is not accurate nor is (A)

24. What is the author's tone in this poem?

(A) She takes the perspective of the bird.

(B) The author's tone is harsh toward potential prey.

(C) The tone is factual, describing the actions of a bird.

(D) Ornithology fascinated the author and she uses flowery language to describe it.

(E) The author's tone is gentle and respectful demeanor regarding nature.

The correct answer is E.

If you know basics about various authors, you would know that Ms. Dickenson wrote during an era of respecting nature and promoting its good features to the masses.

25. What is a potential meaning of the allegory used by the author?

(A) It could reveal the author's perceptions of God.

(B) The allegory could be looking at the author's view of marriage.

(C) The author could reveal the hierarchy between man and beast.

(D) Descriptions of the forces of nature could parallel emotions.

(E) There is no allegory used as a literary device in this poem.

The correct answer is A.

Knowing your definitions, (E) can be removed as correct because you would have identified the allegory previously. While (D) is a fair choice, (A) is a better one—again, known the traits of the era, you would be able to most easily identify the right choice.

Questions 26-32. Read the following selection and answer the questions below, selecting the best choice of the options presented.

A man is born into this world with only a tiny spark of goodness in him. The spark is God, it is the soul; the rest is ugliness and evil, a shell. The spark must be guarded like a treasure, it must be nurtured, it must be fanned into flame. It must learn to seek out other sparks, it must dominate the shell. Anything can be a shell, Reuven. Anything. Indifference, laziness, brutality, and genius. Yes, even a great mind can be a shell and choke the spark.

"Reuven, the Master of the Universe blessed me with a brilliant son. And he cursed me with all the problems of raising him. Ah, what it is to have a Daniel, whose mind is like a pearl, like a sun. Reuben, when my Daniel was four years old, I saw him reading a story from a book. And I was frightened. He did not read the story, he swallowed it, as one swallows food or water. There was no soul in my four-year-old Daniel, there was only his mind. He was a mind in a body without a soul. It was a tory in a Yiddish book about a poor Jew and his struggles to get to Eretz Yisroel before he died. Ah, how that man suffered! And my Daniel enjoyed the story, he enjoyed the last terrible page, because when he finished it he realized for the first time what a memory he had. He looked at me proudly and told me back the story from memory, and I cried inside my heart. I went away and cried to the Master of the Universe, 'What have you done to me? A mind like this I need for a son? A heart I need for a son, a soul I need for a son, compassion I want for my son, righteousness, mercy, strength to suffer and carry pain, that I want from my son, not a mind without a soul!'"

Reb Saunders paused and took a deep, trembling breath. I tried to swallow; my mouth was sand-dry. Danny sat with his right hand over his eyes, his glasses pushed up on his forehead.) He was crying silently, his shoulders quivering. Reb Saunders did not look at him.

26. According to the passage, what was the goal behind raising Danny in silence?

(A) For the speaker to be cruel.

(B) The speaker thought he was being noble.

(C) The narrator believed by being harsh, he was right.

(D) The speaker wanted other people to think they were normal.

(E) He wanted to develop Danny's compassion and soul.

The correct answer is E.

The intention of the speaker wasn't to be cruel or noble, and there was no indication that the speaker wanted to appear "normal" to his neighbors. This is an example of when your ability to infer is tested.) By the repetition of the italics, that should give you an indication those are the important traits that Reb wanted to develop in Danny.

27. **What is the author doing when using italics?**

(A) The author is using short words to mean big things.

(B) The author signifies the important things in a person's life.

(C) The speaker is listing the attributes of his son.

(D) The speaker shows what his son understood in the stories.

(E) None of these things apply to those words.

The correct answer is B.

Option (C) is not correct—it is actually the opposite. It also isn't the explanation of his son's attributes, but the ones Danny was lacking. (A) is not correct, either, and you should know by now to be skeptical of answers like (E)

28. **When Reb's mouth went "sand-dry," this is an example of:**

(A) a parody.

(B) an allusion.

(C) a synecdoche.

(D) a metaphor.

(E) an oxymoron.

The correct answer is B.

These are definitions you should know and thus be able to recognize examples in literature.

29. **Throughout the book, Reuven had been the peripheral narrator. Who is the narrator in this section?**

(A) It is still Reuven.

(B) It is Reb.

(C) It is Danny.

(D) It is a third person narrator.

(E) It is Eretz Yisroel.

The correct answer is B.

This is clear in the beginning of the last paragraph.

30. The passage of this book is written as:

(A) the denouement.

(B) the complication.

(C) the climax.

(D) the suspense.

(E) the introduction.

The correct answer is C.

By knowing the stages used in literature, you should be able to answer the question. You can also infer the meaning from the poignant phrases in the passage to help you pick the right option.

31. What is the theme of this passage?

(A) Recounting the last moments of an old man's life.

(B) The discussion of coming marriage of Danny.

(C) The symbolism of reading as an alternative for family interactions.

(D) The adoption of Reuven by Reb.

(E) Another example of Jews suffering to get further in life.

The correct answer is A.

This question should have been easy to answer. There is no mention of Danny's marriage. Reading was not an alternative for attributes, but Reb believed it was a replacement for personality traits. There is no discussion that supports option (D) and (E) is not correct, either.

32. What is the writing style used by this author in this passage?

(A) Expository

(B) Didactic

(C) Persuasive

(D) Descriptive

(E) Theatrical

The correct answer is C.

If you can't tell from the description being given by the speaker, then if you know the basic definitions of these terms then you would be able to pick the right answer.

Questions 33-40. Read the following selection and answer the questions below, selecting the best choice of the options presented.

Okonkwo and his fellow prisoners were set free as soon as the fine was paid. The District Commissioner spoke to them again about the great queen, and about peace and good government. But the men did not listen. They just sat and looked at him and at his interpreter. In the end they were given back their bags and sheathed machetes and told to go home. They rose and left the courthouse. They neither spoke to anyone nor among themselves.

The courthouse, like the church, was but a little way outside the village. The footpath that linked them was a very busy one because it also led to the stream, beyond the court. It was open and sandy. Footpaths were open and sandy in the dry season. But when the rains came the bush grew thick on either side and closed in on the path. It was now dry season.

As they made their way to the village the six men met women and children going to the stream with their waterpots. But them wore such heavy and fearsome looks to them, but edged out of the way to let them pass. In the village little groups of men joined them until they became a sizable company. They walked silently. As each o the six men got to his compound, he turned in, taking some of the crowd with him. The village was air in a silent, suppressed way.

Ezinma had prepared some food for her father as soon as news spread that the six men would be released. She took it to him in his obi. He ate absent-mindedly. He had no appetite, he only ate to please her. His male relations and friends had gathered in his obi, and Obierika was urging him to eat. Nobody else spoke, but they noticed the log stripes on Okonkwo's back where the warder's whip had cut into his flesh.

33. **Who is the protagonist of this story?**

   (A) Obierika

   (B) Ezinma

   (C) Okonkwo

   (D) The District Commissioner

   (E) Okonkwo's wife

   The correct answer is C.

   If you are unfamiliar with the book, you can still read carefully and pick the right main character. If you didn't recognize the word protagonist, brush up on your literary device vocabulary.

34. What is the name of this book?

(A) Obi

(B) Things Fall Apart

(C) Let the Circle Be Unbroken

(D) Ashes and Dust

(E) The Rainy Season

The correct answer is B.

We mentioned in the chapters that you should have familiarity with era and types of literature, such as some key writers and books in American, British and World Literature.

35. What category of literature does this book represent?

(A) Romantic.

(B) Victorian.

(C) Modernism.

(D) Transcendentalism.

(E) Post Colonial.

The correct answer is C.

Knowing the literary eras are important. If you forget during the test, look at the keys of each word. Romantic era as well as Victorian are much older—and a book about Africa from the native resident's perspective would not likely have been widely published early in literature.Post-colonial refers to British colonies and usually Indian pieces. Narrowed down to Transcendentalism and Modernism, you may recall the first is written by American authors and in particular Ralph Waldo Emerson.

36. The main character of the book appears to have what occur throughout the book?

(A) He is a champion of his village.

(B) He shows that he is good provider for his family.

(C) He represents the disintegration of his society against the change.

(D) The village doesn't support him.

(E) The courthouse is targeting him to get rid of the village.

The correct answer is A.

Neither (D) nor (E) are correct, and that can be known from the passage. He is a tragic hero, and nothing in the passage represents (C) being accurate. Of the two remaining, while both (A) and (B) are true, option A is supported by the characterization in the passage.

37. The narrative structure of this passage is:

(A) simple narrative.

(B) cause and effect.

(C) chronological.

(D) inductive.

(E) deductive.

The correct answer is C.

While it is a narration, and yes because of their release there is food waiting at the village, it is a chronological stepwise piece and that is the best answer.

38. The literary style of the book is:

(A) comedy.

(B) tragedy.

(C) drama.

(D) exploration.

(E) quest.

The correct answer is B.

as it describes the downfall of the main character due to his own choices. While (C) is a tempting answer, it is not the best option.

39. How is this passage narrated?

(A) First person.

(B) Second person.

(C) Third person.

(D) Omniscient observer.

(E) None of these.

The correct answer is D.

Third person may seem like a desirable option, but it only gives the point of view from one particular person and there are two "inside thoughts" here. Omniscient means they see everything. You should have been able to discount (A) and (B) quite easily.

40. What is the main idea of this passage?

(A) The village members continue to carry out the traditions of their ancestors.

(B) There is a drought affecting crops and village life.

(C) The interpreter was sharing with them a new way of life.

(D) The government and church were coming together for the people.

(E) People are resistant to change, and the village and protagonist illustrate it.

The correct answer is A.

This is the best option for the passage and though E may be accurate for the book, you must answer according to what's in the passage.

Questions 41-47. Read the following selection and answer the questions below, selecting the best choice of the options presented.

Mornings, he likes to sit in his new leather chair by his new living room window, looking out across the rooftops and chimney pots, the clotheslines and telegraph lines and office towers. It's the first time Manhattan, from high above, hasn't crushed him with desire. On the contrary the view makes him feel smug. All those people down there, striving, hustling, pushing, shoving, busting to get what Willie's already got. In spades. He lights a cigarette, blows a jet of smoke against the window. Suckers.

41. The subject in this passage is:

(A) a character, and seems to be the lead of the story.

(B) a supporting character.

(C) has an attitude of a criminal.

(D) is female.

(E) has been poor his whole life.

The correct answer is A.

The female pronoun is used, so (D) is inaccurate. (B) is not accurate as he is the focus of the passage. You cannot infer (E) is correct. Of (A) and (C), there is no support for this character being a criminal. Remember not to make assumptions when you answer questions.

42. **What kind of description is the author providing of this scene?**

    (A) Backstory of the character.

    (B) A characterization of what the character is like.

    (C) A narrative in the first person.

    (D) The unreliable narrative about a character.

    (E) The author is using a persuasive argument.

    The correct answer is C.

    Backstory isn't accurate because a current scene is described. (B) uses the same root-word twice, which is usually an indication that it is not a correct guess. There is nothing to suggest the character is unreliable. This leaves options (C) and (E) and neither the author nor character are persuading the reader toward a conclusion.

43. **What types of words are "striving, hustling, pushing, shoving, bustling"?**

    (A) Adjectives

    (B) Adverbs

    (C) Nouns

    (D) Gerunds

    (E) Verbs

    The correct answer is E.

    This is a basic vocabulary situation.

44. **If you had to explain the phrase "crushed him" in the paragraph above and context of the paragraph, what would be the best appropriate explanation?**

    (A) The city sustained him with all the opportunity available.

    (B) The city called to him to be part of its life.

    (C) The city complimented him for everything he has achieved.

    (D) The city had energized him to get what he felt he deserved.

    (E) The city smothered him with all its offerings.

    The correct answer is E.

45. **Replacing the word "smug" with an antonym in context would have which of the following used?**

(A) Sleepy

(B) Prideful

(C) Humble

(D) Self-satisfied

(E) Elated

The correct answer is C.

This involves knowing the words meanings as well as reading carefully as the question asked for antonym.

46. **When the author uses the phrase, "In spades," which of the following is best representing what he is referencing?**

(A) The large apartment in which Willie is living.

(B) The personal satisfaction of accumulated wealth.

(C) Modern comforts in his home.

(D) The loved ones surrounding him.

(E) None of these is representative.

The correct answer is B.

The context and reading comprehension bring you to the correct answer. Nothing implying loved ones, modern comforts or the mere large apartment relate to the question.

47. **By using the introductory word "Mornings," the author achieves what?**

(A) An optimistic tone for the passage.

(B) A simple description of time of day, or chronology for the passage.

(C) It's the start of the book, so he sets the passage at "day one."

(D) A and C

(E) None of these.

The correct answer is A.

Context of the tone of the passage shows the character speaking is in a good mood, but it does not mean that it actually is morning and there is no indication that it is the start of the book.

Questions 48-52. Read the following selection and answer the questions below, selecting the best choice of the options presented.

"Mother," said little Pearl, "the sunshine does not love you. It runs away and hides itself, because it is afraid of something on your bosom. . . . It will not flee from me, for I wear nothing on my bosom yet!"

"Nor ever will, my child, I hope," said Hester.

"And why not, mother?" asked Pearl, stopping short. . . . "Will it not come of its own accord, when I am a woman grown?"

—*The Scarlett Letter*

48. **What kind of description is the author providing of this scene?**

   (A) A symbolic, metaphorical description that provides a backstory of the main character

   (B) A characterization of what the character is like

   (C) A narrative, with the end of the selection giving thoughts in the first person

   (D) The unreliable narrative about a character

   (E) The author is using a persuasive argument

   The correct answer is A.

   You need to determined the meaning of passages in this SAT Literature Test to achieve the "Analyzing" component of the title.

49. **What does the "sunshine" represent?**

   (A) Light

   (B) Hope

   (C) Purity

   (D) Heaven

   (E) Good luck

   The correct answer is C.

   This is an analogy. Being one of Hawthorne's most popular works and frequently used on tests, understanding of the phrase is important.

50. **The author portrays the attitude of the character Pearl as:**

(A) condescending

(B) loving

(C) disrespectful

(D) innocent

(E) resentful

The correct answer is C.

Again, knowing the symbolism of one of the most important novels of that era is important. Understanding some of the plot and having read the book would have occurred in the literature classes at the early stages of college coursework, so you should understand some of the dynamics of the story.

51. **"Will it not come of its own accord, when I am a woman grown?**
    What is the author implying that Pearl is asking for?

(A) If the scarlet letter will be handed down to her when she becomes a woman.

(B) If she will become pregnant when she becomes mature enough.

(C) Whether or not she will get divorced when she marries.

(D) If she will find true love when she grows up.

(E) If her mother will share this symbol with her when she is old enough.

The correct answer is D.

52. **Which of the following best describes the author's message?**

(A) Little girls are oblivious to the world around them.

(B) Daughters always question things that their mothers do.

(C) Growing up means losing your innocence.

(D) The world will know when you have sinned.

(E) None of the above.)

The correct answer is C.

Again, knowing the symbolism of one of the most important novels of that era is important. Understanding some of the plot and having read the book would have occurred in the literature classes at the early stages of college coursework, so you should understand some of the dynamics of the story.

Questions 53-60. Read the following selection and answer the questions below, selecting the best choice of the options presented.

In a village of La Mancha, the name of which I have no desire to call to mind, there lived not long since one of those gentlemen that keep a lance in the lance-rack, an old buckler, a lean hack, and a greyhound for coursing. An olla of rather more beef than mutton, a salad on most nights, scraps on Saturdays, lentils on Fridays, and a pigeon or so extra on Sundays, made away with three-quarters of his incom(E) The rest of it went in a doublet of fine cloth and velvet breeches and shoes to match for holidays, while on week-days he made a brave figure in his best homespun. He had in his house a housekeeper past forty, a niece under twenty, and a lad for the field and market-place, who used to saddle the hack as well as handle the bill-hook. The age of this gentleman of ours was bordering on fifty; he was of a hardy habit, spare, gaunt-featured, a very early riser and a great sportsman. They will have it his surname was Quixada or Quesada (for here there is some difference of opinion among the authors who write on the subject), although from reasonable conjectures it seems plain that he was called Quexana. This, however, is of but little importance to our tale; it will be enough not to stray a hair's breadth from the truth in the telling of it.

You must know, then, that the above-named gentleman whenever he was at leisure (which was mostly all the year round) gave himself up to reading books of chivalry with such ardour and avidity that he almost entirely neglected the pursuit of his field-sports, and even the management of his property; and to such a pitch did his eagerness and infatuation go that he sold many an acre of tillageland to buy books of chivalry to read, and brought home as many of them as he could get. But of all there were none he liked so well as those of the famous Feliciano de Silva's composition, for their lucidity of style and complicated conceits were as pearls in his sight, particularly when in his reading he came upon courtships and cartels, where he often found passages like "the reason of the unreason with which my reason is afflicted so weakens my reason that with reason I murmur at your beauty;" or again, "the high heavens, that of your divinity divinely fortify you with the stars, render you deserving of the desert your greatness deserves." Over conceits of this sort the poor gentleman lost his wits, and used to lie awake striving to understand them and worm the meaning out of them; what Aristotle himself could not have made out or extracted had he come to life again for that special purpose. He was not at all easy about the wounds which Don Belianis gave and took, because it seemed to him that, great as were the surgeons who had cured him, he must have had his face and body covered all over with seams and scars. He commended, however, the author's way of ending his book with the promise of that interminable adventure, and many a time was he tempted to take up his pen and finish it properly as is there proposed, which no doubt he would have done, and made a successful piece of work of it too, had not greater and more absorbing thoughts prevented him.

53. The author's tone in this piece can best be described as...

(A) Heroic

(B) Comedic

(C) Florid

(D) Epic

(E) Mysterious

The correct answer is B.

This is the story of Don Quixote. The author writes about the enthusiasm of the lead character, eliminating options (C), (D) and (E). Between the first and second choice, if you know the story, it is easy to select the correct answer. If you need to infer the meaning, you need to select key words that lead to (B). There are not many depictions of a hero, but there are allusions to entertaining situations, so that is the answer even if you have not read the book.

54. The line "were as pearls to his site" is an example of a...

(A) Metaphor

(B) Analogy

(C) Simile

(D) Allegory

(E) Conceit

The correct answer is C.

Remember to know your literary device terms, and this answer would be apparent.

55. Our main character's attitude towards reading can best be described as...

(A) Lackadaisical

(B) Unusual

(C) Illiterate

(D) Obsessive

(E) Joyous

The correct answer is D.

The phrase "buy books of chivalry to read, and brought home as many of them as he could get" gives some insight as well as other clues to the nature of the lead character. While (may also be true, (D) is the best answer.

56. **The passage "the high heavens, that of your divinity divinely fortify you with the stars, render you deserving of the desert your greatness deserves" contains several examples what poetic device?**

(A) Alliteration

(B) Onomatopoeia

(C) Diction

(D) Resonance

(E) Enjambment

The correct answer is A.

If you review the meaning of any of these terms you didn't know, the right choice will be readily apparent. Make sure you learn them before you take the exam.

57. **According to the text, who is Count Belianis?**

(A) A historical champion

(B) A fictional character

(C) A competing nobleman

(D) A romantic rival

(E) A dead family member

The correct answer is A.

The many scars and wounds are described as well as his grand thoughts in the last sentenc(E) Thus, in context of the passage, (B) is false as well as (D) and (E). While (C) may be true to some degree (or rather, appear true), you need to select the best answer and that is (A).

58. **The passage "it will be enough not to stray a hair's breadth from the truth in the telling of it" characterizes the previous passage as…**

(A) Essential

(B) Metaphorical

(C) Unimportant

(D) Esoteric

(E) Bland

The correct answer is C.

The prior sentence is about the spelling of the main character's name. In perspective and context, that is unimportant as when compared to the events. When given a snippet of the passage, read around the phrase for context to help you—especially when they direct you to a particular area of the passage (such as the "previous passage" in the selection.

59. What are the two defining traits of the main character described above?

(A) Laziness and obsessiveness

(B) Ignorance and piousness

(C) Diligence and valor

(D) Prideful and vain

(E) Curious and kindhearted

The correct answer is A.

This selection refers in part to his compulsiveness on reading (explained earlier). Before selecting (A) and the other half could be blatantly wrong, look at the other options. Perhaps valor in (C) is accurately portrayed in the selection, but none of the others are true. Between (A) and (C), use the context of the passage to determine if laziness or diligence is more appropriate, and you'll note that (A) is the better answer.

60. The final sentence of this excerpt is an example of...

(A) Satire

(B) Foreshadowing

(C) Interstitial

(D) Subtext

(E) Premonition

The correct answer is B.

The ending of the introduction (which this is) sets the stage for the book and what is to follow. Knowing your literary terms is helpful, as you can narrow the possible answers to (B) and (E) in, but the actual definitions show B is more correct. Promotion is a character's particular feeling or description whereas foreshadowing is the casting of mood prior to arriving to a scene.

Sample Test Two

Section I

Multiple Choice Questions. Time: 60 minutes.

This sample exam gives passages from known writings (fiction, poems, non-fiction/history, biographies, drama and more) over the past five hundred years. While the student taking the exam is not expected to have read the material or have familiarity with the passage prior to the exam, the test taker is expected to have the essential knowledge from schoolwork to answer the questions included herein.

At the end of the test passages and answers, there is an answer key and a "rationale" key for each question. Take the test without referencing these guides. For questions that you guess the answers or get wrong, the rationale is provided to help you see how test makers frame answers to questions or explain pieces of information with which you are unfamiliar.

As with the SAT Literature Test, the passages are taken primarily from American and British Literature—though at least one question, just as in the actual exam, is taken from another area of literature. Within the questions of the SAT Literature Test, the mixture of genre types falls typically almost 80-90% between poetry and prose and the remaining on drama. The entire test is balanced between three main eras—Renaissance/17th Century, 18th/19th Century, as well as 20th/21st Century. The test includes three main classifications-American Literature, British Literature, and World Literature. American and British Literature typically account for 80-90%, with 1-2 passages from India, Ireland, Canada, Africa, and/or the Caribbean.

The SAT Literature Test allows 60 minutes to take the exam of approximately 60 questions. Time yourself during the exam, but as you practice, focus more attention on accurately answer-ing questions as the total number of correct answers impacts your score, not how many you skip or get wrong. If you skip any questions, make sure that you also skip that line on the answer sheet—or you may spend a lot of time erasing and redoing your answer key.

These passages do not actually appear on the SAT Literature exam, but are meant to show how the exam is written and the various range of questions, answers, and key knowledge points required in order to pass the SAT Literature exam. Read each question carefully and provide the best answer choice. Good luck!

Questions 1-4 Read the following passage carefully before you decide on your answers to the questions.

I'd like to say here, that I wasn't the only important one. I was part of a family, just like all of my brothers and sisters. The whole community was important. We used to discuss many of the community's problems together, especially when someone was ill and we couldn't buy medicine, because we were getting poorer and poorer. We'd start discussing and heaping insults on the rich who'd made us suffer for so long. It was about then I began learning about politics. I tried to talk to people who could help me sort my ideas out. I wanted to know what the world was like on the other side. I knew the finca, I knew the Altiplano. But what I didn't know was about the other problems of the Indians in Guatemala. I didn't know the problems the other groups had to holding onto their land.I knew there were lots of other Indians in other parts of the country, because I'd been meeting them in the finca since I was a child, but though we all worked together, we didn't know any of the names of the towns they came from, or how they lived, or what they ate. We just imagined that they were like us.

—Rigoberta Menchu, Nobel Peace Prize Winner 1992

1. **From the context of the passage, what is a finca?**

   (A) A farm

   (B) A village or town

   (C) A mountain range

   (D) A house

   (E) It cannot be determined

2. **The author is telling a story about her own life. What is this kind of document called?**

   (A) Autobiography

   (B) Mystery

   (C) Biography

   (D) Narrative

   (E) Romance

3. **Given the information in the passage, the author most likely worked as:**

   (A) a washer woman

   (B) a seamstress

   (C) a farmer

   (D) a teacher

   (E) it cannot be determined from the passage

4. The author describes who is the most important. She defines it as:

(A) herself

(B) her family

(C) her community

(D) the rich people that employed them

(E) the finca

Questions 5-7. Read the following passage carefully before you decide on your answers to the questions.

A marvelous case is it to hear, either the warnings of that he should have voided, or the tokens of that he could not void. For the self night next before his death, the lord Stanley sent a trusty secret messenger unto him at midnight in all the haste, requiring him to rise and ride away with him, for he was disposed utterly no longer to bide; he had so fearful a dream, in which him thought that a boar with his tusks so raced them both by the heads, that the blood ran about both their shoulders. And forasmuch as the protector gave the boar for his cognizance, this dream made so fearful an impression in his heart, that he was thoroughly determined no longer to tarry, but had his horse ready, if the lord Hastings would go with him to ride so far yet the same night, that they should be out of danger ere day. Ay, good lord, quoth the lord Hastings to this messenger, leaneth my lord thy master so much to such trifles, and hath such faith in dreams, which either his own fear fantasieth or do rise in the night's rest by reason of his day thoughts? Tell him it is plain witchcraft to believe in such dreams; which if they were tokens of things to come, why thinketh he not that we might be as likely to make them true by our going if we were caught and brought back (as friends fail fleers), for then had the boar a cause likely to race us with his tusks, as folk that fled for some falsehood, wherefore either is there no peril (nor none there is indeed), or if any be, it is rather in going than biding. And if we should, needs cost, fall in peril one way or other, yet had I livelier that men should see it were by other men's falsehood, than think it were either our own fault or faint heart. And therefore go to thy master, man, and commend me to him, and pray him be merry and have no fear: for I ensure him I am as sure of the man that he wotteth of, as I am of my own hand. God send grace, sir, quoth the messenger, and went his way.

—Sir Thomas More, 1513

5. The beginning of the passage is describing what?

(A) An injury sustained by the main character

(B) A rider that is trying to escape injury

(C) The main character's dream

(D) A witch's story

(E) The boar that the character will grill for dinner

6. **What is the cautionary message that the rider gets when he reaches his destination?**

   (A) Dreams are witchcraft if you believe in them.

   (B) Dreams can come true if you believe in them.

   (C) God sends His grace.

   (D) Those faint of heart do not have dreams.

   (E) Men cannot fall for other men's falsehoods.

7. **Did the main character in this passage believe he could out run bad visions?**

   (A) No, the passage makes it clear you always get what's coming in a dream.

   (B) No, dreams mean nothing, so the main character didn't pay any attention to it.

   (C) Yes, it was possible to escape bad visions on horseback.

   (D) Yes, the main character thought dancing would rid himself of bad dreams.

   (E) There is nothing in the passage that assists in answering this question.

Questions 8-14. Read the following passage carefully before you decide on your answers to the questions.

"I went to work the next day, turning, so to speak, my back on that station. In that way only it seemed to me I could keep my hold on the redeeming facts of life. Still, one must look about sometimes; and then I saw this station, these men strolling aimlessly about in the sunshine of the yard. I asked myself sometimes what it all meant. They wandered here and there with their absurd long staves in their hands, like a lot of faithless pilgrims bewitched inside a rotten fence. The word 'ivory' rang in the air, was whispered, was sighed. You would think they were praying to it. A taint of imbecile rapacity blew through it all, like a whiff from some corpse. By Jove! I've never seen anything so unreal in my life. And outside, the silent wilderness surrounding this cleared speck on the earth struck me as something great and invincible, like evil or truth, waiting patiently for the passing away of this fantastic invasion."

8. **Who wrote this novel?**

   (A) Joseph Conrad

   (B) James Joyce

   (C) Jane Austen

   (D) Charlotte Brontë

   (E) Charles Dickens

9. **What does the following line represent?**
   "I saw this station, these men strolling aimlessly about in the sunshine of the yard."

   (A) Soldiers enjoying their day

   (B) Men being unaware of the negativity that surrounds them

   (C) Positivity is infectious

   (D) The station is a happy place

   (E) Embracing the weather before a storm hits

10. **What does the word staves mean?**

    (A) Machete

    (B) Axe

    (C) Gun

    (D) Bomb

    (E) Wooden club

11. **What does the ivory represent?**

    (A) Death

    (B) Prosperity

    (C) Jewelry

    (D) Trade

    (E) None of the above

12. **What literary device is used when describing the ivory?**

    (A) Alliteration

    (B) Allegory

    (C) Simile

    (D) Personification

    (E) Repetition

13. **What does rapacity represent?**

    (A) Greed

    (B) Rapid movement

    (C) Intelligent

    (D) Affluent

    (E) Generous

14. **What literary device is used in this passage?**

"And outside, the silent wilderness surrounding this cleared speck on the earth struck me as something great and invincible, like evil or truth, waiting patiently for the passing away of this fantastic invasion."

(A) Simile

(B) Metaphor

(C) Illusion

(D) Personification

(E) Onomatopoeia

Questions 15-21. Read the following passage carefully before you decide on your answers to the questions.

"Finished, it's finished, nearly finished, it must be nearly finished. Grain upon grain, one by one, and one day, suddenly, there's a heap, a little heap, the impossible heap. I can't be punished any more. I'll go now to my kitchen, ten feet by ten feet by ten feet, and wait for him to whistle me. Nice dimensions, nice proportions, I'll lean on the table, and look at the wall, and wait for him to whistle me."

—Endgame

15. **What literary device is used throughout this passage?**

(A) Simile

(B) Metaphor

(C) Euphemism

(D) Flashback

(E) Repetition

16. **Who wrote this play?**

(A) Anton Chekov

(B) William Shakespeare

(C) Lillian Hellman

(D) Athol Fugard

(E) Samuel Beckett

17. **What does the impossible heap represent?**

   (A) Life's greatest hurdles

   (B) A pile of grain so tall it cannot be moved

   (C) Death

   (D) A mountain

   (E) Heaven

18. **The whistle symbolizes _____.**

   (A) A referee

   (B) The character's father

   (C) Death

   (D) An angel

   (E) All of the above

19. **What is an endgame?**

   (A) The final play in a game, such as chess

   (B) The end of a negotiation

   (C) A wish

   (D) The final approval for a lease

   (E) None of the above

20. **What is the author trying to portray in this selection?**

   (A) An old man

   (B) A prisoner

   (C) A farmer

   (D) A mill worker

   (E) A plantation

21. **What best describes this selection?**

   (A) Epic

   (B) Foreshadowing

   (C) Cliffhanger

   (D) Flashback

   (E) Irony

Questions 22-29. Read the following passage carefully before you decide on your answers to the questions.

Boys are playing basketball around a telephone pole with a backboard bolted to it. Legs, shouts. The scrape and snap of Keds on loose alley pebbles seems to catapult their voices high into the moist March air blue above the wires. Rabbit Angstrom, coming up the alley in a business suit, stops and watches, though he's twenty-six and six three. So tall, he seems an unlikely rabbit, but the breadth of white face, the pallor of his blue irises, and a nervous flutter under his brief nose as he stabs a cigarette into his mouth partially explain the nickname, which was given to him when he too was a boy. He stands there thinking, the kids keep coming, they keep crowding you up.

His standing there makes the real boys feel strange. Eyeballs slide. They're doing this for themselves, not as a show for some adult walking around town in a double-breasted cocoa suit. It seems funny to them, an adult walking up the alley at all. Where's his car? The cigarette makes it more sinister still. Is this one of those going to offer them cigarettes or money to go out in back of the ice plant with him? They've heard of such things but are not too frightened; there are six of them and one of him.

The ball, rocketing off the crotch of the rim, leaps over the heads of the six and lands at the feet of the one. He catches it on the short bounce with a quickness that startles them. As they stare hushed he sights squinting through blue clouds of weed smoke, a suddenly dark silhouette like a smokestack against the afternoon spring sky, setting his feet with care, wiggling the ball with nervousness in front of his chest, one widespread white hand on top of the ball and the other underneath, jiggling it patiently to get some adjustment in air itself. The cuticle moons on his fingernails are big. Then the ball seems to ride up the right lapel of his coat and comes off his shoulder as his knees dip down, and it appears the ball will miss because though he shot from an angle the ball is not going toward the backboard. It was not aimed there. It drops into the circle of the rim, whipping the net with a ladylike whisper. "Hey!" he shouts in pride.) "Luck," one of the kids says.

22. **The first few sentences establish the scene using**

   (A) Exposition

   (B) Diction

   (C) Asides

   (D) Imager

   (E) Interjections

23. **The second paragraph characterizes the situation as:**

   (A) Humorous

   (B) Banal

   (C) Tense

   (D) Inappropriate

   (E) Enjoyable

24. This passage is written in present tense, suggesting:

(A) Immediacy

(B) Exuberance

(C) Confusion

(D) Terseness

(E) Suspense

25. What is the "dark silhouette"?

(A) Rabbit

(B) The boys

(C) The column of smoke

(D) The telephone pole

(E) The basketball

26. In this passage, the author is most concerned with establishing:

(A) Rabbit's youthfulness and skill

(B) The poor behavior of the boys

(C) The great facility Rabbit has with children

(D) Rabbit's inability to fit in

(E) The necessity for recreation in Rabbit's life

27. "Whipping the net with a ladylike whisper" is an example of:

(A) Foreshadowing

(B) Personification

(C) Parallelism

(D) Metaphor

(E) Characterization

28. Inferring from this passage, what are the primary characteristics of Rabbit?

(A) He is tall and boyish

(B) He is socially inept

(C) He has great skill at various sports

(D) He struggles to connect with the youth

(E) He has great disdain for children

29. **"So tall, he seems an unlikely rabbit," is an example of:**

(A) Symbolism

(B) Foreshadowing

(C) Decontruction

(D) Irony

(E) Personification

Questions 30-37. Read the following passage carefully before you decide on your answers to the questions.

"If people bring so much courage to this world the world has to kill them to break them, so of course it kills them. The world breaks every one and afterward many are strong at the broken places. But those that will not break it kills. It kills the very good and the very gentle and the very brave impartially. If you are none of these you can be sure it will kill you too but there will be no special hurry."

—*Farewell to Arms*

30. **Who wrote this novel?**

(A) Henry David Thoreau

(B) Ernest Hemingway

(C) F. Scott Fitzgerald

(D) Harper Lee

(E) Tom Wolfe

31. **What is the theme of this novel?**

(A) Innocence

(B) War

(C) Love

(D) Death

(E) Grief

32. **What does the title symbolize?**

(A) An amputation caused during war

(B) Being discharged

(C) Saying goodbye to the arms of someone you love

(D) Saying goodbye to weaponry and warfare

(E) Both C & D

33. **Which literary device is used to describe war?**

    (A) Personification

    (B) Alliteration

    (C) Simile

    (D) Metaphor

    (E) Idiom

34. **Which of the following best represents this passage**

    (A) Sarcasm

    (B) Resentment

    (C) Irony

    (D) Sympathy

    (E) Affectionate

35. **What best describes the author's intention in the following line?**
    "It kills the very good and the very gentle and the very brave impartially."

    (A) Everyone will die sooner or later

    (B) Murderers target nice people

    (C) The good, gentle and brave are easier to kill

    (D) The good, gentle and brave die protecting others

    (E) War kills everyone, it doesn't have a bias

36. **How does the world break people?**

    (A) It creates challenging times

    (B) It represents being shot and not dying

    (C) It causes extreme wounds, mentally and physically

    (D) People can have broken bones

    (E) Physical objects and precious belongings can be broken

37. **Which literary period is this from?**

    (A) Romantcism

    (B) Renaissance

    (C) The Enlightenment

    (D) Existentialism

    (E) Modernism

Questions 38-45. Read the following passage carefully before you decide on your answers to the questions.

Mr. Pocket said he was glad to see me, and he hoped I was not sorry to see him. `For, I really am not,' he added, with his son's smile, `an alarming personage.' He was a young-looking man, in spite of his perplexities and his very grey hair, and his manner seemed quite natural. I use the word natural, in the sense of its being unaffected; there was something comic in his distraught way, as though it would have been downright ludicrous but for his own perception that it was very near being so. When he had talked with me a little, he said to Mrs Pocket, with a rather anxious contraction of his eyebrows, which were black and handsome, `Belinda, I hope you have welcomed Mr Pip?' And she looked up from her book, and said, `Yes.' She then smiled upon me in an absent state of mind, and asked me if I liked the taste of orange-flower water? As the question had no bearing, near or remote, on any foregone or subsequent transaction, I consider it to have been thrown out, like her previous approaches, in general conversational condescension.

I found out within a few hours, and may mention at once, that Mrs Pocket was the only daughter of a certain quite accidental deceased Knight, who had invented for himself a conviction that his deceased father would have been made a Baronet but for some- body's determined opposition arising out of entirely personal motives -- I forget whose, if I ever knew -- the Sovereign's, the Prime Minister's, the Lord Chancellor's, the Archbishop of Canterbury's, anybody's -- and had tacked himself on to the nobles of the earth in right of this quite supposititious fact. I believe he had been knighted himself for storming the English grammar at the point of the pen, in a desperate address engrossed on vellum, on the occasion of the laying of the first stone of some building or other, and for handing some Royal Personage either the trowel or the mortar. Be that as it may, he had directed Mrs Pocket to be brought up from her cradle as one who in the nature of things must marry a title, and who was to be guarded from the acquisition of plebeian domestic knowledge.

38. Who is the speaker in this piece?

   (A) Pocket

   (B) An unnamed person

   (C) Belinda

   (D) Pip

   (E) Baronet

39. What do we know about Mrs. Pocket's father?

   (A) He felt cheated by some politician

   (B) He was a liar

   (C) He was dim and uneducated

   (D) He was lower class

   (E) He was very wealthy

40. What best describes Belinda's attitude towards the speaker?

(A) Curiosity

(B) Indifference

(C) Haughtiness

(D) Suspicion

(E) Lewdness

41. What is meant by the sentence "as though it would have been downright ludicrous but for his own perception that it was very near being so"?

(A) He was unbearable to be around, but did not care

(B) He was ashamed of his own lack of grace and finesse

(C) His self-awareness prevents him from being completely awkward

(D) He is unaware of how incompetent he is

(E) He has a striking appearance, carefully maintained

42. What do we learn about Belinda from the phrase "who was to be guarded against the acquisition of plebian domestic knowledge?"

(A) She was raised upper class and has little understanding of working class customs

(B) She has deep contempt for common folk, for her father despised them

(C) She has great skill in interacting with those outside her social class

(D) She resents her sheltered upbringing and wishes to experience more of life

(E) She had little education growing up, like many women of the time

43. Belinda's question to the speaker can best be described as a:

(A) Interjection

(B) Non sequitur

(C) Insult

(D) Aside

(E) Jab

44. The tone of this piece is very:

(A) Humorous

(B) Morose

(C) Bland

(D) Tense

(E) Mysterious

45. Why was Belinda's father knighted?

(A) He wrote a loving address

(B) He won fame in a battle

(C) He wasn't; he was cheated out of knighthood by a rival

(D) He was appointed as such by the Sovereign

(E) He offered nominal help in some construction project

Questions 46–50. Read the following passage carefully before you decide on your answers to the questions.

Knowing that Mrs. Mallard was afflicted with a heart trouble, great care was taken to break to her as gently as possible the news of her husband's death.

It was her sister Josephine who told her, in broken sentences; veiled hints that revealed in half concealing. Her husband's friend Richards was there, too, near her. It was he who had been in the newspaper office when intelligence of the railroad disaster was received, with Brently Mallard's name leading the list of "killed." He had only taken the time to assure himself of its truth by a second telegram, and had hastened to forestall any less careful, less tender friend in bearing the sad message.

She did not hear the story as many women have heard the same, with a paralyzed inability to accept its significance. She wept at once, with sudden, wild abandonment, in her sister's arms. When the storm of grief had spent itself she went away to her room alone. She would have no one follow her.

There stood, facing the open window, a comfortable, roomy armchair. Into this she sank, pressed down by a physical exhaustion that haunted her body and seemed to reach into her soul.

She could see in the open square before her house the tops of trees that were all aquiver with the new spring life. The delicious breath of rain was in the air. In the street below a peddler was crying his wares. The notes of a distant song which some one was singing reached her faintly, and countless sparrows were twittering in the eaves.

There were patches of blue sky showing here and there through the clouds that had met and piled one above the other in the west facing her window.

She sat with her head thrown back upon the cushion of the chair, quite motionless, except when a sob came up into her throat and shook her, as a child who has cried itself to sleep continues to sob in its dreams.

46. What best describes the tone of this piece?

(A) Suspenseful

(B) Somber

(C) Conceited

(D) Bittersweet

(E) Angry

47. The primary contrast in this selection is between:

(A) Mrs. Mallard and Josephine

(B) Mrs. Mallard and her dead husband

(C) Mrs. Mallard's grief and the outside world

(D) Josephine and Richards

(E) Cocealed truths and brutal honesty

48. What can we tell about Mrs. Mallard's relationship with Josephine?

(A) Josephine treats her firmly

(B) They are estranged

(C) Josephine has no idea how to handle her sister's condition

(D) The pair have few things in common

(E) Josephine is reluctant to be around Mrs. Mallard

49. The world outside Mrs. Mallard's window is characterized with all of the senses EXCEPT:

(A) Taste

(B) Smell

(C) Sight

(D) Touch

(E) Sound

50. In context, what can "forestall" be taken to mean?

(A) Hurry forward

(B) Obstruct

(C) Inform

(D) Consider

(E) Explain to

51. Inferring from the text, Mrs. Mallard's grief renders her:

(A) Infntile

(B) Hysterical

(C) Violent

(D) Volatile

(E) Recalcitrant

52. What is the subject of the verb "sank" in paragraph four?

(A) "This"

(B) "She"

(C) "Into"

(D) "Armchair"

(E) "Exhaustion"

53. What best describes the author's characterization of the view from the window?

(A) Dreary

(B) Dreamlike

(C) Yearning

(D) Impactful

(E) Livey

Questions 54-57. Read the following passage carefully before you decide on your answers to the questions.

Bernardo : Welcome, Horatio: welcome, good Marcellus.
Marcellus : What, has this thing appear'd again to-night?
Bernardo : I have seen nothing.
Marcellus : Horatio says 'tis but our fantasy,
And will not let belief take hold of him
Touching this dreaded sight, twice seen of us:
Therefore I have entreated him along
With us to watch the minutes of this night;
That if again this apparition come,
He may approve our eyes and speak to it.
Horatio : Tush, tush, 'twill not appear.
Bernardo : Sit down awhile;
And let us once again assail your ears,
That are so fortified against our story
What we have two nights seen.

—William Shakespeare, 1599-1602

54. The three men in the play can be said, in this passage:

(A) to disagree about a ghost that was seen

(B) to disagree that two days ago they saw people meeting "twice seen of us"

(C) that Horatio and Bernardo are trying to persuade Marcellus they saw something

(D) that Horatio and Marcellus are trying to persuade Bernardo they saw something

(E) to meet for a drink for "fortification"

55. When Marcellus speaks of "approving our eyes", what is he saying?

(A) Marcellus and Bernardo need glasses.

(B) Bernardo didn't believe what Marcellus saw.

(C) Horatio believes what Marcellus saw.

(D) Horatio should see what Bernardo and Marcellus saw.

(E) Marcellus should believe what Bernardo saw.

56. When Bernardo says "once again assail your ears", what does he mean?

(A) He wants to repeat himself to Marcellus to make him believe him.

(B) He wants to repeat himself to Horatio to make him believe him.

(C) He wants to repeat himself to help all three of them believe the story.

(D) He wants Marcellus and Horatio to poke holes in the story.

(E) None of these are the meaning of that phrase in the passag(E)

57. In the context of the passage, entreated means:

(A) invited

(B) engaged

(C) demanded

(D) refused

(E) ignored

Edmund : That's foolishness. You know it's only a bad cold.

Mary : Yes, of course, I know that!

Edmund : But listen, Mama. I want you to promise me that even if it turns out to be something worse, you'll know I'll soon be alright again, anyway, and don't worry yourself sick, and you'll keep on taking care of yourself—

Mary : I won't listen when you talk so silly! There's absolutely no reason to talk as if you expect som thing dreadful! Of course, I promise you I give you my sacred word of honor! But I suppose you're remembering I've promised before on my word of honor.

Edmund : No!

Mary : I'm not blaming you, dear. How can you help it? How can any one of us forget? That's what makes it so hard—for all of us. We can't forget.

Edmund : Mama! Stop it!

Mary : All right, dear. I didn't beam to be so gloomy. Don't mind me. Here. Let me feel your head Why, it's nice and cool. You certainly don't have any fever now.

— Eugene O'Neill, 1955

58. It can be said that this passage of the drama:

(A) puts American dream against American nightmare

(B) describes the normal American family

(C) portrays Americans in a very resilient fashion

(D) was likely written during a war so obviously has negative overtones

(E) has the mother remembering the death of another child

59. Mary changes the direction of the conversation by:

(A) stopping Edmund from talking by taking his temperature

(B) making Edmund feel badly about the death of his brother

(C) walking out of the room

(D) tucking the covers up to his chin

(E) ignoring him

60. This portion of the play is a:

(A) monologue

(B) dialogue

(C) soliloquy

(D) entendre

(E) stichomythia

Sample Test Two

ANSWER KEY

Question Number	Correct Answer	Your Answer
1.	B	
2.	A	
3.	C	
4.	C	
5.	C	
6.	A	
7.	C	
8.	A	
9.	B	
10.	E	
11.	B	
12.	B	
13.	A	
14.	A	
15.	E	
16.	E	
17.	C	
18.	C	
19.	A	
20.	B	
21.	B	
22.	D	
23.	C	
24.	A	
25.	D	
26.	A	
27.	B	
28.	A	
29.	D	
30.	B	

Question Number	Correct Answer	Your Answer
31.	B	
32.	D	
33.	A	
34.	B	
35.	E	
36.	C	
37.	E	
38.	D	
39.	A	
40.	B	
41.	C	
42.	A	
43.	B	
44.	A	
45.	E	
46.	B	
47.	C	
48.	D	
49.	A	
50.	B	
51.	A	
52.	B	
53.	E	
54.	A	
55.	D	
56.	B	
57.	A	
58.	E	
59.	A	
60.	B	

Sample Test 2 Explanation

Questions 1-4   Read the following passage carefully before you decide on your answers to the questions.

I'd like to say here, that I wasn't the only important one. I was part of a family, just like all of my brothers and sisters. The whole community was important. We used to discuss many of the community's problems together, especially when someone was ill and we couldn't buy medicine, because we were getting poorer and poorer. We'd start discussing and heaping insults on the rich who'd made us suffer for so long. It was about then I began learning about politics. I tried to talk to people who could help me sort my ideas out. I wanted to know what the world was like on the other side. I knew the finca, I knew the Altiplano. But what I didn't know was about the other problems of the Indians in Guatemala. I didn't know the problems the other groups had to holding onto their land.I knew there were lots of other Indians in other parts of the country, because I'd been meeting them in the finca since I was a child, but though we all worked together, we didn't know any of the names of the towns they came from, or how they lived, or what they ate. We just imagined that they were like us.

—Rigoberta Menchu, Nobel Peace Prize Winner 1992

1. From the context of the passage, what is a finca?

(A) A farm

(B) A village or town

(C) A mountain range

(D) A house

(E) It cannot be determined

The correct answer is B.

In the passage, only two Spanish words are used. Since the author describes a group of unrelated people The answer is not (D) When offered an option like (E), typically that is not the correct choice in a reading comprehension exam. Of the three remaining choices, since it talks about a gathering at this location, (C) is not an appropriate choice. Either (A) or (B) could apply, but (A) is a workplace not a gathering place. Choose (B) as the best answer—note that it is also mentioned at the end of the paragraph about people living in towns, another clue that this is the best answer.

2. The author is telling a story about her own life. What is this kind of document called?

(A) Autobiography

(B) Mystery

(C) Biography

(D) Narrative

(E) Romance

The correct answer is A.

(A) is the type of story where someone talks about their own life, While narrative could be another possible answer, the best answer is (A).

3. Given the information in the passage, the author most likely worked as:

(A) a washer woman

(B) a seamstress

(C) a farmer

(D) a teacher

(E) it cannot be determined from the passage

The correct answer is C.

There are no indications that the woman washed clothes, worked as a seamstress or a teacher. Thus, (A), (B) and (D) are eliminated. Between choices (C) and (E), you must decide. If you read the book in full, (C) is the correct answer. But because this is about this passage, you do not have enough information to decide and (E) is the best selection—a rare occurrence in this exam, but it does happen.

4. The author describes who is the most important. She defines it as:

(A) herself

(B) her family

(C) her community

(D) the rich people that employed them

(E) the finca

The correct answer is C.

It is clear that the author says the community is important. It is literally part of the passage. She denounces A (herself) and even to an extent her family (option B); she goes on to talk about the community together, so the best answer is (C). (D) is opposite of the intent of the passage and (E) is incongruous, though the translation is town that is just a physical location. Community has stronger meaning and is the best answer.

Questions 5-7. Read the following passage carefully before you decide on your answers to the questions.

A marvelous case is it to hear, either the warnings of that he should have voided, or the tokens of that he could not void. For the self night next before his death, the lord Stanley sent a trusty secret messenger unto him at midnight in all the haste, requiring him to rise and ride away with him, for he was disposed utterly no longer to bide; he had so fearful a dream, in which him thought that a boar with his tusks so raced them both by the heads, that the blood ran about both their shoulders. And forasmuch as the protector gave the boar for his cognizance, this dream made so fearful an impression in his heart, that he was thoroughly determined no longer to tarry, but had his horse ready, if the lord Hastings would go with him to ride so far yet the same night, that they should be out of danger ere day. Ay, good lord, quoth the lord Hastings to this messenger, leaneth my lord thy master so much to such trifles, and hath such faith in dreams, which either his own fear fantasieth or do rise in the night's rest by reason of his day thoughts? Tell him it is plain witchcraft to believe in such dreams; which if they were tokens of things to come, why thinketh he not that we might be as likely to make them true by our going if we were caught and brought back (as friends fail fleers), for then had the boar a cause likely to race us with his tusks, as folk that fled for some falsehood, wherefore either is there no peril (nor none there is indeed), or if any be, it is rather in going than biding. And if we should, needs cost, fall in peril one way or other, yet had I livelier that men should see it were by other men's falsehood, than think it were either our own fault or faint heart. And therefore go to thy master, man, and commend me to him, and pray him be merry and have no fear: for I ensure him I am as sure of the man that he wotteth of, as I am of my own hand. God send grace, sir, quoth the messenger, and went his way.

—Sir Thomas More, 1513

5. **The beginning of the passage is describing what?**

   (A) An injury sustained by the main character

   (B) A rider that is trying to escape injury

   (C) The main character's dream

   (D) A witch's story

   (E) The boar that the character will grill for dinner

   The correct answer is C.

   Discounting the incorrect description of what's in the passage (such as in option (E) and (A) as well as (B), that leaves options (C) and (D) There is no reference to a witch, so the best choice is (C) He even states that it is a dream.

6. What is the cautionary message that the rider gets when he reaches his destination?

(A) Dreams are witchcraft if you believe in them.

(B) Dreams can come true if you believe in them.

(C) God sends His grace.

(D) Those faint of heart do not have dreams.

(E) Men cannot fall for other men's falsehoods.

The correct answer is A.

The rider warns the statement included in (A)

7. Did the main character in this passage believe he could out run bad visions?

(A) No, the passage makes it clear you always get what's coming in a dream.

(B) No, dreams mean nothing, so the main character didn't pay any attention to it.

(C) Yes, it was possible to escape bad visions on horseback.

(D) Yes, the main character thought dancing would rid himself of bad dreams.

(E) There is nothing in the passage that assists in answering this question.

The correct answer is C.

Again, the main character gives indications that the correct answer is (C) The other options of No are wrong, as is the answer given in (E) Answer (D) can be discounted because dancing is not discussed in the passage.

Questions 8-14. Read the following passage carefully before you decide on your answers to the questions.

"I went to work the next day, turning, so to speak, my back on that station. In that way only it seemed to me I could keep my hold on the redeeming facts of life. Still, one must look about sometimes; and then I saw this station, these men strolling aimlessly about in the sunshine of the yard. I asked myself sometimes what it all meant. They wandered here and there with their absurd long staves in their hands, like a lot of faithless pilgrims bewitched inside a rotten fence. The word 'ivory' rang in the air, was whispered, was sighed. You would think they were praying to it. A taint of imbecile rapacity blew through it all, like a whiff from some corpse. By Jove! I've never seen anything so unreal in my life. And outside, the silent wilderness surrounding this cleared speck on the earth struck me as something great and invincible, like evil or truth, waiting patiently for the passing away of this fantastic invasion."

8. **Who wrote this novel?**

(A) Joseph Conrad

(B) James Joyce

(C) Jane Austen

(D) Charlotte Brontë

(E) Charles Dickens

The correct answer is A.

This is another question where you may have to eliminate answers to help you pick the right one. Charles Dickens and Charlotte Bronte could be eliminated as can Jane Austen—they do not write novels in this syntax and manner. Of the two remaining, James Joyce was an Irish poet and novelist, most famous for writing Ulysses and short stories if not poems. Joseph Conrad was a Polish author, writing in English, and this is one of his most famous works.

9. **What does the following line represent?**

"I saw this station, these men strolling aimlessly about in the sunshine of the yard."

(A) Soldiers enjoying their day

(B) Men being unaware of the negativity that surrounds them

(C) Positivity is infectious

(D) The station is a happy place

(E) Embracing the weather before a storm hits

The correct answer is B.

You should eliminate the obvious wrong answers, such as (A) (when the College Board asks questions, there is more meaning than this option is portraying) and (C) (as there is no lead in the sentence that brings you to this conclusion). Of the three remaining choices, (D) and (E) could be true, but the key phrase "strolling aimlessly" makes you believe that there is more meaning than just being in the sunshine.

10. **What does the word staves mean?**

(A) Machete

(B) Axe

(C) Gun

(D) Bomb

(E) Wooden club

The correct answer is E.

Using the context of the passage if you don't know the definition of the word, the clues there are "long" and in their hands. That reduces the likelihood that either gun or bomb are appropriate choices. There is no indication that there are machetes or axes involved, but this is a question where better vocabulary increases the likelihood that you know the right synonym.

11. **What does the ivory represent?**

(A) Death

(B) Prosperity

(C) Jewelry

(D) Trade

(E) None of the above

The correct answer is B.

If an person possessed ivory, it was very expensive and represented wealth, which is another word for prosperity. There are no clues that would lead the other three options are appropriate in the passage. Hint: the College Board very rarely uses "none of these" or "all of these" as appropriate choices.

12. **What literary device is used when describing the ivory?**

(A) Alliteration

(B) Allegory

(C) Simile

(D) Personification

(E) Repetition

The correct answer is B.

From the list, you should be able to easily eliminate (C), (D) and (E) Between the first two, you need to know the definitions presented earlier, but if you forget, you should at least be able to make a 50-50 guess.

13. **What does rapacity represent?**

(A) Greed

(B) Rapid movement

(C) Intelligent

(D) Affluent

(E) Generous

The correct answer is A.

From the context of the passage (a taint that blew through), you should be able to eliminate(C), (D), and (E). There is nothing else in the passage that implies rapid movement, so if you don't know what the word means, you should still be able to eliminate the wrong choices.

14. What literary device is used in this passage?

"And outside, the silent wilderness surrounding this cleared speck on the earth struck me as something great and invincible, like evil or truth, waiting patiently for the passing away of this fantastic invasion."

(A) Simile

(B) Metaphor

(C) Illusion

(D) Personification

(E) Onomatopoeia

The correct answer is A.

Simile means a figure of speech comparing two things, making a vivid description. You should know the other definitions—if you got this wrong, look up the other terms to refresh your memory.

Questions 15-21. Read the following passage carefully before you decide on your answers to the questions.

"Finished, it's finished, nearly finished, it must be nearly finished. Grain upon grain, one by one, and one day, suddenly, there's a heap, a little heap, the impossible heap. I can't be punished any more. I'll go now to my kitchen, ten feet by ten feet by ten feet, and wait for him to whistle me. Nice dimensions, nice proportions, I'll lean on the table, and look at the wall, and wait for him to whistle me."

—*Endgame*

15. What literary device is used throughout this passage?

(A) Simile

(B) Metaphor

(C) Euphemism

(D) Flashback

(E) Repetition

The correct answer is E.

Knowing the definitions would rule out (A), (B) and (C) But seeing the word finished many times should tip you to the correct answer.

16. Who wrote this play?

(A) Anton Chekov

(B) William Shakespeare

(C) Lillian Hellman

(D) Athol Fugard

(E) Samuel Beckett

The correct answer is E.

You should be able to eliminate (A), (B) and (C) as options as soon as you read them. This story, Endgame, is one of the more famous books by Beckett; Athol Fugard is a South African writer mostly working on plays and or films.

17. What does the impossible heap represent?

(A) Life's greatest hurdles

(B) A pile of grain so tall it cannot be moved

(C) Death

(D) A mountain

(E) Heaven

The correct answer is C.

Both (B) and (D) would be a more literal meaning that wasn't present in context of the passage, so they should be eliminated. If it was asking about the whole series, then (A) would be accurate. The answer is (C), the action not the destination (represented by Heaven in E).

18. The whistle symbolizes _____.

(A) A referee

(B) The character's father

(C) Death

(D) An angel

(E) All of the above

The correct answer is C.

The whistle would be a literal representation of a device used by a referee but we have to consider context. That also eliminates (B) and (C) as the passage talks about the characters approach to death.

19. **What is an endgame?**

   (A) The final play in a game, such as chess

   (B) The end of a negotiation

   (C) A wish

   (D) The final approval for a lease

   (E) None of the above

   The correct answer is A.

   The end of a negotiation is an end result, not endgame (which is the final or last move). (C) and (D) are also not appropriate answers and as previously explained, the "none of the above" answer is rarely right, if you are having to guess for a correct answer.

20. **What is the author trying to portray in this selection?**

   (A) An old man

   (B) A prisoner

   (C) A farmer

   (D) A mill worker

   (E) A plantation

   The correct answer is B.

   E is not correct as that is a place and the description is for a person. Of the four remaining, and using other questions (such as the definition of an endgame), and knowing that death is coming for the person, the best answer is (B)

21. **What best describes this selection?**

   (A) Epic

   (B) Foreshadowing

   (C) Cliffhanger

   (D) Flashback

   (E) Irony

   The correct answer is B.

   From the selection, irony is not present, nor is a flashback or cliffhanger (a suspense scene). Of the two remaining selections, you should know what they both are—an epic is a story about a hero, and there are no indications that is who is being describe or is present in the passage.

Questions 22-29. Read the following passage carefully before you decide on your answers to the questions.

Boys are playing basketball around a telephone pole with a backboard bolted to it. Legs, shouts. The scrape and snap of Keds on loose alley pebbles seems to catapult their voices high into the moist March air blue above the wires. Rabbit Angstrom, coming up the alley in a business suit, stops and watches, though he's twenty-six and six three. So tall, he seems an unlikely rabbit, but the breadth of white face, the pallor of his blue irises, and a nervous flutter under his brief nose as he stabs a cigarette into his mouth partially explain the nickname, which was given to him when he too was a boy. He stands there thinking, the kids keep coming, they keep crowding you up.

His standing there makes the real boys feel strange. Eyeballs slide. They're doing this for themselves, not as a show for some adult walking around town in a double-breasted cocoa suit. It seems funny to them, an adult walking up the alley at all. Where's his car? The cigarette makes it more sinister still. Is this one of those going to offer them cigarettes or money to go out in back of the ice plant with him? They've heard of such things but are not too frightened; there are six of them and one of him.

The ball, rocketing off the crotch of the rim, leaps over the heads of the six and lands at the feet of the one. He catches it on the short bounce with a quickness that startles them. As they stare hushed he sights squinting through blue clouds of weed smoke, a suddenly dark silhouette like a smokestack against the afternoon spring sky, setting his feet with care, wiggling the ball with nervousness in front of his chest, one widespread white hand on top of the ball and the other underneath, jiggling it patiently to get some adjustment in air itself. The cuticle moons on his fingernails are big. Then the ball seems to ride up the right lapel of his coat and comes off his shoulder as his knees dip down, and it appears the ball will miss because though he shot from an angle the ball is not going toward the backboard. It was not aimed there. It drops into the circle of the rim, whipping the net with a ladylike whisper. "Hey!" he shouts in pride.) "Luck," one of the kids says.

22. The first few sentences establish the scene using

(A) Exposition

(B) Diction

(C) Asides

(D) Imager

(E) Interjections

The correct answer is D.

The opening sentences of the passage feature brief, powerful descriptions of sensory details – the scrape of pebbles, the shouts of young boys, etc. Diction and asides (B and C) would not apply, and the piece features short sentences, but they don't qualify as interjections (E). The piece also does not feature exposition (A), as there is no backstory nor story detail discussed.

23. The second paragraph characterizes the situation as:

(A) Humorous

(B) Banal

(C) Tense

(D) Inappropriate

(E) Enjoyable

The correct answer is C.

The author clearly describes the "sinister" nature of Rabbit's cigarette, and the unease of the boys. There's a certain absurdity to the proceedings, but not enough to characterize it as humorous (A). Inappropriate (D) is too strong a qualifier for the going's on, and "enjoyable" (E) does not apply given how the action is characterized.

24. This passage is written in present tense, suggesting:

(A) Immediacy

(B) Exuberance

(C) Confusion

(D) Terseness

(E) Suspense

The correct answer is A.

Present tense suggests the actions are happening now, at this moment. Immediately. The piece could hardly be characterized as exuberant (B), and though suspense and confusion may be present in the piece, they aren't served by the present tense narration.

25. What is the "dark silhouette"?

(A) Rabbit

(B) The boys

(C) The column of smoke

(D) The telephone pole

(E) The basketball

The correct answer is D.

Rabbit spies the dark silhouette just before lobbing the basketball at it. It is clearly the telephone pole with the hoop attached to it.

26. In this passage, the author is most concerned with establishing:

(A) Rabbit's youthfulness and skill

(B) The poor behavior of the boys

(C) The great facility Rabbit has with children

(D) Rabbit's inability to fit in

(E) The necessity for recreation in Rabbit's life

The correct answer is A.

The primary purpose of this piece is to illustrate Rabbit's bygone years as a basketball star and his lingering affection for the sport and those simpler times. The boys behave uncouthly, but this is not a primary concern of this passage (B). Rabbit would not be expected to fit in in such a situation, so (D) is not appropriate. (E) relies on assumptions, and (C) does not apply as Rabbit fails to connect with the boys.

27. "Whipping the net with a ladylike whisper" is an example of:

(A) Foreshadowing

(B) Personification

(C) Parallelism

(D) Metaphor

(E) Characterization

The correct answer is B.

The net is given a human quality, the ability to whisper like a lady.

28. Inferring from this passage, what are the primary characteristics of Rabbit?

(A) He is tall and boyish

(B) He is socially inept

(C) He has great skill at various sports

(D) He struggles to connect with the youth

(E) He has great disdain for children

The correct answer is A.

Much is made of Rabbit's unusual height, as well as his boyish skill at basketball. We cannot infer (B) from such an unusual scenario as the one described, and (C) relies on assumptions we cannot prove. (D), likewise, requires assumptions and (E) does not apply as Rabbit seems to be trying to connect with the boys.

29. "So tall, he seems an unlikely rabbit," is an example of:

(A) Symbolism

(B) Foreshadowing

(C) Decontruction

(D) Irony

(E) Personification

The correct answer is D.

The sentence marks the oddness of a man named "Rabbit" being so tall.

Questions 30-37. Read the following passage carefully before you decide on your answers to the questions.

"If people bring so much courage to this world the world has to kill them to break them, so of course it kills them. The world breaks every one and afterward many are strong at the broken places. But those that will not break it kills. It kills the very good and the very gentle and the very brave impartially. If you are none of these you can be sure it will kill you too but there will be no special hurry."

—*Farewell to Arms*

30. Who wrote this novel?

(A) Henry David Thoreau

(B) Ernest Hemingway

(C) F. Scott Fitzgerald

(D) Harper Lee

(E) Tom Wolfe

The correct answer is B.

This is one of his most famous novels.

31. What is the theme of this novel?

(A) Innocence

(B) War

(C) Love

(D) Death

(E) Grief

The correct answer is B.

This is one of the books you should know; but the title also gives clues to the meaning. There are some authors, like those in question 48's options, that you should be able to recognize a few of the more famous works.

32. What does the title symbolize?

(A) An amputation caused during war

(B) Being discharged

(C) Saying goodbye to the arms of someone you love

(D) Saying goodbye to weaponry and warfare

(E) Both C & D

The correct answer is D.

Rarely in multiple choice questions like this are there two correct answers. If you recognize the title of the book and general theme, this will be easier to answer.

33. Which literary device is used to describe war?

(A) Personification

(B) Alliteration

(C) Simile

(D) Metaphor

(E) Idiom

The correct answer is A.

You should know all of these terms and be able to answer questions like this quickly and correctly. Review any terms that are unfamiliar.

34. Which of the following best represents this passage

(A) Sarcasm

(B) Resentment

(C) Irony

(D) Sympathy

(E) Affectionate

The correct answer is B.

This is reading comprehension and interpreting the correct tone from the author's work.

35. **What best describes the author's intention in the following line?**
"**It kills the very good and the very gentle and the very brave impartially.**"

(A) Everyone will die sooner or later

(B) Murderers target nice people

(C) The good, gentle and brave are easier to kill

(D) The good, gentle and brave die protecting others

(E) War kills everyone, it doesn't have a bias

The correct answer is E.

The key word is impartially, meaning without bias. (E) is the only possible answer.

36. **How does the world break people?**

(A) It creates challenging times

(B) It represents being shot and not dying

(C) It causes extreme wounds, mentally and physically

(D) People can have broken bones

(E) Physical objects and precious belongings can be broken

The correct answer is C.

This is not a physical action of breaking only, as there are other ways people are broken described in the passage; therefore, answers with only physical or only mental are not correct, leaving (C) as the only option.

37. **Which literary period is this from?**

(A) Romantcism

(B) Renaissance

(C) The Enlightenment

(D) Existentialism

(E) Modernism

The correct answer is E.

Knowing the dates of when movements happened will help you identify authors or movements, which appear frequently in the exams.

Mr. Pocket said he was glad to see me, and he hoped I was not sorry to see him. `For, I really am not,' he added, with his son's smile, `an alarming personage.' He was a young-looking man, in spite of his perplexities and his very grey hair, and his manner seemed quite natural. I use the word natural, in the sense of its being unaffected; there was something comic in his distraught way, as though it would have been downright ludicrous but for his own perception that it was very near being so. When he had talked with me a little, he said to Mrs Pocket, with a rather anxious contraction of his eyebrows, which were black and handsome, `Belinda, I hope you have welcomed Mr Pip?' And she looked up from her book, and said, `Yes.' She then smiled upon me in an absent state of mind, and asked me if I liked the taste of orange-flower water? As the question had no bearing, near or remote, on any foregone or subsequent transaction, I consider it to have been thrown out, like her previous approaches, in general conversational condescension.

I found out within a few hours, and may mention at once, that Mrs Pocket was the only daughter of a certain quite accidental deceased Knight, who had invented for himself a conviction that his deceased father would have been made a Baronet but for some- body's determined opposition arising out of entirely personal motives -- I forget whose, if I ever knew -- the Sovereign's, the Prime Minister's, the Lord Chancellor's, the Archbishop of Canterbury's, anybody's -- and had tacked himself on to the nobles of the earth in right of this quite supposititious fact. I believe he had been knighted himself for storming the English grammar at the point of the pen, in a desperate address engrossed on vellum, on the occasion of the laying of the first stone of some building or other, and for handing some Royal Personage either the trowel or the mortar. Be that as it may, he had directed Mrs Pocket to be brought up from her cradle as one who in the nature of things must marry a title, and who was to be guarded from the acquisition of plebeian domestic knowledge.

38. Who is the speaker in this piece?

(A) Pocket

(B) An unnamed person

(C) Belinda

(D) Pip

(E) Baronet

The correct answer is D.

Mr. Pocket says to his wife "I hope you have welcomed Mr. Pip", indicating the speaker is Pip.

39. **What do we know about Mrs. Pocket's father?**

(A) He felt cheated by some politician

(B) He was a liar

(C) He was dim and uneducated

(D) He was lower class

(E) He was very wealthy

The correct answer is A.

Mrs. Pocket's father is stated to have had a self-serving feud with some noble or another who prevented his ascension out of spite. The rest of the answers require assumptions we can't support with the text given.

40. **What best describes Belinda's attitude towards the speaker?**

(A) Curiosity

(B) Indifference

(C) Haughtiness

(D) Suspicion

(E) Lewdness

The correct answer is B.

Belinda barely acknowledges Pip, and even then only in a bizarre, obligatory manner.

41. **What is meant by the sentence "as though it would have been downright ludicrous but for his own perception that it was very near being so"?**

(A) He was unbearable to be around, but did not care

(B) He was ashamed of his own lack of grace and finesse

(C) His self-awareness prevents him from being completely awkward

(D) He is unaware of how incompetent he is

(E) He has a striking appearance, carefully maintained

The correct answer is C.

The quote suggests that the very odd Mr. Pocket's only saving grace is his own understanding that he is strange. He does conduct himself with politeness and decorum, so (A) and (B) do not apply. (D) is the opposite of the meaning of the quite, and (E) is not supported.

42. What do we learn about Belinda from the phrase "who was to be guarded against the acquisition of plebian domestic knowledge?"

(A) She was raised upper class and has little understanding of working class customs

(B) She has deep contempt for common folk, for her father despised them

(C) She has great skill in interacting with those outside her social class

(D) She resents her sheltered upbringing and wishes to experience more of life

(E) She had little education growing up, like many women of the time

The correct answer is A.

The quoted section suggests that Belinda was prevented from learning commoner's skills and behaviors.

43. Belinda's question to the speaker can best be described as a:

(A) Interjection

(B) Non sequitur

(C) Insult

(D) Aside

(E) Jab

The correct answer is B.

Belinda asks Pip if he enjoys orange-flower water, which Pip states has nothing to do with any discussion they were having. She does not interject with the question (A), nor does she insult (C). It could not be characterized as an aside (D) or jab (E). (B) is the safest answer.

44. The tone of this piece is very:

(A) Humorous

(B) Morose

(C) Bland

(D) Tense

(E) Mysterious

The correct answer is A.

The inherent absurdity of the situation characterizes the piece as primarily comedic. Pocket's strange mannerisms and his wife's non-sequitors are bizarre in the extreme.

45. Why was Belinda's father knighted?

(A) He wrote a loving address

(B) He won fame in a battle

(C) He wasn't; he was cheated out of knighthood by a rival

(D) He was appointed as such by the Sovereign

(E) He offered nominal help in some construction project

The correct answer is E.

The text states that Belinda's father likely achieved his knighthood by delivering a letter and then handing some noble a shovel or a trowel during a construction project.

Questions 46-50. Read the following passage carefully before you decide on your answers to the questions.

Knowing that Mrs. Mallard was afflicted with a heart trouble, great care was taken to break to her as gently as possible the news of her husband's death.

It was her sister Josephine who told her, in broken sentences; veiled hints that revealed in half concealing. Her husband's friend Richards was there, too, near her. It was he who had been in the newspaper office when intelligence of the railroad disaster was received, with Brently Mallard's name leading the list of "killed." He had only taken the time to assure himself of its truth by a second telegram, and had hastened to forestall any less careful, less tender friend in bearing the sad message.

She did not hear the story as many women have heard the same, with a paralyzed inability to accept its significance. She wept at once, with sudden, wild abandonment, in her sister's arms. When the storm of grief had spent itself she went away to her room alone. She would have no one follow her.

There stood, facing the open window, a comfortable, roomy armchair. Into this she sank, pressed down by a physical exhaustion that haunted her body and seemed to reach into her soul.

She could see in the open square before her house the tops of trees that were all aquiver with the new spring life. The delicious breath of rain was in the air. In the street below a peddler was crying his wares. The notes of a distant song which some one was singing reached her faintly, and countless sparrows were twittering in the eaves.

There were patches of blue sky showing here and there through the clouds that had met and piled one above the other in the west facing her window.

She sat with her head thrown back upon the cushion of the chair, quite motionless, except when a sob came up into her throat and shook her, as a child who has cried itself to sleep continues to sob in its dreams.

46. What best describes the tone of this piece?

(A) Suspenseful

(B) Somber

(C) Conceited

(D) Bittersweet

(E) Angry

The correct answer is B.

The piece deals with death and the grief of Mrs. Mallard. The death has already occurred, so there is little in the way of suspense (A), and there is no uplifting sweetness (D) to counteract the gloom. (C) and (E) could not apply.

47. The primary contrast in this selection is between:

(A) Mrs. Mallard and Josephine

(B) Mrs. Mallard and her dead husband

(C) Mrs. Mallard's grief and the outside world

(D) Josephine and Richards

(E) Cocealed truths and brutal honesty

The correct answer is C.

The piece primarily concerns itself with Mallard's grief and the ironic joyousness of the world outside her window. All the rest of the descriptions lead up to this primary contrast.

48. What can we tell about Mrs. Mallard's relationship with Josephine?

(A) Josephine treats her firmly

(B) They are estranged

(C) Josephine has no idea how to handle her sister's condition

(D) The pair have few things in common

(E) Josephine is reluctant to be around Mrs. Mallard

The correct answer is D.

(A) and (C) would not apply, Josephine knows how to handle her sister, and she does this with tenderness. We have no indication that they are estranged (B), and they seem to interact regularly so (E) does not apply.

49. The world outside Mrs. Mallard's window is characterized with all of the senses EXCEPT:

(A) Taste

(B) Smell

(C) Sight

(D) Touch

(E) Sound

The correct answer is A.

There are no tastes described in the piece.

50. In context, what can "forestall" be taken to mean?

(A) Hurry forward

(B) Obstruct

(C) Inform

(D) Consider

(E) Explain to

The correct answer is B.

Richards, it is explained, has taken great care to make sure a less tender friend does not deliver the message of the death. He "forestalls" or obstructs these people.

51. Inferring from the text, Mrs. Mallard's grief renders her:

(A) Infntile

(B) Hysterical

(C) Violent

(D) Volatile

(E) Recalcitrant

The correct answer is A.

All the other answers suggest an opposite reaction. The text even explains Mallard has cried herself into exhaustion as a child might.

52. What is the subject of the verb "sank" in paragraph four?

(A) "This"

(B) "She"

(C) "Into"

(D) "Armchair"

(E) "Exhaustion"

The correct answer is B.

The subject is "She" and the object is "This".

53. What best describes the author's characterization of the view from the window?

(A) Dreary

(B) Dreamlike

(C) Yearning

(D) Impactful

(E) Livey

The correct answer is E.

This liveliness contrasts with Mrs. Mallard's depression.

Questions 54-57. Read the following passage carefully before you decide on your answers to the questions.

Bernardo : Welcome, Horatio: welcome, good Marcellus.
Marcellus : What, has this thing appear'd again to-night?
Bernardo : I have seen nothing.
Marcellus : Horatio says 'tis but our fantasy,
And will not let belief take hold of him
Touching this dreaded sight, twice seen of us:
Therefore I have entreated him along
With us to watch the minutes of this night;
That if again this apparition come,
He may approve our eyes and speak to it.
Horatio : Tush, tush, 'twill not appear.
Bernardo : Sit down awhile;
And let us once again assail your ears,
That are so fortified against our story
What we have two nights seen.

—William Shakespeare, 1599-1602

54. The three men in the play can be said, in this passage:

(A) to disagree about a ghost that was seen

(B) to disagree that two days ago they saw people meeting "twice seen of us"

(C) that Horatio and Bernardo are trying to persuade Marcellus they saw something

(D) that Horatio and Marcellus are trying to persuade Bernardo they saw something

(E) to meet for a drink for "fortification"

The correct answer is A.

Drama selections need you to pay close attention to the characters and who says what. (B) is not true—the two men don't disagree about what they saw. (C) and (D) do not list the characters correctly about who sees what. (E) isn't correct at all, so (A) is the correct answer.

55. When Marcellus speaks of "approving our eyes", what is he saying?

(A) Marcellus and Bernardo need glasses.

(B) Bernardo didn't believe what Marcellus saw.

(C) Horatio believes what Marcellus saw.

(D) Horatio should see what Bernardo and Marcellus saw.

(E) Marcellus should believe what Bernardo saw.

The correct answer is D.

You need to review the members of the scene if you got this inaccurate. The only correct choice about who saw what and who needs to see what they saw is (D)

56. When Bernardo says "once again assail your ears", what does he mean?

(A) He wants to repeat himself to Marcellus to make him believe him.

(B) He wants to repeat himself to Horatio to make him believe him.

(C) He wants to repeat himself to help all three of them believe the story.

(D) He wants Marcellus and Horatio to poke holes in the story.

(E) None of these are the meaning of that phrase in the passag(E)

The correct answer is B.

Pay attention to the characters. Answer choices can be confusing.

57. In the context of the passage, entreated means:

(A) invited

(B) engaged

(C) demanded

(D) refused

(E) ignored

The correct answer is A.

Picking the best synonym should get easier at the end of the exam. A is correct.

Questions 58-60. Read the following passage carefully before you decide on your answers to the questions.

Edmund : That's foolishness. You know it's only a bad cold.
Mary : Yes, of course, I know that!
Edmund : But listen, Mama. I want you to promise me that even if it turns out to be something worse, you'll know I'll soon be alright again, anyway, and don't worry yourself sick, and you'll keep on taking care of yourself—
Mary : I won't listen when you talk so silly! There's absolutely no reason to talk as if you expect som thing dreadful! Of course, I promise you I give you my sacred word of honor! But I suppose you're remembering I've promised before on my word of honor.
Edmund : No!
Mary : I'm not blaming you, dear. How can you help it? How can any one of us forget? That's what makes it so hard—for all of us. We can't forget.
Edmund : Mama! Stop it!
Mary : All right, dear. I didn't beam to be so gloomy. Don't mind me. Here. Let me feel your head.Why, it's nice and cool. You certainly don't have any fever now.

> — Eugene O'Neill, 1955

58. It can be said that this passage of the drama:

(A) puts American dream against American nightmare

(B) describes the normal American family

(C) portrays Americans in a very resilient fashion

(D) was likely written during a war so obviously has negative overtones

(E) has the mother remembering the death of another child

The correct answer is E.

You have to limit your answers to the passage; therefore, (A) is not correct. (B) invites the reader to make assumptions about normal, and that does not usually happen in the exam. There is not enough information in the passage to presume (C) is correct. (E) is the best answer.

59. Mary changes the direction of the conversation by:

(A) stopping Edmund from talking by taking his temperature

(B) making Edmund feel badly about the death of his brother

(C) walking out of the room

(D) tucking the covers up to his chin

(E) ignoring him

The correct answer is A.

You need to read the scene to make sure to pick the right answer. (A) is correct.

60. This portion of the play is a:

(A) monologue

(B) dialogue

(C) soliloquy

(D) entendre

(E) stichomythia

The correct answer is B.

By definition, since there are two people, (A) and (C) are incorrect. While (D) is possible, (E) is wrong; (B) is the best choice. Look up the words if you are unfamiliar with them.

Sample Test Three
Section I

Multiple Choice Questions. Time: 60 minutes.

Instructions: This sample exam gives passages from known writings (fiction, poems, non-fiction/history, biographies, drama and more) over the past five hundred years. While the student taking the exam is not expected to have read the material or have familiarity with the passage prior to the exam, the test taker is expected to have the essential knowledge from schoolwork to answer the questions included herein.

At the end of the test passages and answers, there is an answer key and a "rationale" key for each question. Take the test without referencing these guides. For questions that you guess the answers or get wrong, the rationale is provided to help you see how test makers frame answers to questions or explain pieces of information with which you are unfamiliar.

As with the SAT Literature Test, the passages are taken primarily from American and British Literature—though at least one question, just as in the actual exam, is taken from another area of literature. Within the questions of the SAT Literature Test, the mixture of genre types falls typically almost 80-90% between poetry and prose and the remain-ing on drama. The entire test is balanced between three main eras—Renaissance/17th Century, 18th/19th Century, as well as 20th/21st Century. The test includes three main classifications — American Literature, British Literature, and World Literature. Ameri-can and British Literature typically account for 80-90%, with 1-2 passages from India, Ireland, Canada, Africa, and/or the Caribbean.

The SAT Literature Test allows 60 minutes to take the exam of approximately 60 ques-tions. Time yourself during the exam, but as you practice, focus more attention on ac-curately answering questions as the total number of correct answers impacts your score, not how many you skip or get wrong. If you skip any questions, make sure that you also skip that line on the answer sheet—or you may spend a lot of time erasing and redoing your answer key.

These passages do not actually appear on the SAT Literature exam, but are meant to show how the exam is written and the various range of questions, answers, and key knowledge points required in order to pass the SAT Literature exam. Read each ques-tion carefully and provide the best answer choice. Good luck!

Questions 1-5. Read the following passage carefully before you decide on your answers to the questions.

THE BROAD-BACKED hippopotamus
Rests on his belly in the mud;
Although he seems so firm to us
He is merely flesh and blood.

Flesh and blood is weak and frail,
Susceptible to nervous shock;
While the True Church can never fail
For it is based upon a rock.

The hippo's feeble steps may err
In compassing material ends,
While the True Church need never stir
To gather in its dividends.

The potamus can never reach
The mango on the mango-tree;
But fruits of pomegranate and peach
Refresh the Church from over sea.

At mating time the hippos voice
Betrays inflexions hoarse and odd,
But every week we hear rejoice
The Church, at being one with God.

The hippopotamus's day
Is passed in sleep; at night he hunts;
God works in a mysterious way;
The Church can sleep and feed at once.

I saw the potamus take wing
Ascending from the damp savannas,
And quiring angels round him sing
The praise of God, in loud hosannas.

Blood of the Lamb shall wash him clean
And him shall heavenly arms enfold,
Among the saints he shall be seen
Performing on a harp of gold.)

He shall be washed as white as snow,
By all the martyrd virgins kist,
While the True Church remains below
Wrapt in the old miasmal mist.

1. **Who is the author of this poem?**

   (A) William Faulkner

   (B) T.S. Eliot

   (C) William Blake

   (D) C.S. Lewis

   (E) William Shakespeare

2. **What is the rhyme scheme in the second stanza?**

   (A) ABAB

   (B) ABCD

   (C) ABCA

   (D) ADDA

   (E) None of the above

3. **What does the hippo represent?**

   (A) The devil

   (B) Sinners

   (C) Animals

   (D) Heaven

   (E) Good luck

4. **What does the mud represent?**

   (A) Sin

   (B) Dirt

   (C) Home

   (D) Comfort

   (E) All of the above

5. **What does "take wing" symbolize in the following line?**
   "I saw the potamus take wing"

   (A) Hunting a bird

   (B) Flying in a plane

   (C) Laying down on its side

   (D) Going to heaven

   (E) None of the above

Two roads diverged in a yellow wood,
And sorry I could not travel both
And be one traveler, long I stood
And looked down one as far as I could
To where it bent in the undergrowth;

Then took the other, as just as fair,
And having perhaps the better claim,
Because it was grassy and wanted wear;
Though as for that the passing there
Had worn them really about the same,

And both that morning equally lay
In leaves no step had trodden black.
Oh, I kept the first for another day!
Yet knowing how way leads on to way,
I doubted if I should ever come back.

I shall be telling this with a sigh
Somewhere ages and ages hence:
Two roads diverged in a wood, and I—
I took the one less traveled by,
And that has made all the difference.

6. **Who wrote this poem?**

   (A) Robert Frost

   (B) Emily Dickinson

   (C) John Keats

   (D) William Wadsworth

   (E) Emily Bronte

7. **The author says that he "took the one less traveled by"; what does that mean?**

   (A) The other path looked like it was used more.

   (B) He did the right thing when others chose the wrong one.

   (C) He took the one on the left.

   (D) He took the one on the right.

   (E) It cannot be determined what the author meant by this short selection.

8. **What does the author imply since he took the path less traveled?**

   (A) He has run into fewer people that try to bully him into doing what they want.

   (B) Life is tougher getting to see the light.

   (C) He was sorry he didn't chose to go the more well-trod path.

   (D) He didn't make as much money as the people that took the other path.

   (E) His life is better for choosing to go his own path.

9. **What is the rhyme scheme?**

   (A) ABBAB

   (B) ABABA

   (C) ABAAC

   (D) ABCAB

   (E) ABAAB

10. **Taking the road less traveled by made all the difference because _____.**

    (A) the decision shaped his life

    (B) it was a good hike

    (C) the character was able to find peace

    (D) he created a new path on the road

    (E) he will always be able to go back to walk on the more traveled path if he chooses to

Questions 11-15. Read the following passage carefully before you decide on your answers to the questions.

American black music was going along like an express train. But white cats, after Buddy Holly died and Eddie Cochran died, and Elvis was in the army gone wonky, white American music when I arrived was the Beach Boys and Bobby Vee. They were still stuck in the past. The past was six months ago; it wasn't a long time. But things changed. The Beatles were the milestone. And then they got stuck inside their own cage. "The Fab Four." Hence, eventually, you got the Monkees, all this ersatz stuff. But I think there was a vacuum somewhere in white American music at the time.

When we first got to America and to LA, there was a lot of Beach Boys on the radio, which was pretty funny to us—it was before Pet Sounds—it was hot rod songs and surfing songs, pretty lousily played, familiar Chuck Berry licks going on. "Round, round get around / I get around," I though that was brilliant. It was later on, but Brian Wilson had something. "In My Room," "Don't Worry Baby." I was more interested in their B-sides, the ones he slipped in. There was no particular correlation with what we were doing so I could just listen to it on another level. I thought these are very well-constructed songs. I took easily to the pop song idiom. I'd always listened to everything, and America opened it all out—we were hearing records there that were regional hits. We'd get to know local labels and local acts, which is how we came across "Time Is on My

Side," in LA, sung by Irma Thomas. It was a B-side of a record on Imperial Records, a label we'd have been aware of because it was independent and successful and based on Sunset Strip.

—Keith Richards, 2010

11. **How many unique singers versus unique bands, respectively, are named in the passage above?**

(A) Seven and Four

(B) Six and Three

(C) Eight and Three

(D) Seven and Three

(E) Six and Four

12. **How many songs are referenced in the passage above?**

(A) Two

(B) Three

(C) Four

(D) Five

(E) Six

13. **In the context of the selection's first paragraph, how many white singers or groups are named by the author?**

(A) Four

(B) Five

(C) Three

(D) Seven

(E) One

14. **Given what the author says about the B-side of a record, which of the following sentences is closest to the author's opinion?**

(A) The B-side had more creativity and outlets for artists, making it unique

(B) It was called the B-side because the songs were generally not as good

(C) Only regional labels took the time to press B-sides.

(D) The B-side was where all the surfing songs were recorded

(E) Labels were strict about the contents of the B-sides.

15. When the author talks about the Beatles and says "they got stuck inside their own cage," the author most likely means:

(A) that the Beatles always had to hide in hotels because they were so famous

(B) that successful musical groups could never enjoy the publicity

(C) that the Beatles were trapped on planes all the time

(D) that the Beatles couldn't perform with anyone outside of their four members

(E) the Beatles outgrew the standard previously set for successful musicians, and were trapped in their own famous sensation

Questions 16-20. Read the following passage carefully before you decide on your answers.

> There is no frigate like a book
> To take us lands away,
> Nor any coursers like a page
> Of prancing poetry;
> This traverse may the poorest take
> Without oppress of toll;
> How frugal is the chariot
> That bears the human soul!
>   —Emily Dickinson

16. Authors use particular literary structures for descriptions. What best explains the one that Emily Dickinson employs in this poem?

(A) A literary allegory

(B) Personification

(C) Idioms

(D) Similes

(E) Flashbacks

17. How many types of transport types does the author incorporate?

(A) Two

(B) Three

(C) Four

(D) Five

(E) None

18. If the words "frigate, coursers, and chariot" were replaced with synonyms, what would the best choice of the following options include?

(A) Train, car, carriage

(B) Train, horse, carriage

(C) Ship, car, carriage

(D) Ship, car, train

(E) Ship, horse, carriage

19. Which of the following descriptions more closely describes the author's intended meaning of poem?

(A) Difficulties at work

(B) The importance of books

(C) Confessions for the soul

(D) Poverty makes things difficult

(E) Describing modes of transportation

20. What is a good paraphrase of "To take us lands away" that Ms. Dickinson writes in this poem?

(A) War makes it unsafe to travel, so we can just read about places.

(B) Poems will drive us to save our souls.

(C) Books can engage us to see new things.

(D) Authors can show us how to go on vacation.

(E) It shows poems are short and fun.

Questions 21-24. Read the following passage carefully before you decide on your answers.

Fever 103°

Pure? What does it mean?
The tongues of hell
Are dull, dull as the triple

Tongues of dull, fat Cerberus
Who wheezes at the gat(E) Incapable
Of licking clean

The aguey tendon, the sin, the sin.
The tinder cries.
The indelible smell

Of a snuffed candle!
Love, love, the low smokes roll
From me like Isadora's scarves, I'm in a fright

One scarf will catch and anchor in the wheel,
Such yellow sullen smokes
Make their own element. They will not rise,

But trundle round the globe
Choking the aged and the meek,
The weak

Hothouse baby in its crib,
The ghastly orchid
Hanging its hanging garden in the air,
Devilish leopard!
Radiation turned it white
And killed it in an hour.

Greasing the bodies of adulterers
Like Hiroshima ash and eating in.
The sin. The sin.

21. The word trundle is significant because _____.

(A) It represents moving very slowly.

(B) It is a roll out bed, used for camping.

(C) it is not dark nor light.

(D) it represents being instinctive.

(E) None of the above.

22. What literary device is used in this poem?

(A) Repetition

(B) Onomatopoeia

(C) Alliteration

(D) Flashback

(E) Flash forward

23. Which of the following best describes the setting?

(A) Utopia

(B) Dystopia

(C) Promised land

(D) Eden

(E) Erotic

24. Why is the title substantial?

(A) You can sweat out sins with a fever

(B) It's the temperature in the underworld

(C) This level of a fever would kill you

(D) This is the temperature of fire

(E) All of the above

Questions 25-32. Read the following passage carefully before you decide on your answers to the questions.

Jason threw into the fire. It hissed, uncurled, turning black. Then it was gray. Then it was gone. Caddy and Father and Jason were in Mother's chair. Jason's eyes were puffed shut and his mouth moved, like tasting. Caddy's head was on Father's shoulder. Her hair was like fire, and little points of fire were in her eyes, and I went and Father lifted me into the chair too, and Caddy held me. She smelled like trees.

She smelled like trees. In the corner it was dark, but I could see the window. I squatted there, holding the slipper. I couldn't see it, but my hands saw it, and I could hear it getting night, and my hands saw the slipper but I couldn't see myself, but my hands could see the slipper, and I squatted there, hearing it getting dark.

Here you is, Luster said. Look what I got. He showed it to me. You know where I got it. Miss Quentin give it to me. I knowed they couldn't keep me out. What you doing, off in here. I thought you done slipped back out doors. Aint you done enough moaning and slobbering today, without hiding off in this here empty room, mumbling and taking on. Come on here to bed, so I can get up there before it starts. I cant fool with you all night tonight. Just let them horns toot the first toot and I done gone.

25. The subject in this passage is:

(A) is female

(B) a supporting character.

(C) has an attitude of a criminal.

(D) a character, and seems to be the lead of the story.

(E) is well-educated

26. **What kind of description is the author providing of this scene?**

(A) Backstory of the environment of one of the characters.

(B) A narrative in the first person.

(C) Information about a dream she had.

(D) An unreliable narrative about a character.

(E) The author is using a persuasive argument.

27. **What are types of narration style is used in this passage?**

(A) Defamiliarization.

(B) Audience surrogate, trying to convey the audience's confusion.

(C) A stream of consciousness of one character's opinion of another's situation.

(D) Unreliable narrator.

(E) Hamartia style.

28. **One of the themes of the book is**

(A) changes in family values away from chastity and sin strain families.

(B) that people are all the same, rich or poor.

(C) rivers of emotion run deep.

(D) religion can hold a family together.

(E) obstacles can be overcome with hard work.

29. **The phrase, "Her hair was like fire," is what kind of literary device?**

(A) Simile.

(B) Metaphor.

(C) Reverse Personification.

(D) Allusion.

(E) Denotation.

30. **The phrase, "little points of fire were in her eyes," is what kind of literary device?**

(A) Simile

(B) Metaphor.

(C) Reverse Personification.

(D) Allusion.

(E) Denotation.

31. By using incorrect speech patterns, the author achieves what?

(A) An optimistic tone for the passage

(B) Changing of the time in history for this character.

(C) An indicator of internal thoughts, not "scrubbed" for other's hearing.

(D) (A) and (D).

(E) None of these

32. By repeating the phrase "She smelled like trees,", the author

(A) uses anaphora.

(B) uses pleonasm.

(C) changes pace through repetition.

(D) uses consonance.

(E) uses the lacan technique.

Questions 33-36. Read the following passage carefully before you decide on your answers to the questions.

But though thus largely indebted to fortune, to nature she had yet greater obligation: her form was elegant, her heart was liberal. Her countenance announced the intelligence of her mind, her complexion varied with every emotion of her foul, and her eyes, the heralds of her speech, now beamed with understanding and now glistened with sensibility.

For the short period of her minority, the management of her fortune and the care of her person, had by the Dean been entrusted to three guardians, among whom her own choice was to settle to her residence: but her mind, saddened by the lots of all her natural friends, coveted to regain its serenity in the quietness of the country, and in the bosom of an aged and maternal counsellor, whom she loved as her mother, and to whom she had been known from her childhood.

—Fanny Burney, 1782

33. From the context of this passage, which of the following statements is the most likely to be true?

(A) The main character is poor.

(B) The main character is an orphan.

(C) The setting of the story is in England.

(D) The main character is going to live with her aunt.

(E) The main character doesn't like to live in town.

34. In the quote, "her heart was liberal", what is the author trying to express?

(A) The author implies that the main character is of loose morals.

(B) The author implies that while ladylike, she has a wild streak.

(C) The author alludes that the woman is more open than her demeanor.

(D) The author makes it clear that she is alone.

(E) The author shows how she was older than her natural friends.

35. What does the word "minority" mean in the context of the passage?

(A) The woman in the passage is a Native American.

(B) The character is not yet an adult.

(C) The group of people in the story are members of the minority political party.

(D) The character has less money than her friends.

(E) None of the given options explain "minority" in this passage.

36. What is another word for serenity in this passage?

(A) Peacefulness

(B) Counsellor

(C) Bosom

(D) Rambunctiousness

(E) Prayerful

Questions 37-43. Read the following passage carefully before you decide on your answers to the questions.

"Then you must tell 'em dat love ain't somethin' lak uh grindstone dat's de same thing everywhere and do de same thing tuh everything it touch. Love is lak de sea. It's uh movin' thing, but still and all, it takes its shape from de shore it meets, and it's different with every shore."

—*Their Eyes Were Watching God*

37. Who wrote this novel?

(A) Toni Morrison

(B) Zora Neal Hurston

(C) W.E.B. Dubois

(D) Maya Angelou

(E) Richard Wright

38. **What literary device is used to show the similarity between love and the sea?**

   (A) Simile

   (B) Metaphor

   (C) Euphemism

   (D) Flashback

   (E) Foreshadowing

39. **In what form is this written?**

   (A) Phonetic

   (B) Informal

   (C) With an accent

   (D) Vernacular

   (E) Stream of consciousness

40. **_____ is used to describe the sea**

   (A) Imagery

   (B) Alliteration

   (C) Action

   (D) Personification

   (E) All of the above

41. **How does the author portray love?**

   (A) It's different for each relationship.

   (B) It's unobtainable.

   (C) It causes waves in your life.

   (D) It comes and goes like the tide.

   (E) None of the above.

42. **What is a grindstone?**

   (A) A stone made of sand

   (B) A workday

   (C) A square stone used to grind sediment

   (D) A round stone used to sharpen tools

   (E) A plantation

43. What best describes love in this passage?

(A) Grindstone

(B) Uh movin' thing

(C) Still

(D) Same thing

(E) Everyone

Questions 44-51. Read the following passage carefully before you decide on your answers to the questions.

"And if she thought anything, it was No. No. Nono. Nonono. Simple. She just flew. Collected every bit of life she had made, all the parts of her that were precious and fine and beautiful, and carried, pushed, dragged them through the veil, out, away, over there where no one could hurt them. Over there. Outside this place, where they would be safe."

—*Beloved*

44. Who wrote Beloved?

(A) Martin Luther King

(B) Frederick Douglass

(C) Maya Angelou

(D) Toni Morrison

(E) Zora Neal Hurston

45. What does "No. No. Nono. Nonono." represent?

(A) Children fighting with their parents

(B) Parents defending discipline

(C) Teachers arguing with parents

(D) Children being defiant

(E) Parents defending their children

46. What are "bits of life"?

(A) Children

(B) Belongings

(C) Crops

(D) Flowers

(E) Poems

47. What does the veil represent?

    (A) A screen of oppression

    (B) A funeral

    (C) Birth

    (D) Puberty

    (E) None of the above

48. Where is "over there"?

    (A) Africa

    (B) The Underground Railroad

    (C) The slaves quarters

    (D) The afterlife

    (E) The garden

49. Where would they be safe?

    (A) Nowhere on this earth

    (B) Off the plantation

    (C) Back in Africa

    (D) In school

    (E) Up North

50. The author implies that the main character _____.

    (A) would rather see her children die than watch them suffer.

    (B) is trying to hide her children from the master.

    (C) is planning on escaping on the Underground Railroad.

    (D) would like to return to Africa.

    (E) is hiding her belongings from fellow slaves.

51. What literary device is used in this passage?

    (A) Alliteration

    (B) Allegory

    (C) Analogy

    (D) Anecdote

    (E) Anagram

Questions 52-56. Read the following passage carefully before you decide on your answers to the questions.

Since brass, nor stone, nor earth, nor boundless sea,
But sad mortality o'ersways their power,
How with this rage shall beauty hold a plea,
Whose action is no stronger than a flower? (line 4)
O how shall summer's honey breath hold out
Against the wrackful siege of batt'ring days,
When rocks impregnable are not so stout,
Nor gates of steel so strong, but Time decays? (line 8)
O fearful meditation! where, alack,
Shall Time's best jewel from Time's chest lie hid?
Or what strong hand can hold his swift foot back?
Or who his spoil of beauty can forbid? (line 12)
O none, unless this miracle have might,
That in black ink my love may still shine bright.
                              —William Shakespeare, 1609

52. **In line four, what is the strength of a flower describing?**

    (A) Beauty (beauty line above)

    (B) Time

    (C) Summer's honey breath

    (D) Strong hand

    (E) Meditation

53. **The first line of the poem tries to explain _____.**

    (A) that there are a lot of things discussed in the poem.

    (B) that the strongest natural things are no match for beauty.

    (C) where you can find love.

    (D) what the author went through to write this poem.

    (E) that prayer can solve any problems.

54. **"Black ink" references what in the last line?**

    (A) Written poems

    (B) Street signs

    (C) Black diamonds

    (D) Summer flowers dying

    (E) Graffiti

55. The main idea of this poem is describing all of the following except:

(A) hope

(B) time, aging and death overthrow beauty

(C) marriage

(D) things that time cannot destroy

(E) the author's victory

56. Shakespeare creates emotions in this poem, and expresses all of the following except:

(A) rage

(B) defeat

(C) love

(D) devotion

(E) mortality

Questions 57-60. Read the following passage carefully before you decide on your answers to the questions.

There is likewise another diversion, which is only shown before the Emperor and Empress, and first minister, upon particular occasions. The Emperor lays on a table three fine silken threads of six inches long. One is blue, the other red, and the third green. These threads are proposed as prizes for those persons whom the Emperor hath a mind to distinguish by a peculiar mark of his favor. The ceremony is performed in his Majesty's great chamber of state; where the candidates are to undergo a trial of dexterity very different from the former, and such as I have not observed the least resemblance of in any other country of the old or the new world. The Emperor holds a stick in his hands, both ends parallel to the horizon, while the candidates, advancing one by one, sometimes leap over the stick, sometimes creep under it backwards and forwards several times, according as the stick is advanced or depressed. Sometimes the Emperor holds one end of the stick, and his first minister holds the other; sometimes the minister has it entirely to himself. Whoever performs his part with most agility, and holds out the longest in leaping and creeping, is rewarded with the blue-colored silk; the red is given to the next, and the green is given to the third, which they all wear girt twice round the middle; and you see few great persons about this court who are not adorned with one of these girdles.

—Jonathan Swift, 1704

57. The stick game described by the author in this passage is an allusion to what?

(A) Jumping to the tune of the Emperor's (his boss') direction

(B) Baseball

(C) War games

(D) A circus

(E) Tennis

58. Why are the silk threads highly valued?

(A) Silk is a common material.

(B) Green is the Empress' favorite color.

(C) People don't give gifts very often.

(D) Silk was very expensive in the 1700s, when the story was written.

(E) All great persons wear silk.

59. Using the information only in the passage, are the colors of the silk threads significant?

(A) Yes, because they are royal colors.

(B) Yes, because they represent places of winners.

(C) No, because everyone has them.

(D) No, because hardly everyone has them.

(E) You cannot determine from the passage if the colors are important.

60. Why is the word girdle significant?

(A) It represents weight loss.

(B) It represents being tied to loyalty.

(C) It represents sexuality as a corset.

(D) It represents compliance

(E) B & D

ANSWER KEY

Question Number	Correct Answer	Your Answer
1.	B	
2.	A	
3.	B	
4.	A	
5.	D	
6.	A	
7.	A	
8.	E	
9.	E	
10.	A	
11.	D	
12.	C	
13.	D	
14.	A	
15.	E	
16.	A	
17.	B	
18.	E	
19.	B	
20.	C	
21.	A	
22.	A	
23.	B	
24.	A	
25.	B	
26.	A	
27.	C	
28.	A	
29.	A	
30.	B	

Question Number	Correct Answer	Your Answer
31.	C	
32.	A	
33.	B	
34.	C	
35.	B	
36.	A	
37.	B	
38.	A	
39.	D	
40.	A	
41.	D	
42.	D	
43.	B	
44.	D	
45.	B	
46.	A	
47.	A	
48.	D	
49.	A	
50.	A	
51.	B	
52.	A	
53.	B	
54.	A	
55.	C	
56.	B	
57.	A	
58.	D	
59.	B	
60.	E	

Sample Test Three

Questions 1-5. Read the following passage carefully before you decide on your answers to the questions.

THE BROAD-BACKED hippopotamus
Rests on his belly in the mud;
Although he seems so firm to us
He is merely flesh and blood.
Flesh and blood is weak and frail,
Susceptible to nervous shock;
While the True Church can never fail
For it is based upon a rock.

The hippo's feeble steps may err
In compassing material ends,
While the True Church need never stir
To gather in its dividends.

The potamus can never reach
The mango on the mango-tree;
But fruits of pomegranate and peach
Refresh the Church from over sea.

At mating time the hippos voice
Betrays inflexions hoarse and odd,
But every week we hear rejoice
The Church, at being one with God.

The hippopotamus's day
Is passed in sleep; at night he hunts;
God works in a mysterious way;
The Church can sleep and feed at once.

I saw the potamus take wing
Ascending from the damp savannas,
And quiring angels round him sing
The praise of God, in loud hosannas.

Blood of the Lamb shall wash him clean
And him shall heavenly arms enfold,
Among the saints he shall be seen
Performing on a harp of gold.)

He shall be washed as white as snow,
By all the martyrd virgins kist,
While the True Church remains below
Wrapt in the old miasmal mist.

1. **Who is the author of this poem?**

   (A) William Faulkner

   (B) T.S. Eliot

   (C) William Blake

   (D) C.S. Lewis

   (E) William Shakespeare

   The correct answer is B.

   T.S. Eliot is the author of this poem.

2. **What is the rhyme scheme in the second stanza?**

   (A) ABAB

   (B) ABCD

   (C) ABCA

   (D) ADDA

   (E) None of the above

   The correct answer is A.

   The rhyme scheme in the second stanza follows ABAB. The first and third lines rhyme, and the second and fourth lines rhyme.

3. **What does the hippo represent?**

   (A) The devil

   (B) Sinners

   (C) Animals

   (D) Heaven

   (E) Good luck

   The correct answer is B.

   The hippo represents sinners in this poem. Given the religious context of the poem, sinners is the most appropriate answer.

4. What does the mud represent?

(A) Sin

(B) Dirt

(C) Home

(D) Comfort

(E) All of the above

The correct answer is A.

Because the hippo represents sinners, the mud represents sin. The hippo may be dirty (B), and could feel at home (C) or comforted by the mud (D), but this does not parallel the symbolism within the writing.

5. What does "take wing" symbolize in the following line?
"I saw the potamus take wing"

(A) Hunting a bird

(B) Flying in a plane

(C) Laying down on its side

(D) Going to heaven

(E) None of the above

The correct answer is D.

Taking wing is a representation of going to the heavens in the sky. Flying a plane and laying on its side are obviously incorrect and it's easy to narrow down to (A) and (D) The literal interpretation, (A), is incorrect and does not represent the symbolism embedded in the writing.

Questions 6-10. Read the following passage carefully before you decide on your answers to the questions.

Two roads diverged in a yellow wood,
And sorry I could not travel both
And be one traveler, long I stood
And looked down one as far as I could
To where it bent in the undergrowth;

Then took the other, as just as fair,
And having perhaps the better claim,
Because it was grassy and wanted wear;
Though as for that the passing there
Had worn them really about the same,

And both that morning equally lay
In leaves no step had trodden black.
Oh, I kept the first for another day!
Yet knowing how way leads on to way,
I doubted if I should ever come back.

I shall be telling this with a sigh
Somewhere ages and ages hence:
Two roads diverged in a wood, and I—
I took the one less traveled by,
And that has made all the difference.

6. **Who wrote this poem?**

    (A) Robert Frost

    (B) Emily Dickinson

    (C) John Keats

    (D) William Wadsworth

    (E) Emily Bronte

    The correct answer is A.

    Robert Frost is the author of this poem.

7. **The author says that he "took the one less traveled by"; what does that mean?**

    (A) The other path looked like it was used more.

    (B) He did the right thing when others chose the wrong one.

    (C) He took the one on the left.

    (D) He took the one on the right.

    (E) It cannot be determined what the author meant by this short selection.

    The correct answer is A.

    One of the paths had a path from people walking on it. The path that he chose "wanted wear," meaning, there was no path because not many people had walked on it. The character took the path less traveled by, which was used less than the other option that he had.

8. **What does the author imply since he took the path less traveled?**

(A) He has run into fewer people that try to bully him into doing what they want.

(B) Life is tougher getting to see the light.

(C) He was sorry he didn't chose to go the more well-trod path.

(D) He didn't make as much money as the people that took the other path.

(E) His life is better for choosing to go his own path.

The correct answer is E.

The author implies that he has had a better life due to the decisions that he's made on his own. He believes his life is better for choosing to go his own path.

9. **What is the rhyme scheme?**

(A) ABBAB

(B) ABABA

(C) ABAAC

(D) ABCAB

(E) ABAAB

The correct answer is E.

This poem follows the ABAAB rhyme scheme

10. **Taking the road less traveled by made all the difference because _____.**

(A) the decision shaped his life

(B) it was a good hike

(C) the character was able to find peace

(D) he created a new path on the road

(E) he will always be able to go back to walk on the more traveled path if he chooses to

The correct answer is A.

Going on the other path would have led to a different life for this character. The best answer is (A) because choosing the road less traveled by has been a decision that has shaped his life.

Questions 11-15. Read the following passage carefully before you decide on your answers to the questions.

American black music was going along like an express train. But white cats, after Buddy Holly died and Eddie Cochran died, and Elvis was in the army gone wonky, white American music when I arrived was the Beach Boys and Bobby Vee. They were still stuck in the past. The past was six months ago; it wasn't a long time. But things changed. The Beatles were the milestone. And then they got stuck inside their own cage. "The Fab Four." Hence, eventually, you got the Monkees, all this ersatz stuff. But I think there was a vacuum somewhere in white American music at the time.

When we first got to America and to LA, there was a lot of Beach Boys on the radio, which was pretty funny to us—it was before Pet Sounds—it was hot rod songs and surfing songs, pretty lousily played, familiar Chuck Berry licks going on. "Round, round get around / I get around," I though that was brilliant. It was later on, but Brian Wilson had something. "In My Room," "Don't Worry Baby." I was more interested in their B-sides, the ones he slipped in. There was no particular correlation with what we were doing so I could just listen to it on another level. I thought these are very well-constructed songs. I took easily to the pop song idiom. I'd always listened to everything, and America opened it all out—we were hearing records there that were regional hits. We'd get to know local labels and local acts, which is how we came across "Time Is on My Side," in LA, sung by Irma Thomas. It was a B-side of a record on Imperial Records, a label we'd have been aware of because it was independent and successful and based on Sunset Strip.

—Keith Richards, 2010

11. How many unique singers versus unique bands, respectively, are named in the passage above?

(A) Seven and Four

(B) Six and Three

(C) Eight and Three

(D) Seven and Three

(E) Six and Four

The correct answer is D.

This is merely counting. There are Seven singers (Buddy Holly, Eddie Cochran, Elivs, Bobby Vee, Chuck Berry, Brian Wilson, Irma Thomas) and three bands (Beatles, Monkeys, Beach Boys). The "Fab Four" is referring to the Beatles. (Note the author's group is not named in the passage, and neither is he.)

12. **How many songs are referenced in the passage above?**

(A) Two

(B) Three

(C) Four

(D) Five

(E) Six

The correct answer is C.

Count them - In My Room, Don't Worry Baby and Time Is On My Side. (B) (note "Round, round get around/I get around" are lyrics and not the name of a song.)

13. **In the context of the selection's first paragraph, how many white singers or groups are named by the author?**

(A) Four

(B) Five

(C) Three

(D) Seven

(E) One

The correct answer is D.

The whole passage is about white male singers except Irma Thomas, but her name is in the second paragraph. This question is limited to the first paragraph. Seven singers or bands are named after the author's "white cats" comment.

14. **Given what the author says about the B-side of a record, which of the following sentences is closest to the author's opinion?**

(A) The B-side had more creativity and outlets for artists, making it unique

(B) It was called the B-side because the songs were generally not as good

(C) Only regional labels took the time to press B-sides.

(D) The B-side was where all the surfing songs were recorded

(E) Labels were strict about the contents of the B-sides.

The correct answer is A.

You need to read the passage to understand which is the most appropriat(E) (A) is the best answer. The others are wrong because (B) is opposite of what he expresses as his opinion, (C) is factually not what the author writes, (D) is the opposite of what he says about the Beach Boys, and (E) is also the opposite of what the author writes.

15. **When the author talks about the Beatles and says "they got stuck inside their own cage," the author most likely means:**

(A) that the Beatles always had to hide in hotels because they were so famous

(B) that successful musical groups could never enjoy the publicity

(C) that the Beatles were trapped on planes all the time

(D) that the Beatles couldn't perform with anyone outside of their four members

(E) the Beatles outgrew the standard previously set for successful musicians, and were trapped in their own famous sensation

The correct answer is E.

For this answer, you need to interpret the author's intention from the context of the passage. The first four options are not supported by the passage at all; (E) is the best interpretation of the author's phrase.

Questions 16-20. Read the following passage carefully before you decide on your answers.

There is no frigate like a book
To take us lands away,
Nor any coursers like a page
Of prancing poetry;
This traverse may the poorest take
Without oppress of toll;
How frugal is the chariot
That bears the human soul!
            —Emily Dickinson

16. **Authors use particular literary structures for descriptions. What best explains the one that Emily Dickinson employs in this poem?**

(A) A literary allegory

(B) Personification

(C) Idioms

(D) Similes

(E) Flashbacks

The correct answer is A.

This is another definition type of question, and the correct choice is (A).

17. How many types of transport types does the author incorporate?

(A) Two

(B) Three

(C) Four

(D) Five

(E) None

The correct answer is B.

This is a counting exercise - (B), for three, as listed in the next question.

18. If the words "frigate, coursers, and chariot" were replaced with synonyms, what would the best choice of the following options include?

(A) Train, car, carriage

(B) Train, horse, carriage

(C) Ship, car, carriage

(D) Ship, car, train

(E) Ship, horse, carriage

The correct answer is E.

Defining frigate (ship), coursers (horses) and chariots (similar to a carriage drawn by a horse), the best choice is (E)

19. Which of the following descriptions more closely describes the author's intended meaning of poem?

(A) Difficulties at work

(B) The importance of books

(C) Confessions for the soul

(D) Poverty makes things difficult

(E) Describing modes of transportation

The correct answer is B.

This poem is about the journeys available through stories and books. From the first sentence, the author lays forth the meaning of the poem is (B)

20. **What is a good paraphrase of "To take us lands away" that Ms. Dickinson writes in this poem?**

(A) War makes it unsafe to travel, so we can just read about places.

(B) Poems will drive us to save our souls.

(C) Books can engage us to see new things.

(D) Authors can show us how to go on vacation.

(E) It shows poems are short and fun.

The correct answer is C.

Option (A) is very abrupt and makes too many assumptions; Option (E) is not relevant to the subject of the poem - both of these are obviously out. Of the choices remaining, using the references with the different ways people traveled in her earlier lines, the best answer is (C)

Questions 21-24. Read the following passage carefully before you decide on your answers.

Fever 103°

Pure? What does it mean?
The tongues of hell
Are dull, dull as the triple

Tongues of dull, fat Cerberus
Who wheezes at the gat(E) Incapable
Of licking clean

The aguey tendon, the sin, the sin.
The tinder cries.
The indelible smell

Of a snuffed candle!
Love, love, the low smokes roll
From me like Isadora's scarves, I'm in a fright

One scarf will catch and anchor in the wheel,
Such yellow sullen smokes
Make their own element. They will not rise,

But trundle round the globe
Choking the aged and the meek,
The weak

Hothouse baby in its crib,
The ghastly orchid
Hanging its hanging garden in the air,
Devilish leopard!
Radiation turned it white
And killed it in an hour.

Greasing the bodies of adulterers
Like Hiroshima ash and eating in.
The sin. The sin.

21. **The word trundle is significant because ____.**

(A) It represents moving very slowly.

(B) It is a roll out bed, used for camping.

(C) it is not dark nor light.

(D) it represents being instinctive.

(E) None of the above.

The correct answer is A.

Trundle is the word for a bed that is used for camping, but it also represents moving very slowly. In the context of this piece, trundle represents traveling around the world very slowly. (C) and (D) are easy to mark off as incorrect for this question.

22. **What literary device is used in this poem?**

(A) Repetition

(B) Onomatopoeia

(C) Alliteration

(D) Flashback

(E) Flash forward

The correct answer is A.

This is an obvious answer. "The sin." is repeated several times.

23. **Which of the following best describes the setting?**

(A) Utopia

(B) Dystopia

(C) Promised land

(D) Eden

(E) Erotic

The correct answer is B.

Unlike utopia, where everything is perceived to be beautiful and happy, dystopia is the complete opposite.) It represents a very negative, unpleasant environment. Because the poem represents a hell-like environment, it's easy to eliminate (C) and (D) There are no sexual references, so E can also be eliminated. This leaves (B) as the best answer.

24. Why is the title substantial?

(A) You can sweat out sins with a fever

(B) It's the temperature in the underworld

(C) This level of a fever would kill you

(D) This is the temperature of fire

(E) All of the above

The correct answer is A.

While it's assumed that the underworld is a hot place, we are not aware of the exact temperature; therefore, (B) can be eliminated. The temperature of fire is much higher, and can reach as high as 1500 degrees. This level of a fever would be dangerous, but not necessarily deadly. This leaves (A) as the best answer, as it represents a cleanse of sins by sweating them out with a fever.

Questions 25-32. Read the following passage carefully before you decide on your answers to the questions.

Jason threw into the fire. It hissed, uncurled, turning black. Then it was gray. Then it was gone. Caddy and Father and Jason were in Mother's chair. Jason's eyes were puffed shut and his mouth moved, like tasting. Caddy's head was on Father's shoulder. Her hair was like fire, and little points of fire were in her eyes, and I went and Father lifted me into the chair too, and Caddy held me. She smelled like trees.

She smelled like trees. In the corner it was dark, but I could see the window. I squatted there, holding the slipper. I couldn't see it, but my hands saw it, and I could hear it getting night, and my hands saw the slipper but I couldn't see myself, but my hands could see the slipper, and I squatted there, hearing it getting dark.

Here you is, Luster said. Look what I got. He showed it to me. You know where I got it. Miss Quentin give it to me. I knowed they couldn't keep me out. What you doing, off in here. I thought you done slipped back out doors. Aint you done enough moaning and slobbering today, without hiding off in this here empty room, mumbling and taking on. Come on here to bed, so I can get up there before it starts. I cant fool with you all night tonight. Just let them horns toot the first toot and I done gone.

25. The subject in this passage is:

(A) is female

(B) a supporting character.

(C) has an attitude of a criminal.

(D) a character, and seems to be the lead of the story.

(E) is well-educated

The correct answer is B.

You cannot determine the gender of the character. The attitude of the character described shows no criminal intent, nor is there overwhelming evidence to show that the character is well-educated. Between (B) and (C), you need to understand the context of the passage to pick the right answer.

26. What kind of description is the author providing of this scene?

(A) Backstory of the environment of one of the characters.

(B) A narrative in the first person.

(C) Information about a dream she had.

(D) An unreliable narrative about a character.

(E) The author is using a persuasive argument.

The correct answer is A.

It provides backstory of a character. There is no evidence that any of the other options would be correct.

27. What are types of narration style is used in this passage?

(A) Defamiliarization.

(B) Audience surrogate, trying to convey the audience's confusion.

(C) A stream of consciousness of one character's opinion of another's situation.

(D) Unreliable narrator.

(E) Hamartia style.

The correct answer is C.

There is no attempt in the passage to confuse readers. (A) and (B) are similar answers in this respect and there is no context to show the narrator is unreliable. If you don't know Hamartia, describing a fatal flaw, you can't eliminate this option, but you should be able to follow the passage that is like a stream of the character's thoughts.

28. One of the themes of the book is

(A) changes in family values away from chastity and sin strain families.

(B) that people are all the same, rich or poor.

(C) rivers of emotion run deep.

(D) religion can hold a family together.

(E) obstacles can be overcome with hard work.

The correct answer is A.

as the description shows changes away from family values. It may be true that (B), (C), and (E) are true, but remember you need to use clues from the book to pick the right answer.

29. The phrase, "Her hair was like fire," is what kind of literary device?

(A) Simile.

(B) Metaphor.

(C) Reverse Personification.

(D) Allusion.

(E) Denotation.

The correct answer is A.

You need to know these definitions, and that describing an object like another is a simile.

30. The phrase, "little points of fire were in her eyes," is what kind of literary device?

(A) Simile

(B) Metaphor.

(C) Reverse Personification.

(D) Allusion.

(E) Denotation.

The correct answer is B.

Again, knowing the definitions will show you that metaphor is the correct choice as the eyes are being described like something for rhetorical effect using a common characteristic.

31. By using incorrect speech patterns, the author achieves what?

(A) An optimistic tone for the passage

(B) Changing of the time in history for this character.

(C) An indicator of internal thoughts, not "scrubbed" for other's hearing.

(D) (A) and (D).

(E) None of these

The correct answer is C.

As this is a stream of consciousness, that also contributes to you picking the right answer on this one. Speech patterns wouldn't reflect time changes, and there is no overly optimistic tone of the passage.

32. By repeating the phrase "She smelled like trees,", the author

(A) uses anaphora.

(B) uses pleonasm.

(C) changes pace through repetition.

(D) uses consonance.

(E) uses the lacan technique.

The correct answer is A.

You can eliminate (C) as it uses reputation but not to change pace. Consonance is not appropriate here, the agreement between actions. Lecan deals with psychoanalysis, and doesn't apply here, either. Between (A) and (B), (B) is incorrect as it uses too many words to convey meaning.

Questions 33-36. Read the following passage carefully before you decide on your answers to the questions.

But though thus largely indebted to fortune, to nature she had yet greater obligation: her form was elegant, her heart was liberal. Her countenance announced the intelligence of her mind, her complexion varied with every emotion of her foul, and her eyes, the heralds of her speech, now beamed with under-standing and now glistened with sensibility.

For the short period of her minority, the management of her fortune and the care of her person, had by the Dean been entrusted to three guardians, among whom her own choice was to settle to her residence: but her mind, saddened by the lots of all her natural friends, coveted to regain its serenity in the quietness of the country, and in the bosom of an aged and maternal counsellor, whom she loved as her mother, and to whom she had been known from her childhood.

—Fanny Burney, 1782

33. From the context of this passage, which of the following statements is the most likely to be true?

(A) The main character is poor.

(B) The main character is an orphan.

(C) The setting of the story is in England.

(D) The main character is going to live with her aunt.

(E) The main character doesn't like to live in town.

The correct answer is B.

The female character seems to have inherited money, so (A) is not correct. There is no way to know in what country the setting takes place, and remember that all answers are dependent on the passage; so (C) is incorrect. (D) is also incorrect because the passage explicitly talks about her wanting to set up her own house. (B) is the right answer.

34. In the quote, "her heart was liberal", what is the author trying to express?

(A) The author implies that the main character is of loose morals.

(B) The author implies that while ladylike, she has a wild streak.

(C) The author alludes that the woman is more open than her demeanor.

(D) The author makes it clear that she is alone.

(E) The author shows how she was older than her natural friends.

The correct answer is C.

While this one may seem difficult, if you take each statement apart, the answer comes quickly. A is wrong because nowhere does the author talk about morals being questionable. (B) implies an overly outward exuberance by the main character, and that is overstating what is written. (D) is simply not accurate, and while there seems to be a difference between her and her friends, nowhere does the passage indicate she is older. (C) is correct. Also, when the author describes her "heart", it can mean that her inward thoughts, and since her demeanor is so proper, the outward indications of her character, (C) again is shown to be the right answer.

35. What does the word "minority" mean in the context of the passage?

(A) The woman in the passage is a Native American.

(B) The character is not yet an adult.

(C) The group of people in the story are members of the minority political party.

(D) The character has less money than her friends.

(E) None of the given options explain "minority" in this passage.

The correct answer is B.

This passage does not talk about race or ethnicity or religion; (A) is wrong. (C) talks about politics and that is not within the passage, so it, too, is wrong. (D) is the opposite of what is implied by the author about the main character; and as you have learned, (E) is likely the wrong choice.

36. What is another word for serenity in this passage?

(A) Peacefulness

(B) Counsellor

(C) Bosom

(D) Rambunctiousness

(E) Prayerful

The correct answer is A.

Another synonym choice - (A) is correct.

Questions 37-43. Read the following passage carefully before you decide on your answers to the questions.

"Then you must tell 'em dat love ain't somethin' lak uh grindstone dat's de same thing everywhere and do de same thing tuh everything it touch. Love is lak de sea. It's uh movin' thing, but still and all, it takes its shape from de shore it meets, and it's different with every shore."

—*Their Eyes Were Watching God*

37. **Who wrote this novel?**

   (A) Toni Morrison

   (B) Zora Neal Hurston

   (C) W.E.B. Dubois

   (D) Maya Angelou

   (E) Richard Wright

   The correct answer is B.

   There are many questions like this in past tests; reviewing the literature lists as previously suggested helps you score more points easily and quickly!

38. **What literary device is used to show the similarity between love and the sea?**

   (A) Simile

   (B) Metaphor

   (C) Euphemism

   (D) Flashback

   (E) Foreshadowing

   The correct answer is A.

   Remember to review your literary terms!

39. **In what form is this written?**

   (A) Phonetic

   (B) Informal

   (C) With an accent

   (D) Vernacular

   (E) Stream of consciousness

   The correct answer is D.

   Some of the words listed are literary devices, but this option is a word you should be able to recognize - both its use and meaning.

40. _____ is used to describe the sea

    (A) Imagery

    (B) Alliteration

    (C) Action

    (D) Personification

    (E) All of the above

The correct answer is A.

Remember, "all of the above" and "none of the above" are rarely right when given as options by The College Board. Action is not a literary term applicable in this instance. Of the three remaining, you need to know your literary terms.

41. **How does the author portray love?**

    (A) It's different for each relationship.

    (B) It's unobtainable.

    (C) It causes waves in your life.

    (D) It comes and goes like the tide.

    (E) None of the above.

The correct answer is D.

The selection describes lobe being like the sea, and the next phrase is nearly identical to this correct option.

42. **What is a grindstone?**

    (A) A stone made of sand

    (B) A workday

    (C) A square stone used to grind sediment

    (D) A round stone used to sharpen tools

    (E) A plantation

The correct answer is D.

Sometimes, The College Board will ask questions to make sure you know definitions of literary terms, but other times - like this - they ask for definitions of routine/regular words. This allows them to determine if you know the actual words and can then extrapolate to determine the meaning of a passage in the literary sense.

43. What best describes love in this passage?

(A) Grindstone

(B) Uh movin' thing

(C) Still

(D) Same thing

(E) Everyone

The correct answer is B.

Option (C) and even (D) are the opposite of the phrasing used to describe love. Choice (E) gives an answer as to who can experience love but it doesn't answer the question - always make sure you are answering the question they ask, not just selecting something that is accurate from the passage; it's a favorite trick to give a statement that is true in the passage but not applicable to the question asked! Of (A) and (B), the correct choice should be clear to you given the emotional description of love from the passage.

Questions 44-51. Read the following passage carefully before you decide on your answers to the questions.

"And if she thought anything, it was No. No. Nono. Nonono. Simple. She just flew. Collected every bit of life she had made, all the parts of her that were precious and fine and beautiful, and carried, pushed, dragged them through the veil, out, away, over there where no one could hurt them. Over there. Outside this place, where they would be safe."

—Beloved

44. Who wrote Beloved?

(A) Martin Luther King

(B) Frederick Douglass

(C) Maya Angelou

(D) Toni Morrison

(E) Zora Neal Hurston

The correct answer is D.

Again, one of her most famous pieces and highly used in college literary courses, you should know the answer to this. Review famous literary works and their authors so you can recognize simple questions such as this.

45. **What does "No. No. Nono. Nonono." represent?**

(A) Children fighting with their parents

(B) Parents defending discipline

(C) Teachers arguing with parents

(D) Children being defiant

(E) Parents defending their children

The correct answer is B.

If you are unfamiliar with the novel, this would be a harder question to answer accurately. However, you can use analysis on the answer choices to derive the correction one. (A) and (D) are the same, so eliminate them. In this context, there is no mention of teachers or situations that can be construed to have teachers represented by some other words, so (C) is eliminated. Of (B) and (E), there is no indication that a parent is fighting someone/something, so it too can be eliminated.

46. **What are "bits of life"?**

(A) Children

(B) Belongings

(C) Crops

(D) Flowers

(E) Poems

The correct answer is A.

In context, it's "every bit of life she had made". While it could mean objects she actually made, if you had familiarity with the plot and characters in the novel, this would be an easy question. If you have to logic your way through options, crops and flowers do not make sense (as people cannot make crops or flowers) and poems is possible, but (A) and (B) are better possibilities. (A) is the best choice because you don't make belongings - you buy them.

47. **What does the veil represent?**

(A) A screen of oppression

(B) A funeral

(C) Birth

(D) Puberty

(E) None of the above

The correct answer is A.

 The novel is about white oppression/white dominance and a wall (or veil) against opportunities for people of color. She thinks about breaking through the veil and coming out victorious on the other side.

48. **Where is "over there"?**

(A) Africa

(B) The Underground Railroad

(C) The slaves quarters

(D) The afterlife

(E) The garden

The correct answer is D.

Knowing the novel is helpful in this case, but not require(D) "Over there" is away from this place - so you know (B), (C), and (E) are not accurate because they are part of "this place." There is nothing to suggest Africa is the right choice. If you know the novel, it is easier to select (D), but not necessary - this is another test of your analyzing skills.

49. **Where would they be safe?**

(A) Nowhere on this earth

(B) Off the plantation

(C) Back in Africa

(D) In school

(E) Up North

The correct answer is A.

Using the same logic as described in the previous rationale, the choices other than (A) are incorrect. If you know the book, these last two questions are easy points for you. If you don't know the book, you can review the top literature pieces in British and American literature, find reviews to explain the books and plots.

50. **The author implies that the main character _____.**

(A) would rather see her children die than watch them suffer.

(B) is trying to hide her children from the master.

(C) is planning on escaping on the Underground Railroad.

(D) would like to return to Africa.

(E) is hiding her belongings from fellow slaves.

The correct answer is A.

Options (B) through (E) are all relatively similar, so even if you didn't know the answer, you may be able to pick the right choice by reviewing the possible selections. But if you know this book, you can pick the right answer quickly. Even reviewing the past three questions may help you see a theme of the book's storyline.

51. What literary device is used in this passage?

(A) Alliteration

(B) Allegory

(C) Analogy

(D) Anecdote

(E) Anagram

The correct answer is B.

This is a matter of knowing your literary terms, so make sure you review the terms for poetry and for literary devices.

Questions 52-56. Read the following passage carefully before you decide on your answers to the questions.

Since brass, nor stone, nor earth, nor boundless sea,
But sad mortality o'ersways their power,
How with this rage shall beauty hold a plea,
Whose action is no stronger than a flower? (line 4)
O how shall summer's honey breath hold out
Against the wrackful siege of batt'ring days,
When rocks impregnable are not so stout,
Nor gates of steel so strong, but Time decays? (line 8)
O fearful meditation! where, alack,
Shall Time's best jewel from Time's chest lie hid?
Or what strong hand can hold his swift foot back?
Or who his spoil of beauty can forbid? (line 12)
O none, unless this miracle have might,
That in black ink my love may still shine bright.
                    —William Shakespeare, 1609

52. In line four, what is the strength of a flower describing?

(A) Beauty (beauty line above)

(B) Time

(C) Summer's honey breath

(D) Strong hand

(E) Meditation

The correct answer is A.

This is a direct answer from line three.

53. The first line of the poem tries to explain _____.

(A) that there are a lot of things discussed in the poem.

(B) that the strongest natural things are no match for beauty.

(C) where you can find love.

(D) what the author went through to write this poem.

(E) that prayer can solve any problems.

The correct answer is B.

The author does not mention love, personal struggles, or prayer in this poem. Of the remaining answers, (A) is too general and (B) is the correct answer (using many of the lines about strength that cannot compare to beauty).

54. "Black ink" references what in the last line?

(A) Written poems

(B) Street signs

(C) Black diamonds

(D) Summer flowers dying

(E) Graffiti

The correct answer is A.

(A) is the best answer, as all others are not pertaining to the time period or not mentioned even indirectly with the poem.

55. The main idea of this poem is describing all of the following except:

(A) hope

(B) time, aging and death overthrow beauty

(C) marriage

(D) things that time cannot destroy

(E) the author's victory

The correct answer is C.

This is another question where you must read carefully. All of the items are mentioned or alluded to with the exception of (C); therefore, that is the answer that is NOT in the poem.

56. Shakespeare creates emotions in this poem, and expresses all of the following except:

(A) rage

(B) defeat

(C) love

(D) devotion

(E) mortality

The correct answer is B.

Again, another question to make sure you are reading and not just going with the first answer that matches a word in the passage, making (B) the correct answer.

Questions 57-60. Read the following passage carefully before you decide on your answers to the questions.

There is likewise another diversion, which is only shown before the Emperor and Empress, and first minister, upon particular occasions. The Emperor lays on a table three fine silken threads of six inches long. One is blue, the other red, and the third green. These threads are proposed as prizes for those persons whom the Emperor hath a mind to distinguish by a peculiar mark of his favor. The ceremony is performed in his Majesty's great chamber of state; where the candidates are to undergo a trial of dexterity very different from the former, and such as I have not observed the least resemblance of in any other country of the old or the new world. The Emperor holds a stick in his hands, both ends parallel to the horizon, while the candidates, advancing one by one, sometimes leap over the stick, sometimes creep under it backwards and forwards several times, according as the stick is advanced or depressed. Sometimes the Emperor holds one end of the stick, and his first minister holds the other; sometimes the minister has it entirely to himself. Whoever performs his part with most agility, and holds out the longest in leaping and creeping, is rewarded with the blue-colored silk; the red is given to the next, and the green is given to the third, which they all wear girt twice round the middle; and you see few great persons about this court who are not adorned with one of these girdles.

—Jonathan Swift, 1704

57. The stick game described by the author in this passage is an allusion to what?

(A) Jumping to the tune of the Emperor's (his boss') direction

(B) Baseball

(C) War games

(D) A circus

(E) Tennis

The correct answer is A.

This is another passage where it makes sense to check the year the item was written. Baseball was not yet invented, and tennis as we know it today was not yet played - so both (B) and (E) are wrong. A circus doesn't have anything to do with a straight line, so (D) is also wrong. While (A) and (C) are both possible, only A is probable and directly connects to the passage.

58. Why are the silk threads highly valued?

(A) Silk is a common material.

(B) Green is the Empress' favorite color.

(C) People don't give gifts very often.

(D) Silk was very expensive in the 1700s, when the story was written.

(E) All great persons wear silk.

The correct answer is D.

A is not true, so it can be eliminate(D) B has no basis of support in the passage, so it is not true. (E) has some reference in the passage, but it uses one of those extreme words, so it can be eliminated. Between (C) and (D), (C) has no mention in the passage whereas (D) references the time period of the story and is the best answer.

59. Using the information only in the passage, are the colors of the silk threads significant?

(A) Yes, because they are royal colors.

(B) Yes, because they represent places of winners.

(C) No, because everyone has them.

(D) No, because hardly everyone has them.

(E) You cannot determine from the passage if the colors are important.

The correct answer is B.

This question is straight from the passage and is explained in the third sentence.

60. Why is the word girdle significant?

(A) It represents weight loss.

(B) It represents being tied to loyalty.

(C) It represents sexuality as a corset.

(D) It represents compliance

(E) B & D

The correct answer is E.

A girdle is worn around the waste or under the bosom. It has a historical reference to loyalty towards leadership. (A) can be quickly eliminated along with (C), as this passage has nothing to do with sexuality or weight loss. (E) is the best answer because it represents the way an emperor must earn trust, respect, and loyalty.

Sample Test Four

Section I

Multiple Choice Questions. Time: 60 minutes.

Instructions: This sample exam gives passages from known writings (fiction, poems, non-fiction/history, biographies, drama and more) over the past five hundred years. While the student taking the exam is not expected to have read the material or have familiarity with the passage prior to the exam, the test taker is expected to have the essential knowledge from schoolwork to answer the questions included herein.

At the end of the test passages and answers, there is an answer key and a "rationale" key for each question. Take the test without referencing these guides. For questions that you guess the answers or get wrong, the rationale is provided to help you see how test makers frame answers to questions or explain pieces of information with which you are unfamiliar.

As with the SAT Literature Test, the passages are taken primarily from American and British Literature—though at least one question, just as in the actual exam, is taken from another area of literature. Within the questions of the SAT Literature Test, the mixture of genre types falls typically almost 80-90% between poetry and prose and the remaining on drama. The entire test is balanced between three main eras—Renaissance/17th Century, 18th/19th Century, as well as 20th/21st Century. The test includes three main classifications — American Literature, British Literature, and World Literature. American and British Literature passages typically include 80-90%, with India, Ireland, Canada, Africa, and/or the Caribbean.

The SAT Literature Test allows 60 minutes to take the exam of approximately 60 ques-tions. Time yourself during the exam, but as you practice, focus more attention on accurately answering questions as the total number of correct answers impacts your score, not how many you skip or get wrong. If you skip any questions, make sure that you also skip that line on the answer sheet—or you may spend a lot of time erasing and redoing your answer key.

These passages do not actually appear on the SAT Literature exam, but are meant to show how the exam is written and the various range of questions, answers, and key knowledge points required in order to pass the SAT Literature exam. Read each question carefully and provide the best answer choice. Good luck!

Questions 1-6. Read the following passage carefully before you decide on your answers to the questions.

Tyger! Tyger! burning bright
In the forests of the night,
What immortal hand or eye
Could frame thy fearful symmetry?
In what distant deeps or skies
Burnt the fire of thine eyes?
On what wings dare he aspire?
What the hand dare seize the flame?

And what shoulder, & what art,
Could twist the sinews of they heart?
And when thy heart began to beat,
What dread hand? & what dread feet?
　　　—Excerpt, William Blake, 1794

1. **Which of the topics below is this best description of the poem's main idea?**

   (A) Strength, as sinews of the heart are strong.

   (B) Creationism, and the author asks what immortal being created the tiger.

   (C) Flying, because it talks about wings.

   (D) Fire, with references to flames and burning forests.

   (E) Love, describing the heart and how it beats.

2. **Sinews, in the third stanza, can be best compared to:**

   (A) thread

   (B) a cage

   (C) rope

   (D) heart strings or emotions

   (E) burnt fire, from the second stanza

3. **Another phrase for "deeps or skies" that would fit in this poem could be:**

   (A) caves or planes

   (B) trees or forests

   (C) seas or air

   (D) waves or wind

   (E) oceans or lakes

4. **What is personified in the poem?**

   (A) A lion

   (B) Birds

   (C) Candle

   (D) A tiger

   (E) The sky

5. **In line 7 of this poem, what word below most nearly means "aspire"?**

   (A) Soar

   (B) Plunge

   (C) Scheme

   (D) Travel

   (E) Admire

6. **The poet, William Blake, uses all of the following literary tools to convey his message, except:**

   (A) metaphors

   (B) rhymed couplets

   (C) personification

   (D) symbols

   (E) lyrics

Questions 7-14. Read the following passage carefully before you decide on your answers to the questions.

"Where, in Heaven's name, could anyone even be alone in Calcutta? What hanky-panky business, in my mother's words, could go on? Everyone knew the rules and the rules stated caste and community narrowed the range of intimate contact."

—Desirable Daughters by Bharati Mukherjee

7. **Where is Calcutta?**

   (A) Indonesia

   (B) China

   (C) New Zealand

   (D) Jamaica

   (E) India

8. **Why is it abnormal for someone to be alone in Calcutta?**

    (A) Everyone travels with their spouses

    (B) It's a very busy city

    (C) The city is very dangerous

    (D) It's sarcastic because it's such a rural place

    (E) None of the above

9. **What is hanky-panky business?**

    (A) Dancing

    (B) Illegal trade

    (C) Corruption

    (D) A romantic kiss

    (E) Sexual activity

10. **What does the word caste mean?**

    (A) Division of the classes

    (B) Enclosed

    (C) Oppression

    (D) Sin

    (E) Sexualized

11. **What form of speech is in heaven's name?**

    (A) Analogy

    (B) Definition

    (C) Idiom

    (D) Quotation

    (E) Allegory

12. **What is the author implying in this passage?**

    (A) Sexual abuse

    (B) Adultery

    (C) Secret lovers

    (D) Pregnancy

    (E) All of the above

13. **This novel represents _____.**

    (A) Feminism

    (B) Nature

    (C) Misogyny

    (D) City life

    (E) None of the above

14. **How could community narrow the range of intimate contact?**

    (A) Arranged marriage is common

    (B) Rural areas limit physical contact

    (C) People do not associate with others outside of their class

    (D) Communities are not tightknit

    (E) Men and women attend same-sex schools

Questions 15-19. Read the following passage carefully before you decide on your answers to the questions.

"Without their visits you cannot hope to shun the path I tread. Expect the first tomorrow night, when the bell tolls One. Expect the second on the next night at the same hour. The third, upon the next night, when the last stroke of Twelve has ceased to vibrate Look to see me no more; and look that, for your own sake, you remember what has passed between us!"

It walked backward from him; and at every step it took, the window raised itself a little, so that, when the apparition reached it, it was wide open.

Scrooge closed the window, and examined the door by which the Ghost had entered. It was double-locked, as he had locked it with his own hands, and the bolts were undisturbed. Scrooge tried to say "Humbug!" but stopped at the first syllable. And being, from the emotion he had undergone, or the fatigues of the day, or his glimpse of the invisible world, or the dull conversation of the Ghost, or the lateness of the hour, much in need of repose, he went straight to bed, without undressing, and fell asleep on the instant.

—Charles Dickens, 1843

15. **What quality of the Ghost is the most likely trait that Scrooge dislikes the most?**

    (A) The Ghost's old fashioned speech bothers Scrooge the most.

    (B) The authoritative nature the Ghost takes with Scrooge is the quality disliked the most.

    (C) The fact that the Ghost could break into his house is the trait that Scrooge dislikes.

    (D) The Ghost is taller than Scrooge, and that bothers him.

    (E) Scrooge dislikes that his bedtime was later than usual.

16. **The way Scrooge's reaction to the Ghost is portrayed could mean that according to this passage that Scrooge is:**

(A) tired

(B) angry

(C) looking for excuses

(D) forgetful

(E) planning to ignore the Ghost

17. **The Ghost's remarks listed in the passage can most likely be inferred as:**

(A) a warning to Scrooge

(B) the Ghost is talking to the wrong person

(C) Scrooge is hallucinating

(D) a friend was playing a joke on Scrooge

(E) no inference can be made

18. **Scrooge's reaction to the Ghost in this passage leads a reader to conclude:**

(A) that Scrooge was just conducting a normal nighttime house-check

(B) when the Ghost comes back for him, Scrooge will go along willingly

(C) even wealthy people like Scrooge lock their houses

(D) that Scrooge does not believe in the supernatural

(E) Scrooge is likely overcome with exhaustion

19. **The tone of the passage is intended to:**

(A) serve as a warning to Scrooge about things he will be shown

(B) serve as a reminder that Scrooge has forgotten appointments

(C) describe how disconcerted Scrooge felt after the warning was given by the Ghost

(D) provide backstory

(E) explain why Scrooge is so stingy

Questions 20-27. Read the following passage carefully before you decide on your answers to the questions.

Death, Be Not Proud

Death, be not proud, though some have called thee
Mighty and dreadful, for thou art not so;
For those whom thou think'st thou dost overthrow
Die not, poor Death, nor yet canst thou kill m(E)
From rest and sleep, which but thy pictures be,
Much pleasure; then from thee much more must flow,
And soonest our best men with thee do go,
Rest of their bones, and soul's delivery.

Thou art slave to fate, chance, kings, and desperate men,
And dost with poison, war, and sickness dwell,
And poppy or charms can make us sleep as well
And better than thy stroke; why swell'st thou then?
One short sleep past, we wake eternally
And death shall be no more; Death, thou shalt di(E)

20. **Who wrote this poem, titled "Death, be not Proud?**

    (A) John Donne

    (B) William Shakespeare

    (C) Emily Dickinson

    (D) Edgar Allen Poe

    (E) William Wordsworth

21. **What type of poem is this?**

    (A) Ballad

    (B) Epic

    (C) Haiku

    (D) Prose

    (E) Sonnet

22. **What is the rhyme scheme in the first stanza?**

   (A) ABBAABBA

   (B) AABBABBA

   (C) ABCABCBC

   (D) AABBCCAA

   (E) ABBBAAAB

23. **What is the author implying in the following line?**
   "Die not, poor Death, nor yet canst thou kill me."

   (A) He/She is invincible.

   (B) His/Her soul will go to heaven; therefore, death does not end life.

   (C) Death does not decide when he/she will die.

   (D) Poor people do not decide when they will die.

   (E) He/she will defend themselves against a murderer.

24. **What does the following line represent?**
   "One short sleep past, we wake eternally"

   (A) Being buried

   (B) A coma

   (C) Fighting off disease

   (D) A dream

   (E) Resurrection

25. **The last line of the poem tries to explain _____.**

   (A) that heaven/the afterlife defeats death.

   (B) that death dies when the human body dies.

   (C) that death can be defeated with death.

   (D) that death is only a threat to those that are alive.

   (E) None of the above.

26. Why are poison, war, and sickness mentioned?

(A) To give examples of cowardly death scenarios.

(B) To show that you can be killed by others or in a passive way.

(C) To provoke memories from the reader.

(D) To personify death as a bully.

(E) None of the above.)

27. The author speaks about death as if it's a/an _____.

(A) theory

(B) legacy

(C) person

(D) threat

(E) imaginary concept

Questions 28-35. Read the following passage carefully before you decide on your answers to the questions.

"You boys know what tropism is, it's what makes a plant grow toward the light. Everything aspires to the light. You don't have to chase down a fly to get rid of it - you just darken the room, leave a crack of light in a window, and out he goes. Works every time. We all have that instinct, that aspiration. Science can't – what was your word? Dim? – science can't dim that. All science can do is turn out the false lights so the true light can get us home."

—Old School

28. Who is the author of the novel Old School?

(A) Ernest Hemmingway

(B) Tobias Wolff

(C) Geoffrey Chaucer

(D) William Blake

(E) William Wordsworth

29. Which point of view is this written in?

(A) First-person

(B) Second-person

(C) Third-person

(D) Third-person plural

(E) None of the above

30. Tropism is _____.

(A) photosynthesis

(B) always caused by light

(C) the moving of an organism in response to a stimulus

(D) an imaginary concept

(E) survival of the fittest

31. Why would the author mention tropism as an instinct or aspiration?

(A) All organisms are instinctive when they are hunting.

(B) All organisms use strategies like this to attract prey.

(C) It represents being able to flee.

(D) Everyone wants to be attractive.

(E) It represents moving towards a goal.

32. The word dim is significant because _____.

(A) light is necessary for tropism to occur.

(B) it represents a dimming of faith.

(C) it is not dark nor light.

(D) it represents being instinctive.

(E) None of the above.

33. What do the false lights mentioned in the last line represent?

(A) Bad influences

(B) Dim lights

(C) Lights that prompt tropism

(D) Parents

(E) All great persons wear silk.

34. What does this passage imply about the main character?

(A) He questions scientific theories.

(B) He doesn't believe science has all the answers.

(C) He is highly intelligent.

(D) Science is his favorite subject.

(E) All of the above.

35. The literal interpretation of this passage is science. The symbolic interpretation is:

(A) Religion

(B) Motivation

(C) Instinct

(D) Aspiration

(E) Economics

Questions 36-38. Read the following passage carefully before you decide on your answers to the questions.

To go into solitude, a man needs to retire as much from his chamber as from society. I am not solitary whilst I read and write, though nobody is with me. But if a man would be alone, let him look at the stars. The rays that come from those heavenly worlds, will separate between him and what he touches. One might think the atmosphere was made transparent with this design, to give man, in the heavenly bodies, the perpetual presence of the sublime. Seen in the streets of cities, how great they are! If the stars should appear one night in a thousand years, how would men believe and adore; and preserve for many generations the remembrance of the city of God which had been shown! But every night come out these envoys of beauty, and light the universe with their admonishing smile.

—— Ralph Waldo Emerson, 1836

36. The first two lines of this passage imply what?

(A) A man is never alone.

(B) A man is always alone.

(C) A man can be alone if he turns his back on people.

(D) A man can be alone if he makes his mind focus.

(E) A man who is lonely is considered alone.

37. Given the whole passage, which of the following is the best match for the author's opinion about nature?

(A) The author prefers to seek to retire in his chamber.

(B) The author sees wonder in the sky and beauty at night.

(C) The author does not like trees.

(D) The author can only see stars one night in a thousand years.

(E) You cannot tell the author's opinion from this passage.

38. The phrase "light the universe with their admonishing smile" is an example of:

(A) personification

(B) a simile

(C) a metaphor

(D) irony

(E) satire

Questions 39-46. Read the following passage carefully before you decide on your answers to the questions.

A Dream Within a Dream

Take this kiss upon the brow!
And, in parting from you now,
Thus much let me avow —
You are not wrong, who deem
That my days have been a dream;
Yet if hope has flown away
In a night, or in a day,
In a vision, or in none,
Is it therefore the less gone?
All that we see or seem
Is but a dream within a dream.

I stand amid the roar
Of a surf-tormented shore,
And I hold within my hand
Grains of the golden sand —
How few! yet how they creep
Through my fingers to the deep,
While I weep — while I weep!
O God! Can I not grasp
Them with a tighter clasp?
O God! can I not save
One from the pitiless wave?
Is all that we see or seem
But a dream within a dream?

39. **Who wrote A Dream Within a Dream?**

   (A) Emily Dickinson

   (B) William Shakespeare

   (C) Edgar Allen Poe

   (D) Jamaica Kincaid

   (E) Robert Frost

40. **What is the rhyme scheme?**

   (A) AAABBAACCDD

   (B) AAABBCCDDBB

   (C) AABBCDCDAAB

   (D) ABABABABCCD

   (E) ABBABBACCAB

41. **Why is there an exclamation point in the first line?**

   (A) To portray an unwanted kiss

   (B) To demonstrate a demand

   (C) To show excitement

   (D) To explain a romantic kiss

   (E) To show a sense of urgency

42. **What is the significance of the line "And, in parting from you now"**

   (A) It represents a goodbye before traveling

   (B) A little boy is running away from home

   (C) A parent is abandoning their child

   (D) It represents a breakup

   (E) It symbolizes an abortion

43. **What element is described with personification?**

   (A) Love

   (B) The ocean

   (C) Sand

   (D) The night

   (E) All of the above

44. What is the difference between the first and second stanza?

(A) The first stanza describes love, and the second stanza describes hate

(B) The first stanza is calm, and the second stanza has action.

(C) The first stanza has action, and the second stanza is calm.

(D) The first stanza represents hope, and the second stanza represents losing hope

(E) There are no major differences.

45. What is the similarity between the ocean and his tears?

(A) Salt water

(B) They're both parts of nature

(C) He cannot control either

(D) They're both unpredictable

(E) None of the above

46. What is the similarity between the sand and his love?

(A) He dreams about both.

(B) They are both beautiful parts of nature.

(C) They are both unobtainable.

(D) They both happen in waves.

(E) All of the above.

Questions 47-49. Read the following passage carefully before you decide on your answers to the questions.

His memories of the Boston Society Contralto were nebulous and musical. She was a lady who sang, sang, sang in the music room on their house on Washington Square - sometimes with guests all about her, the men with their arms folded, balanced breathlessly on the edges of sofas, the women with their hands in their laps, occasionally making little whispers to the men and always clapping very briskly and uttering cooing cries after each song - and she often sang to Anthony alone, in Italian or French or in a strange and terrible dialect . . . .

Oblivious to the social system, he lived for a while alone and unsought in a high room in Beck Hall — a slim dark boy of medium height with a shy sensitive mouth. His allowance was more than liberal. He laid the foundations for a library by purchasing from a wandering bibliophile first editions of Swinburne, Meredith, and Hardy, and a yellowed illegible autograph letter of Keats', finding later he had been amazingly overcharged. He became an exquisite dandy, amassed a rather pathetic collection of silk pajamas, brocaded dressing-gowns, and neckties too flamboyant to wear; in this secret finery he would parade before a mirror in his room or lie stretched in satin along the window-seat looking down on the yard and realizing this clamor, breathless and immediate, in which it seemed he was to never have a part.

—F. Scott Fitzgerald, 1922

47. Based on the information in the passage, what is a "contralto"?

(A) A Boston slang term for a high class man

(B) A female singer

(C) A female dancer

(D) A writer

(E) A bibliophile

48. Based on the information in the passage, an "exquisite dandy" refers to:

(A) the first editions of the books listed in the passage

(B) anyone who wears silk pajamas

(C) a gentleman who has money to spend extravagantly on fancy things

(D) someone who likes to parade before a mirror

(E) someone who likes candy

49. Why would the social system be important in this reading selection?

(A) Richer classes don't have dandies, so the main character can't be dandy.

(B) A rich man with no female friends is called a dandy, and it helps explain the story.

(C) The character seems ostracized and that can't happen in certain social classes.

(D) If the main character was of a lower class, he could not live the life described.

(E) No one lives the luxurious life described in the passage.

Questions 50-54. Read the following passage carefully before you decide on your answers to the questions.

These are morning matters, pictures you dream as the final wave heaves you up on the sand in the bright light and drying air. You remember pressure, and a curved sleep you rested against, soft, like a scallop in its shell. But the air hardens your skin; you stand; you leave the lighted shore to explore some dim headland, and soon you're lost in the leafy interior, intent, remembering nothing.

I still think of that old tomcat, mornings, when I wake. Things are tamer now; I sleep with the window shut. The cats and our rites are gone and my life is changed, but the memory remains of something powerful playing over me. I wake expectant, hoping to see a new thing. If I'm lucky I might be jogged awake by a strange bird call. I dress in a hurry, imagining the yard flapping with auks, or flamingos. This morning it was a wood duck, down at the creek. It flew away.

—Annie Dillard, 1975 Pulitzer Prize

50. The tone of the selection is:

(A) reflective

(B) indulgent

(C) indifferent

(D) dishonest

(E) ironic

51. The author uses _____ to describe the setting.

(A) personification

(B) ambivalence

(C) satire

(D) allusion

(E) clichés

52. The phrase, "like a scallop in its shell" is an example of:

(A) irony

(B) a simile

(C) a metaphor

(D) personification

(E) euphemism

53. The author describes many of her feelings and situations by focusing the conversation on animals. Based on the information in the passage, one reason could be:

(A) animals are comforting and relax the reader

(B) birds are flighty and the center of her story

(C) the setting of this story is a farm

(D) the lead character doesn't have many human friends

(E) it is the backstory of how animals and nature are always present in the character's life

54. The phrase "the air hardens your skin" within the context of the passage most likely refers to what?

(A) The morning air woke the character up from dreaming.

(B) The scallop shell bed the character sleeps in has opened.

(C) The air dries out the character's skin.

(D) The coldness of the room turns off the brain of the character.

(E) The air turns the character's skin cold when the cat leaves the bed.

Questions 55-60. Read the following passage carefully before you decide on your answers to the questions.

"Oh, Jake," Brett said, "we could have had such a damned good time together."

Ahead was a mounted policeman in khaki directing traffi(C) He raised his baton. The car slowed suddenly pressing Brett against me.

"Yes," I said. "Isn't it pretty to think so?"

—*The Sun Also Rises* by Ernest Hemingway

55. What is the significance of the policeman waiting his baton?

(A) It symbolizes that it's time to move along

(B) Their love will never be legal

(C) If they get caught they will go to jail

(D) It shows their love stuck, as if in traffic

(E) All of the above

56. Which is true about Brett?

(A) She has always been in love with Jak.e.

(B) She refuses to go anywhere without Jake.

(C) She sees Jake in her future.

(D) She regrets the past.

(E) All of the above.

57. Which is true about Jake?

(A) He sees Brett in his future.

(B) He wants to marry Brett.

(C) He doesn't think their relationship would ever work out.

(D) He loves Brett as a friend.

(E) He thinks Brett is pretty.

58. Which literary device would be most appropriate before this dialogue?

(A) Flashforward

(B) Foreshadowing

(C) Backflash

(D) Metaphor

(E) Flashback

59. Which is the best description of this dialogue and its placement in the story?

(A) Introduction

(B) Cliffhanger

(C) Frame story

(D) Backstory

(E) Setting

60. Why did the car slow down?

(A) There was traffic.

(B) The policeman waved his baton.

(C) The driver needed directions.

(D) The driver was picking up another passenger.

(E) It was time to get out.

ANSWER KEY

Question Number	Correct Answer	Your Answer
1.	B	
2.	D	
3.	C	
4.	D	
5.	A	
6.	C	
7.	E	
8.	B	
9.	E	
10.	A	
11.	C	
12.	A	
13.	A	
14.	C	
15.	B	
16.	C	
17.	A	
18.	D	
19.	C	
20.	A	
21.	E	
22.	A	
23.	C	
24.	E	
25.	A	
26.	B	
27.	C	
28.	B	
29.	B	
30.	C	

Question Number	Correct Answer	Your Answer
31.	E	
32.	B	
33.	A	
34.	B	
35.	A	
36.	D	
37.	B	
38.	A	
39.	C	
40.	A	
41.	E	
42.	D	
43.	C	
44.	B	
45.	C	
46.	C	
47.	B	
48.	C	
49.	D	
50.	A	
51.	D	
52.	C	
53.	E	
54.	A	
55.	A	
56.	D	
57.	C	
58.	E	
59.	B	
60.	A	

Sample Test 4 Explanation _____

Questions 1-6. Read the following passage carefully before you decide on your answers to the questions.

Tyger! Tyger! burning bright
In the forests of the night,
What immortal hand or eye
Could frame thy fearful symmetry?
In what distant deeps or skies
Burnt the fire of thine eyes?
On what wings dare he aspire?
What the hand dare seize the flame?

And what shoulder, & what art,
Could twist the sinews of they heart?
And when thy heart began to beat,
What dread hand? & what dread feet?
　　　—Excerpt, William Blake, 1794

1. **Which of the topics below is this best description of the poem's main idea?**

　(A) Strength, as sinews of the heart are strong.

　(B) Creationism, and the author asks what immortal being created the tiger.

　(C) Flying, because it talks about wings.

　(D) Fire, with references to flames and burning forests.

　(E) Love, describing the heart and how it beats.

The correct answer is B.

This passage references the first word of each answer, but only one explanation for the excerpt can be correct. Remember this is about the main idea, not just one idea of the passage. If all of these were right, you need to find the option that is the best choice of all the options - one that can be seen in all of the other options. (B) represents the best choice.

2. **Sinews, in the third stanza, can be best compared to:**

(A) thread

(B) a cage

(C) rope

(D) heart strings or emotions

(E) burnt fire, from the second stanza

The correct answer is D.

Sinews are like tendons. They are strong binding fibers. So, (A) is not correct, nor is (E) The closest two options are (C) and (D); however, since this is poetry, sinews are figurative and the meaning is emotions, choice (D)

3. **Another phrase for "deeps or skies" that would fit in this poem could be:**

(A) caves or planes

(B) trees or forests

(C) seas or air

(D) waves or wind

(E) oceans or lakes

The correct answer is C.

In this selection, synonyms - or similar words - need to be used in the same order as the original passage. Knowing this, (C) is the best option. While (D) could be considered, the original words do not describe movement, so it is not the best selection.

4. **What is personified in the poem?**

(A) A lion

(B) Birds

(C) Candle

(D) A tiger

(E) The sky

The correct answer is D.

This should be a fairly straightforward question, with the correct answer (D)

5. In line 7 of this poem, what word below most nearly means "aspire"?

(A) Soar

(B) Plunge

(C) Scheme

(D) Travel

(E) Admire

The correct answer is A.

Again, look for synonym in the list. Plunge is an antonym. (A) is the right choice.

6. The poet, William Blake, uses all of the following literary tools to convey his message, except:

(A) metaphors

(B) rhymed couplets

(C) personification

(D) symbols

(E) lyrics

The correct answer is C.

For this question, you need to know your literary terms. Look them up if there are any unfamiliar to you. (C) - personification - is the right answer. It was also hinted in question four for this passage.

Questions 7-14. Read the following passage carefully before you decide on your answers to the questions.

"Where, in Heaven's name, could anyone even be alone in Calcutta? What hanky-panky business, in my mother's words, could go on? Everyone knew the rules and the rules stated caste and community narrowed the range of intimate contact."

—Desirable Daughters by Bharati Mukherjee

7. Where is Calcutta?

(A) Indonesia

(B) China

(C) New Zealand

(D) Jamaica

(E) India

The correct answer is E.

While it is a geography question, it is important for the understanding of the book.

8. **Why is it abnormal for someone to be alone in Calcutta?**

(A) Everyone travels with their spouses

(B) It's a very busy city

(C) The city is very dangerous

(D) It's sarcastic because it's such a rural place

(E) None of the above

The correct answer is B.

When the author asks how could anyone be alone there, it implies that it is a very busy place. You need to decipher implied information in these passages.

9. **What is hanky-panky business?**

(A) Dancing

(B) Illegal trade

(C) Corruption

(D) A romantic kiss

(E) Sexual activity

The correct answer is E.

You have likely heard this before, but when the character discusses this, you should be able to infer the meaning.

10. **What does the word caste mean?**

(A) Division of the classes

(B) Enclosed

(C) Oppression

(D) Sin

(E) Sexualized

The correct answer is A.

You likely have heard this discussed before, as a mechanism for dividing communities on income and race or ethnicity.

11. What form of speech is in heaven's name?

(A) Analogy

(B) Definition

(C) Idiom

(D) Quotation

(E) Allegory

The correct answer is C.

You need to be familiar with literary terms.

12. What is the author implying in this passage?

(A) Sexual abuse

(B) Adultery

(C) Secret lovers

(D) Pregnancy

(E) All of the above

The correct answer is A.

By referencing the hanky-panky business and difficulty in having any time alone, you need to infer this is the best answer.

13. This novel represents _____.

(A) Feminism

(B) Nature

(C) Misogyny

(D) City life

(E) None of the above

The correct answer is A.

You should be able to eliminate (B) and (C) as options. Also, (E) is rarely used as a correct answer when "none of the above" appears. Since the passage doesn't describe only busy scenes or what you see in the city, the correct option is (A)

14. How could community narrow the range of intimate contact?

(A) Arranged marriage is common

(B) Rural areas limit physical contact

(C) People do not associate with others outside of their class

(D) Communities are not tightknit

(E) Men and women attend same-sex schools

The correct answer is C.

This is part of the inherent definition in Caste. It's more than physical contact of (B) While (A) is true and (D) is false, you cannot also make the conclusion listed in (E).

Questions 15-19. Read the following passage carefully before you decide on your answers to the questions.

"Without their visits you cannot hope to shun the path I tread. Expect the first tomorrow night, when the bell tolls One. Expect the second on the next night at the same hour. The third, upon the next night, when the last stroke of Twelve has ceased to vibrate Look to see me no more; and look that, for your own sake, you remember what has passed between us!"

It walked backward from him; and at every step it took, the window raised itself a little, so that, when the apparition reached it, it was wide open.

Scrooge closed the window, and examined the door by which the Ghost had entered. It was double-locked, as he had locked it with his own hands, and the bolts were undisturbed. Scrooge tried to say "Humbug!" but stopped at the first syllable. And being, from the emotion he had undergone, or the fatigues of the day, or his glimpse of the invisible world, or the dull conversation of the Ghost, or the lateness of the hour, much in need of repose, he went straight to bed, without undressing, and fell asleep on the instant.

—Charles Dickens, 1843

15. What quality of the Ghost is the most likely trait that Scrooge dislikes the most?

(A) The Ghost's old fashioned speech bothers Scrooge the most.

(B) The authoritative nature the Ghost takes with Scrooge is the quality disliked the most.

(C) The fact that the Ghost could break into his house is the trait that Scrooge dislikes.

(D) The Ghost is taller than Scrooge, and that bothers him.

(E) Scrooge dislikes that his bedtime was later than usual.

The correct answer is B.

There is no indication in the passage that the other items are correct, but there are clues in the reading that the direct speech and authority of the Ghost bothers him.

16. **The way Scrooge's reaction to the Ghost is portrayed could mean that according to this passage that Scrooge is:**

    (A) tired

    (B) angry

    (C) looking for excuses

    (D) forgetful

    (E) planning to ignore the Ghost

    The correct answer is C.

    The continued answers for what is possible or not is most parallel to (C)

17. **The Ghost's remarks listed in the passage can most likely be inferred as:**

    (A) a warning to Scrooge

    (B) the Ghost is talking to the wrong person

    (C) Scrooge is hallucinating

    (D) a friend was playing a joke on Scrooge

    (E) no inference can be made

    The correct answer is A.

    If you know this story, it also makes it easier to answer the questions. Remember to use caution with answers like (E); and there is no proof of (B), (C) or (D).

18. **Scrooge's reaction to the Ghost in this passage leads a reader to conclude:**

    (A) that Scrooge was just conducting a normal nighttime house-check

    (B) when the Ghost comes back for him, Scrooge will go along willingly

    (C) even wealthy people like Scrooge lock their houses

    (D) that Scrooge does not believe in the supernatural

    (E) Scrooge is likely overcome with exhaustion

    The correct answer is D.

    The passage includes clues that there is not a "normal" element to the conversation (in A). The pushback Scrooge gives shows that (B) is not likely. The option (C) may be true but is not supported in the passage, and while E is possibly true, that requires a lot of supposition, not intuitive reasoning.

19. The tone of the passage is intended to:

(A) serve as a warning to Scrooge about things he will be shown

(B) serve as a reminder that Scrooge has forgotten appointments

(C) describe how disconcerted Scrooge felt after the warning was given by the Ghost

(D) provide backstory

(E) explain why Scrooge is so stingy

The correct answer is C.

While (A) may be true, it is not the best answer. There is no proof for (B), and (D) is not accurate. Also, there is no support for (E), either.

Questions 20-27. Read the following passage carefully before you decide on your answers to the questions.

Death, Be Not Proud

Death, be not proud, though some have called thee
Mighty and dreadful, for thou art not so;
For those whom thou think'st thou dost overthrow
Die not, poor Death, nor yet canst thou kill m(E)
From rest and sleep, which but thy pictures be,
Much pleasure; then from thee much more must flow,
And soonest our best men with thee do go,
Rest of their bones, and soul's delivery.

Thou art slave to fate, chance, kings, and desperate men,
And dost with poison, war, and sickness dwell,
And poppy or charms can make us sleep as well
And better than thy stroke; why swell'st thou then?
One short sleep past, we wake eternally
And death shall be no more; Death, thou shalt di(E)

20. Who wrote this poem, titled "Death, be not Proud?

(A) John Donne

(B) William Shakespeare

(C) Emily Dickinson

(D) Edgar Allen Poe

(E) William Wordsworth

The correct answer is A.

You should be able to recognize some of the more famous works by these authors, or at least the style in which they wrote for various questions on the SAT.

21. What type of poem is this?

(A) Ballad

(B) Epic

(C) Haiku

(D) Prose

(E) Sonnet

The correct answer is E.

Again, knowing definitions will help you quickly and accurately answer certain questions when "comprehension" isn't applicable, but it is about recall and identification.

22. What is the rhyme scheme in the first stanza?

(A) ABBAABBA

(B) AABBABBA

(C) ABCABCBC

(D) AABBCCAA

(E) ABBBAAAB

The correct answer is A.

By looking over the words that rhyme in the first stanza, it's easy to determine the rhyme scheme as ABBAABBA.

23. What is the author implying in the following line?
"Die not, poor Death, nor yet canst thou kill me."

(A) He/She is invincible.

(B) His/Her soul will go to heaven; therefore, death does not end life.

(C) Death does not decide when he/she will die.

(D) Poor people do not decide when they will die.

(E) He/she will defend themselves against a murderer.

The correct answer is C.

The author implies that although death may be the end of their body on earth, their soul will live on in heaven. Therefore, (B) is the best option.

24. **What does the following line represent?**
"One short sleep past, we wake eternally"

(A) Being buried

(B) A coma

(C) Fighting off disease

(D) A dream

(E) Resurrection

The correct answer is E.

This is a straightforward question: the words "wake" and "eternally" are direct connections to resurrection.

25. **The last line of the poem tries to explain _____.**

(A) that heaven/the afterlife defeats death.

(B) that death dies when the human body dies.

(C) that death can be defeated with death.

(D) that death is only a threat to those that are alive.

(E) None of the above.

The correct answer is A.

Because we know the poem views death as inferior to the afterlife, and the author believes heaven is a place their soul will live eternally, (A) is the best answer.

26. **Why are poison, war, and sickness mentioned?**

(A) To give examples of cowardly death scenarios.

(B) To show that you can be killed by others or in a passive way.

(C) To provoke memories from the reader.

(D) To personify death as a bully.

(E) None of the above.

The correct answer is B.

Poison, war, and sickness are all practical ways to die and mentioning them displays death as something that can happen to anyone. Each of these scenarios are nearly impossible to avoid and can be related to by the reader, regardless of their stature.

27. The author speaks about death as if it's a/an _____.

(A) theory

(B) legacy

(C) person

(D) threat

(E) imaginary concept

The correct answer is C.

This poem uses personification to describe death. It's viewed as something that tries to take away from others. Therefore, (C) is the best answer.

Questions 28-35. Read the following passage carefully before you decide on your answers to the questions.

"You boys know what tropism is, it's what makes a plant grow toward the light. Everything aspires to the light. You don't have to chase down a fly to get rid of it - you just darken the room, leave a crack of light in a window, and out he goes. Works every time. We all have that instinct, that aspiration. Science can't – what was your word? Dim? – science can't dim that. All science can do is turn out the false lights so the true light can get us home."

—*Old School*

28. Who is the author of the novel Old School?

(A) Ernest Hemmingway

(B) Tobias Wolff

(C) Geoffrey Chaucer

(D) William Blake

(E) William Wordsworth

The correct answer is B.

The novel Old School was written by Tobias Wolff.

29. Which point of view is this written in?

(A) First-person

(B) Second-person

(C) Third-person

(D) Third-person plural

(E) None of the above

The correct answer is B.

Throughout the poem, the author uses the word "you," which is a direct indicator of second-person point of view.

30. **Tropism is ____.**

   (A) photosynthesis

   (B) always caused by light

   (C) the moving of an organism in response to a stimulus

   (D) an imaginary concept

   (E) survival of the fittest

   The correct answer is C.

   Context clues are needed to determine this answer, as tropism is not a common vocabulary word.) Using the first and second sentences, you can determine that (C) is the best answer.

31. **Why would the author mention tropism as an instinct or aspiration?**

   (A) All organisms are instinctive when they are hunting.

   (B) All organisms use strategies like this to attract prey.

   (C) It represents being able to flee.

   (D) Everyone wants to be attractive.

   (E) It represents moving towards a goal.

   The correct answer is E.

   Again, context clues are critical for zeroing in on the correct answer. Similar to moving in response to a stimulus, the author mentions tropism as an instinct or aspiration because a goal can be viewed as the stimulus.

32. **The word dim is significant because ____.**

   (A) light is necessary for tropism to occur.

   (B) it represents a dimming of faith.

   (C) it is not dark nor light.

   (D) it represents being instinctive.

   (E) None of the above.

   The correct answer is B.

   Symbolism is important for narrowing in on the answer for this particular question. (D) has no connection and can easily be eliminated. (A) and (C) are literal interpretations, whereas (B) connects the representation of the dimming of faith.

33. **What do the false lights mentioned in the last line represent?**

    (A) Bad influences

    (B) Dim lights

    (C) Lights that prompt tropism

    (D) Parents

    (E) All great persons wear silk.

    The correct answer is A.

    The best connection to the false lights in the last line is bad influences.

34. **What does this passage imply about the main character?**

    (A) He questions scientific theories.

    (B) He doesn't believe science has all the answers.

    (C) He is highly intelligent.

    (D) Science is his favorite subject.

    (E) All of the above.

    The correct answer is B.

    The author is very skeptical of science and its abilities. While (A), (C), and (D), may all be possible, (B) is the most apparent.

35. **The literal interpretation of this passage is science. The symbolic interpretation is:**

    (A) Religion

    (B) Motivation

    (C) Instinct

    (D) Aspiration

    (E) Economics

    The correct answer is A.

    The best symbolic interpretation for this passage is religion.

Questions 36-38. Read the following passage carefully before you decide on your answers to the questions.

To go into solitude, a man needs to retire as much from his chamber as from society. I am not solitary whilst I read and write, though nobody is with me. But if a man would be alone, let him look at the stars. The rays that come from those heavenly worlds, will separate between him and what he touches. One might think the atmosphere was made transparent with this design, to give man, in the heavenly bodies, the perpetual presence of the sublime. Seen in the streets of cities, how great they are! If the stars should appear one night in a thousand years, how would men believe and adore; and preserve for many generations the remembrance of the city of God which had been shown! But every night come out these envoys of beauty, and light the universe with their admonishing smile.

—— Ralph Waldo Emerson, 1836

36. **The first two lines of this passage imply what?**

(A) A man is never alone.

(B) A man is always alone.

(C) A man can be alone if he turns his back on people.

(D) A man can be alone if he makes his mind focus.

(E) A man who is lonely is considered alone.

The correct answer is D.

Given this is fiction and nearly a poem, you need to interpret what the author intends. The first two options use those extreme words, so they are not the best choices. The literal description of turning a back on people is not discussed. The difference between lonely and being alone is not discussed, either. So, (D) is the answer you should choose.

37. **Given the whole passage, which of the following is the best match for the author's opinion about nature?**

(A) The author prefers to seek to retire in his chamber.

(B) The author sees wonder in the sky and beauty at night.

(C) The author does not like trees.

(D) The author can only see stars one night in a thousand years.

(E) You cannot tell the author's opinion from this passage.

The correct answer is B.

You should realize by now - especially when understanding poems - that it would be extremely rare to select option (E) as the right answer. Option (D) is a misstatement of a phrase in the passage. There is no mention of the author even hinting that he does not like trees, so (C) is incorrect. When considering (A) or (B), (A) does not resound as strongly as (B), which is the right answer.

38. The phrase "light the universe with their admonishing smile" is an example of:

(A) personification

(B) a simile

(C) a metaphor

(D) irony

(E) satire

The correct answer is A.

Remember, the definition of personification is to give an inanimate object the attributes of a human, so (A) is correct. If you are unfamiliar with the other options in this example, it would be a good idea to look them up and learn them, as at least one of these five will be included on the exam.

Questions 39-46. Read the following passage carefully before you decide on your answers to the questions.

A Dream Within a Dream

Take this kiss upon the brow!
And, in parting from you now,
Thus much let me avow —
You are not wrong, who deem
That my days have been a dream;
Yet if hope has flown away
In a night, or in a day,
In a vision, or in none,
Is it therefore the less gone?
All that we see or seem
Is but a dream within a dream.

I stand amid the roar
Of a surf-tormented shore,
And I hold within my hand
Grains of the golden sand —
How few! yet how they creep
Through my fingers to the deep,
While I weep — while I weep!
O God! Can I not grasp
Them with a tighter clasp?
O God! can I not save
One from the pitiless wave?
Is all that we see or seem
But a dream within a dream?

39. **Who wrote A Dream Within a Dream?**

   (A) Emily Dickinson

   (B) William Shakespeare

   (C) Edgar Allen Poe

   (D) Jamaica Kincaid

   (E) Robert Frost

   The correct answer is C.

   Edgar Allen Poe wrote A Dream Within A Dream.

40. **What is the rhyme scheme?**

   (A) AAABBAACCDD

   (B) AAABBCCDDBB

   (C) AABBCDCDAAB

   (D) ABABABABCCD

   (E) ABBABBACCAB

   The correct answer is A.

   Just like the other poems in this practice test, looking through the last words in each sentence can help zero in on the correct option for rhyme scheme. The correct answer for this question is (A)

41. **Why is there an exclamation point in the first line?**

   (A) To portray an unwanted kiss

   (B) To demonstrate a demand

   (C) To show excitement

   (D) To explain a romantic kiss

   (E) To show a sense of urgency

   The correct answer is E.

   Exclamation points are a way to represent an extreme situation. For the first line in this poem, the punctuation mark shows a sense of urgency, making E the best answer.

42. **What is the significance of the line "And, in parting from you now"**

    (A) It represents a goodbye before traveling

    (B) A little boy is running away from home

    (C) A parent is abandoning their child

    (D) It represents a breakup

    (E) It symbolizes an abortion

    The correct answer is D.

    (D) is the best option because "parting" represents ending a relationship.

43. **What element is described with personification?**

    (A) Love

    (B) The ocean

    (C) Sand

    (D) The night

    (E) All of the above

    The correct answer is C.

    The word "creep" is a dead giveaway in trying to find personification. (C) is the best answer for this question.

44. **What is the difference between the first and second stanza?**

    (A) The first stanza describes love, and the second stanza describes hate

    (B) The first stanza is calm, and the second stanza has action.

    (C) The first stanza has action, and the second stanza is calm.

    (D) The first stanza represents hope, and the second stanza represents losing hope

    (E) There are no major differences.

    The correct answer is B.

    Looking at the punctuation and the action within the writing, it's easy to determine that (B) is the best answer.

45. What is the similarity between the ocean and his tears?

(A) Salt water

(B) They're both parts of nature

(C) He cannot control either

(D) They're both unpredictable

(E) None of the above

The correct answer is C.

Waves are caused by the moon's pull on the earth, and his tears are caused naturally. (D) can quickly be eliminated because they are predictable. While it is true that the ocean and his tears are made of salt water and they are both parts of nature, (C) is the best answer given the context of the poem.

46. What is the similarity between the sand and his love?

(A) He dreams about both.

(B) They are both beautiful parts of nature.

(C) They are both unobtainable.

(D) They both happen in waves.

(E) All of the above.

The correct answer is C.

The sand and his love are both slipping away from his fingers. (C) is the best answer because he portrays both at unobtainable.

Questions 47-49. Read the following passage carefully before you decide on your answers to the questions.

His memories of the Boston Society Contralto were nebulous and musical. She was a lady who sang, sang, sang in the music room on their house on Washington Square - sometimes with guests all about her, the men with their arms folded, balanced breathlessly on the edges of sofas, the women with their hands in their laps, occasionally making little whispers to the men and always clapping very briskly and uttering cooing cries after each song - and she often sang to Anthony alone, in Italian or French or in a strange and terrible dialect . . . .

Oblivious to the social system, he lived for a while alone and unsought in a high room in Beck Hall — a slim dark boy of medium height with a shy sensitive mouth. His allowance was more than liberal. He laid the foundations for a library by purchasing from a wandering bibliophile first editions of Swinburne, Meredith, and Hardy, and a yellowed illegible autograph letter of Keats', finding later he had been amazingly overcharged. He became an exquisite dandy, amassed a rather pathetic collection of silk pajamas, brocaded dressing-gowns, and neckties too flamboyant to wear; in this secret finery he would parade before a mirror in his room or lie stretched in satin along the window-seat looking down on the yard and realizing this clamor, breathless and immediate, in which it seemed he was to never have a part.

—F. Scott Fitzgerald, 1922

47. **Based on the information in the passage, what is a "contralto"?**

    (A) A Boston slang term for a high class man

    (B) A female singer

    (C) A female dancer

    (D) A writer

    (E) A bibliophile

    The correct answer is B.

    Using the pronouns in the passage, contralto is a female - so (A) is obviously wrong. While any of the remaining options may be true, in the passage it talks about the woman singing, so (B) is the correct choice.

48. **Based on the information in the passage, an "exquisite dandy" refers to:**

    (A) the first editions of the books listed in the passage

    (B) anyone who wears silk pajamas

    (C) a gentleman who has money to spend extravagantly on fancy things

    (D) someone who likes to parade before a mirror

    (E) someone who likes candy

    The correct answer is C.

    The term "dandy" references a person, so (A) is out. (E) is also out because candy is not mentioned in the passage; it is merely a rhyme for dandy. (B) is mentioned in the passage that the man like to wear silk pajamas and so is (D), when it talks about the mirror. However, you have to look at the whole passage and the thing the man does, so (C) is the best answer if you do not know what "dandy" means.

49. Why would the social system be important in this reading selection?

(A) Richer classes don't have dandies, so the main character can't be dandy.

(B) A rich man with no female friends is called a dandy, and it helps explain the story.

(C) The character seems ostracized and that can't happen in certain social classes.

(D) If the main character was of a lower class, he could not live the life described.

(E) No one lives the luxurious life described in the passage.

The correct answer is D.

In this question, it helps to know the meaning of dandy, which you may use from the previous answer if you do not know it. Since the man described in the passage seems to have a lot of money, (A) cannot be the right answer. (E) also is not a choice because it uses an extreme phrase - "no one". (D) is not correct because anyone can be excluded from a group (it also has an extreme contraction of "can't". Between (B) and (D), there are two reasons why (B) isn't a good choice.) First, no female friends could be read as an extreme description, using "no". Another tip that this may not be the right choice is that if you removed the part of the passage about dandy, the story still works. Therefore, if you don't know that dandies are rarely lower classes, you can reason your way that (D) is correct.

Questions 50-54. Read the following passage carefully before you decide on your answers to the questions.

These are morning matters, pictures you dream as the final wave heaves you up on the sand in the bright light and drying air. You remember pressure, and a curved sleep you rested against, soft, like a scallop in its shell. But the air hardens your skin; you stand; you leave the lighted shore to explore some dim headland, and soon you're lost in the leafy interior, intent, remembering nothing.

I still think of that old tomcat, mornings, when I wake. Things are tamer now; I sleep with the window shut. The cats and our rites are gone and my life is changed, but the memory remains of something powerful playing over me. I wake expectant, hoping to see a new thing. If I'm lucky I might be jogged awake by a strange bird call. I dress in a hurry, imagining the yard flapping with auks, or flamingos. This morning it was a wood duck, down at the creek. It flew away.

—Annie Dillard, 1975 Pulitzer Prize

50. The tone of the selection is:

(A) reflective

(B) indulgent

(C) indifferent

(D) dishonest

(E) ironic

The correct answer is A.

This is knowing what the different words mean. (A) is the correct answer. Review the definitions of these words if you don't know them, to make sure they won't trip you up on the exam.

51. The author uses _____ to describe the setting.

(A) personification

(B) ambivalence

(C) satire

(D) allusion

(E) clichés

The correct answer is D.

Definitions are a large part of reading comprehension answer possibilities, as they like to know that you understand more than just what the passage says. (D) is the correct answer.

52. The phrase, "like a scallop in its shell" is an example of:

(A) irony

(B) a simile

(C) a metaphor

(D) personification

(E) euphemism

The correct answer is C.

Again, this is about definitions. When you use the word "like" in a comparison, which is one hint that the phrase is a metaphor. The answer is (C)

53. The author describes many of her feelings and situations by focusing the conversation on animals. Based on the information in the passage, one reason could be:

(A) animals are comforting and relax the reader

(B) birds are flighty and the center of her story

(C) the setting of this story is a farm

(D) the lead character doesn't have many human friends

(E) it is the backstory of how animals and nature are always present in the character's life

The correct answer is E.

There are some weigh out options for these answers! (A), (B), (C) and (D) make great leaps if you were to make those conclusions.

54. **The phrase "the air hardens your skin" within the context of the passage most likely refers to what?**

(A) The morning air woke the character up from dreaming.

(B) The scallop shell bed the character sleeps in has opened.

(C) The air dries out the character's skin.

(D) The coldness of the room turns off the brain of the character.

(E) The air turns the character's skin cold when the cat leaves the bed.

The correct answer is A.

This question looks at ensuring you understand the suggestions made by the author. (B) is totally made up. (D) is a bit far-fetched, to turn off her brain (what does that have to do with skin?) (E) gives the impression cats are extremely warm and somehow leaving the bed is related with her description, slightly implausible.) (A) and (C) remain; but in the context of fiction, A is the better choice.

Questions 55-60. Read the following passage carefully before you decide on your answers to the questions.

"Oh, Jake," Brett said, "we could have had such a damned good time together."

Ahead was a mounted policeman in khaki directing traffi(C) He raised his baton. The car slowed suddenly pressing Brett against me.

"Yes," I said. "Isn't it pretty to think so?"

—*The Sun Also Rises* by Ernest Hemingway

55. **What is the significance of the policeman waiting his baton?**

(A) It symbolizes that it's time to move along

(B) Their love will never be legal

(C) If they get caught they will go to jail

(D) It shows their love stuck, as if in traffic

(E) All of the above

The correct answer is A.

Using the phrase "could have" shows that the characters are thinking their time is finished and their relationship will never be. The policeman raising his baton symbolizes moving along in a literal sense, which draws a strong (and deliberate from the author) connection to the situation Brett and Jake are in.

56. Which is true about Brett?

(A) She has always been in love with Jak.e.

(B) She refuses to go anywhere without Jake.

(C) She sees Jake in her future.

(D) She regrets the past.

(E) All of the above.

The correct answer is D.

As mentioned in the previous question, this particular passage sets a scene of looking backwards. It's implied that if she really did love Jake, she would have fought harder for him instead of simply letting him go. (D) is the best answer for this question because it's most obvious that she has regrets.

57. Which is true about Jake?

(A) He sees Brett in his future.

(B) He wants to marry Brett.

(C) He doesn't think their relationship would ever work out.

(D) He loves Brett as a friend.

(E) He thinks Brett is pretty.

The correct answer is C.

While Brett is thinking of the "what if" in their relationship, Jake has already come to terms with the fact that it will never work out. He may have loved her in the past, but he has accepted their relationship not moving forwar(D) Because of this, (C) is the best answer.

58. Which literary device would be most appropriate before this dialogue?

(A) Flashforward

(B) Foreshadowing

(C) Backflash

(D) Metaphor

(E) Flashback

The correct answer is E.

This passage makes the reader question what has happened in their relationship in the past to make them question why it would never work out. A flashback would be most appropriate to give the reader context and more details about what they've been through. This makes (E) the best answer for this question.

59. Which is the best description of this dialogue and its placement in the story?

(A) Introduction

(B) Cliffhanger

(C) Frame story

(D) Backstory

(E) Setting

The correct answer is B.

There is obvious action in this piece, and the author is trying to provoke emotion in the reader by making them think of the possible outcomes for Brett and Jake's relationship. Because of the rising action, B is the best answer.

60. Why did the car slow down?

(A) There was traffic.

(B) The policeman waved his baton.

(C) The driver needed directions.

(D) The driver was picking up another passenger.

(E) It was time to get out.

The correct answer is A.

Just like Brett and Jake's relationship, their cab ride has come to an end. The literal interpretation of their cab ride ending ties in with the symbolism of their decision to end all thoughts of being together in the future. Knowing the context of this story, (E) is the correct answer.

SAT

SAT Subject Tests are college admission exams on specific subjects. These tests are generally given six times in any given school year, on the same days and in the same test centers as the SAT — but not all 20 tests are offered on every SAT date. When you take an SAT Subject Test, you are doing more than showing off your strengths.

If the college decides to give you credit, it will record the number of credits on your permanent record, thereby indicating that you have completed work equivalent to a course in that subject. If the college decides to grant exemption without giving you credit for a course, you will be permitted to omit a course that would normally be required of you and to take a course of your choice instead.

SAT Math 1
ISBN 978-1-60787-571-0 $16.99

SAT Math 2
ISNB 978-1-60787-572-7 $14.99

SAT Biology
ISBN 978-1-60787-569-7 $18.99

SAT Chemistry
ISBN 978-1-60787-568-0 $14.99

SAT Literature
ISBN 978-1-60787-573-4 $16.99

SAT Spanish
ISBN 978-1-60787-570-3 $19.99

www.ingramcontent.com/pod-product-compliance
Lightning Source LLC
Chambersburg PA
CBHW081323090426
42737CB00017B/3020